WINTER ROSES after FALL

ALSO BY
ROBERT M. DRAKE

Chaos Theory

Star Theory

Light Theory

Moon Theory

Beautiful and Damned

Gravity: A Novel

Seeds of Chaos

Beautiful Chaos

A Brilliant Madness

Black Butterfly

Broken Flowers

Spaceship

Science

Beautiful Chaos 2

Dead Pop Art

The Great Artist

Moon Matrix

Seeds of Wrath

Dawn of Mayhem

The King is Dead

Empty Bottles Full of Stories

Falling Toward the Moon

She Fits Inside These Words

also by r.h. Sin

Whiskey Words & a Shovel

Whiskey Words & a Shovel II

Whiskey Words & a Shovel III

Rest in the Mourning

A Beautiful Composition of Broken

Algedonic

Planting Gardens in Graves

*Planting Gardens in
Graves Volume Two*

*Planting Gardens in
Graves Volume Three*

She Felt Like Feeling Nothing

Empty Bottles Full of Stories

She Just Wants to Forget

Falling Toward the Moon

We Hope This Reaches You in Time

A Crowded Loneliness

She's Strong, but She's Tired

She Fits Inside These Words

ROBERT M. DRAKE

WINTER ROSES after FALL

r.h. Sin

*Cover illustration
by Hannah Olson*

Andrews McMeel
PUBLISHING®

ROBERT M. DRAKE
contents

AGAINST THE ROPES 27

ALL ABOARD 30

ALL THE MAPS I FOUND ALWAYS LEAD ME TO YOU 65

A PINCH OF LIGHT 47

AT NIGHT, IT ALL MAKES SENSE 74

BEFORE IT BEGINS 7

BLESSINGS COME IN ALL FORMS 76

BORN WITH CAPES ON 10

BROKEN THINGS LEAD TO NEW THINGS 62

CHASING WATERFALLS 66

HOW IT FEELS WHEN YOU FEEL LIKE YOU CAN'T LET GO 96

HOW THINGS BECOME COLD 77

I DO NOT MAKE THE RULES 83

I MET A GIRL AND SHE BROKE MY HEART
AND I WAS NEVER THE SAME AFTER 69

IT COMES LIKE A THIEF IN THE NIGHT 56

RERUNS NEVER GET OLD 58

RUN WITH THE HUNTED 5

SOMETIMES YOU'RE THE HERO
SOMETIMES YOU SAVE YOURSELF 68

THE DAY YOU GET YOUR WINGS 54

THE DOORS ARE OPEN 39

THE GARDEN OF PEOPLE 48

THE GIFT AND THE CURSE 46

THE INVITATION 34

THE LAST MESSAGE TO MY FRIEND 87

THE LAST TIME YOU SAW EACH OTHER 23

THE MOMENT YOU REALIZE THE LIGHT IN YOUR BODY 49

THE MOMENT YOU WAKE UP 28

THE PLAYBACK 9

THERE IS ALWAYS A LITTLE MORE TIME 88

THE SEARCH IS NEVER OVER 84

THE THINGS WE SHARE 11

THE TIMES YOU'VE LEARNED TO LET GO 82

THE WINDOWS ARE OPEN 81

THINGS FALL APART 57

THINGS THAT JUST HURT 61

TO BEGIN 2

UNTITLED ONE 25

UNTITLED TWO 43

UNTITLED THREE 103

WHAT HAPPENS IF I THINK TOO MUCH 75

WHEN A HELPING HAND IS YOUR SAVIOR 90

WHEN FEELINGS BECOME DAGGERS 15

WHEN HOPE CLEARS YOUR HEART 89

WHEN MIRACLES HAPPEN 51

WHEN POEMS SPEAK MORE THAN THE TRUTH 98

WHEN THE GLASS IS HALF FULL 13

WHEN THE SUN RISES 38

WHEN WHAT YOU FEEL WITHIN OUTGROWS YOUR BODY 64

WHEN YOU APPRECIATE PEOPLE
BETTER THAN YOU DID THE NIGHT BEFORE 52

WHEN YOU FEEL LIKE YOU CAN'T MOVE 53

WHEN YOU REEK OF LOVE 21

WHEN YOUR HEART IS BIGGER THAN YOUR BODY 73

WHEN YOUR HOME DOESN'T FEEL LIKE HOME 94

WHEN YOUR LEGS REFUSE TO FALL 40

WHEN YOUR MOUTH DOESN'T MATTER 95

WHEN YOU THOUGHT OTHERWISE 92

WHERE THE FLOWERS GROW 42

WHY DO THEY LEAVE AND NEVER RETURN? 111

YOU GIVE THEM THE WORLD 18

YOUR CHEST IS A POT OF GOLD 32

YOU, TOO, CAN HEAL THEM 71

ROBERT M. DRAKE

TO BEGIN

Don't be
so hard on yourself.

Be kind
to yourself.

No one knows
what you've been through

better than
you.

And no one
is going to give you

the kind of love
you deserve

other than
yourself.

Be kind to yourself.
Be good to yourself.
Take care
of yourself.

It may take
some time.

And it may take
some trials and tribulations

to get
to that point.

But believe me
when I say

in the end,

it will be
the greatest gift

you have ever
received.

Be kind to yourself.
Love yourself.

And be patient
with yourself.

You deserve these types
of soft things

and a lot more
than you think.

You know it.
And I know it, too.

RUN WITH THE HUNTED

They told you
not to run back

to them.

And so you did.
But little did you know.

That, too,
would be

your undoing.

That, too,
would be

your own demise.

Silence.
Moving on.
And isolation.

Is sometimes a slow killer.
And sometimes
these types of things

heal you
while other times

they do not.

BEFORE IT BEGINS

That's the thing.

Not a lot of people
know

what it's like
to be in love.

Because not a lot of people
have received it.

That's just
the way things are.

So don't be surprised
if they don't know

what to do
with your heart.

Don't be surprised
if they've never

experienced it.

Be kind with them.
Be patient.

Maybe you'll be the one
to show them

the way.

Maybe you'll be
the real one

who teaches them
how to love.

What a beautiful process
it can be.

THE PLAYBACK

There's no
correct way

to love someone.

You just love them
and hope

that they, too,
love you

the same way.

This is how it happens.
The cycle of pain.

The reoccurrence
of healing.

And it goes on
And on.
And on.

BORN WITH CAPES ON

You can be
your own hero.

The thing is,
society has taught us

that we *must*
be saved

by someone we love

rather than

teaching us
that we have

our own power
and we are capable

of saving
ourselves.

THE THINGS WE SHARE

Sometimes
the sound of silence

hurts
even more

when you're alone.

And sometimes
it's the loudest sound
you can ever make.

It is just
some people

don't have
the ears for it.

While others
know what to listen for.

They know, just know.

Maybe that's why
only a few

relate to you
more
than most.

WHEN THE GLASS IS HALF FULL

Because we want
to make ourselves

feel things
we know

aren't there anymore.

And that's why
it hurts

sometimes.

We want to love
the people

who've done us wrong,
but we've had enough.

We really want
to try.

But in the end,
we just discover
how we have nothing.

Left.
To give.

And that's why
we feel
so goddamn empty

sometimes.

That's all.

WHEN FEELINGS BECOME DAGGERS

It stings hard.

The fact
that you lost her.

And it wasn't
because

you didn't understand her.
Or you didn't

love her.

Or anything like that.

No.
You lost her
because you didn't

give her
the attention she needed.

You didn't
listen to her
when she wanted to talk.

You didn't
comfort her
when she felt empty.

You didn't
calm her down

when she was
breaking down.

You didn't fill her soul
when she felt lost.

You lost her.

And it wasn't
because

you didn't want what was
best for her.

It was because
you made her feel
even more alone

when she needed you
the most.

You ignored her.
You let her down.

You were absent.

And that's
what hurts

the most.

YOU GIVE THEM THE WORLD

Maybe he didn't
love you.

Maybe he just
loved

the attention
you gave him.

The healing
you helped him with.

And the peace you put
inside of his heart.

He took all of you with him
And left you alone.

Sometimes you give
someone the world

and in return
they take
what you gave them
and never

do they thank you.

They just take
it all

for granted
and only
think about themselves.

And that kind
of wound

cuts far deeper
than any sword

you can imagine.

To be taken
for granted

and feel unappreciated
when you put

so much
time and effort into them.

This kind of pain
never really

goes away.

WHEN YOU REEK OF LOVE

Sometimes
the people you love

will not
love you back.

I know
it's a hard thing

to swallow,
but it's the truth.

Sometimes
you don't get

what you want.

Sometimes
you're forced

to let go.

No matter how hard
you worked
on the relationship.

And sometimes
it just doesn't

work out,
no matter how much

love you gave them.

Sometimes you give
while other times

you give
some more.

And in the end,
it just doesn't add up.

People slip away.
That's what they do.

No matter how much
you tried.

THE LAST TIME YOU SAW EACH OTHER

Sometimes
you wake up,

and they
just aren't there

anymore.

And from one day
to the next.

Without warning.
Without fair words.

Without anything
left behind.

Or any kind
of remorse.

Because that's just
how people are.

They get to the end
of their line.

They get
to their last straw.

To the point
where they just can't take it

anymore.

And vanish.
Just like that, too.

In an instant.

Faster than you can blink.
So don't feel too bad

for moving on.

For wanting a better life.
A new start.

Sometimes people leave
without an explanation.
And sometimes
that's the only way

we say good-bye.

ROBERT M. DRAKE   24

UNTITLED ONE

That's the thing.

Relationships are supposed
to be effortless

and simple.

They're supposed
to give you confidence.

Give you
the self-esteem

you need
to carry on.

They're not supposed
to break you down.

Or make you feel
as if

it's the end of the world.
No.
And no.
And no.

They're supposed
to lift you.

To give you blessings.
Give you love.

Companionship.

And teach you
about patience

and kindness.

If it's anything else,
then it isn't worth

your love.
It isn't worth
your time.

Love shouldn't be that hard.

AGAINST THE ROPES

And when you think
you have nothing left

to give.

No love left
to offer.

That's when you realize
you've only scratched

the surface
of what your heart

is really
capable of.

THE MOMENT YOU WAKE UP

You know it hurts
when you believed them.

And then
you discover

that everything they did
was complete

bullshit.

Everything they said
and did

was a *fucking* lie.

Realizing this
is one of the hardest

things
to go through.

Realizing that
part of your life

was a lie.
Damn.

Sometimes
you wake up,

and when you do,
it is in

the harshest way.

ALL ABOARD

We only
remember the ones

who moved us.

The ones
who meant something

to us.

The special ones.
The ones who made

the best of things.

Who made us laugh
when we were down.

Who lifted our spirits
when we felt

broken.

Who took the time
to be there for us.

That's who
we remember.

That's who we keep
in our hearts.

Forever.

No matter where we end up.
No matter who we meet

and fall in love with.

It's those people
who spoke to us

who we take
with us.

No matter what.

YOUR CHEST IS A POT OF GOLD

Sooner or later.

You have got
to let go

of all that pain.

You cannot hold
on to it forever.

You are not
built to carry

a mountain
on your back.

And you are not
meant to collect

so many ghosts
during your journey.

You are not meant
for that!

You are not meant
to go through

so much fucked-up shit
and hold it all

within.

THE INVITATION

I want to love you.

It is just
I do not know how.

And look.
I am not asking

for your sympathy.

I am not asking
for your help.

Or for your guidance.

I am just asking
for your patience.

Because I know
I will learn

how to love you
the right way.
I know
I will learn

how to be there
for you

when you feel broken.

I know
I will learn

how to be
a better listener.

How to be
a better lover.

A better friend.
A better person.

For you.
And only for you.

And I know
because I can feel it

in my soul.

I can feel it
in the core

of my bones
like a flaming ball

waiting to burst
out.

Waiting to explode
out of me.

I feel it.
I feel you.

It is just
I have a hard time

expressing
all that I have

within me.

I've never been here
before.

All of this
is new to me.

And I am trying
to learn

how to be
that person for you.

The one you deserve.
The one you need.

The one you can
count on.

Just be patient with me.
That's all

I ask.

WHEN THE SUN RISES

I'm moving on.

Not just
from the people

who've done me wrong.

But
from my own doubts.

My own fears.
My own heaviness.

I'm learning
how to appreciate

my flaws.

And I'm willing
to let things go

in order
to grow.

THE DOORS ARE OPEN

May the people
you want to love

love you.

Especially
when you feel broken.

When you need them
the most.

WHEN YOUR LEGS REFUSE TO FALL

I know
you are exhausted.

But you are still
here.

And you are still
moving forward.

Pushing.
Grinding.

And against
the odds, as well.

You are proving
to yourself

that you still
have a fight

in you.

That you are well capable
of love.

That everything
that brings you pain

does not define you.

This is the definition
of strength.

The fact
that you can't take it

anymore
and yet

still find it deep
within your heart

to stand up
and keep going.

WHERE THE FLOWERS GROW

Your greatest lovers
will always teach you

something new
about yourself.

And that is why
you won't forget them.

UNTITLED TWO

Be kinder
to yourself.

Softer.
Lighter.

The world is hard.
Lovers are hard.

People are hard.

And your thoughts
are even harder.

But there is no need
for you

to be
so goddamn tough
on yourself.

No need
to criticize
and be so diminishing
to who you are.

You are you.

A being full of love.
Full of light

and hope.

Believe in yourself
when you are in doubt.

Remember your scars
when you are in

a hard situation.

And know
what you want

when opportunity
presents itself.

Know yourself.
Be kind to yourself.
Be gentle
and understanding.

There's no need
to submit.

No need
to be defeated.

To be wounded
by your own mind.

Be patient
with yourself

and with your feelings.

Remember.
You are love.

And when the doubts end.
And the *overthinking*

is under control,
that is when

you begin.
Take this as a sign.

Take every hard moment
you've been through

since the beginning
as a sign.

THE GIFT AND THE CURSE

You have to expect
brokenness.

Emptiness.
Sadness.

Not everything
is going to perfect.

You cannot love
someone

without any kind
of pain.

You cannot be vulnerable
with anyone

without putting your heart
at risk.

A PINCH OF LIGHT

You have to
love yourself.

Even if
you don't know

where to begin.

THE GARDEN OF PEOPLE

You belong.

Do not let them
make you feel

as if
you do not.

THE MOMENT YOU REALIZE
THE LIGHT IN YOUR BODY

You're in a relationship
with yourself.

Therefore,
it is in your best

interest
to be good

to yourself.

Don't disrespect yourself
by giving into

half-assed love.

And half-assed lovers.

You deserve better.
This

you owe to yourself
before
anything else.

Always know this.

The relationship you have
with yourself

will be
the most important one

you will ever
have.

WHEN MIRACLES HAPPEN

Remember.

That with the right amount
of love.

Anything
is possible.

WHEN YOU APPRECIATE PEOPLE BETTER THAN YOU DID THE NIGHT BEFORE

Sometimes you meet
the perfect girl.

And she gives you
the right amount

of love.

And sadly
you let her slip away.

And that's something
that haunts you.

Something
you have to live with.

Forever.

WHEN YOU FEEL LIKE YOU
CAN'T MOVE

You want to love.
But you're terrified

of getting
your heart broken again.

You're terrified
of being back there.

In that lonely.
Cold.

Dark place.

So I get you
when you say

you want to be
alone.

'Cause those types of things
weigh heavily.

THE DAY YOU GET YOUR WINGS

Yes.

I can agree
that the right person

can really
turn things around

in your life.

But that doesn't mean
you need them.

You have everything
you need

within.

Search within
for love.

Search within
for guidance.
For truth.
For compassion.

For advice.
For growth.

For lessons.

Trust yourself.

The moment you do
is the moment

you will be free.

IT COMES LIKE A THIEF
IN THE NIGHT

People change
for several different reasons.

But nothing
is worse

than when they change
and you don't

even know
why.

THINGS FALL APART

That's the thing.

They didn't know
how to love you.

And that's why
they let you

down.

RERUNS NEVER GET OLD

People will tell you
to be alone.

To
use all of this

new time
on yourself.

But the facts
are facts.

And if you
fall in love again.

Back-to-back.

Right after
you got out

of a relationship.

Then you must understand.
That there is nothing
you can do

about it.

That nine
out of ten times

you'll lose
that battle.

Because the heart
demands

what it demands.

And it always gets
what it wants.

No matter what
or who it is.

Once your heart
is involved.

It's over.
You'll fall in love
again.

Get hurt
again.

And your life
will continue.

No matter what.

THINGS THAT JUST HURT

Maybe

"I'll see you around"

is just another way
of telling someone

good-bye.

BROKEN THINGS LEAD
TO NEW THINGS

Maybe
I never had you.

And to think
that perhaps

it was me
who lost you.

When in reality
you were never mine

to begin with.

I never stood a chance.
And the realization hurts

because at one point
I actually believed

that you loved me.

But that was
my mistake,
and that's where

things began
to fall apart.

But also

where things began
to make sense.

WHEN WHAT YOU FEEL WITHIN
OUTGROWS YOUR BODY

Remember.

Whatever happens
from here on out.

I will still
be there for you.

No matter what.

Believe this.

Place this
under your skin.

ALL THE MAPS I FOUND ALWAYS
LEAD ME TO YOU

It's the way
you make me feel.

That alone
makes all

the difference.

That alone
is why I choose

to stay.

CHASING WATERFALLS

I want
to be yours.

And you want
to be his.

And he wants
to be someone else's.

And in a strange way.

This is
what sums us up.

We never get
what we want.

And we always chase
the people

we know
we *don't* deserve.

And that's why
our fucking hearts

break
the way

they break.

SOMETIMES YOU'RE THE HERO
SOMETIMES YOU SAVE YOURSELF

It took me years
to understand.

That I
was my own hero.

That only I
could save myself.

And only I
could give myself

the kind of love
I deserved.

I MET A GIRL AND SHE BROKE MY HEART AND I WAS NEVER THE SAME AFTER

You have to
be careful

with your feelings.

'Cause in the end.
No matter what happens.

That's all
you're left with.

Feelings.
Memories.

The bad.
The good.

And the sound
of silence.

Those are the things
you feel

when there's nothing
left anymore.

*When you no longer
have anything*

to give.

YOU, TOO, CAN HEAL THEM

You can't just tell
someone

to move on.

That's not
how it works.

You have to
be there for them.

Take the time
to listen to them.

To talk to them.

To comfort them.
Do little things

to help them
get their mind

off the person
who hurt them.

And it can take weeks.

Months.
Years.

No one is the same.
And no one heals

the same way,
either.

We have to
understand this.

Keep this
in mind

when someone you care about
is broken down.

Be patient with them.

Help them.
That's how
they'll move on.

That's how
they'll learn

to let go.

ROBERT M. DRAKE   72

WHEN YOUR HEART IS BIGGER THAN YOUR BODY

I saw you
in such a way

that I wouldn't be able
to describe it

with words.

I felt it
that deeply.

I loved you
that much.

AT NIGHT, IT ALL MAKES SENSE

Some of the best
feelings

I've ever felt
didn't involve you.

They involved me,

flowers,
and the relationship

I have
with the moon.

WHAT HAPPENS IF I THINK TOO MUCH

Maybe
I *overthink*

so much
that I don't

give myself
a chance to love.

BLESSINGS COME IN ALL FORMS

Don't take
your grieving

for granted.

For sadness,
too,

is sometimes
a gift.

It can be
healing.

And that's all
I have to say

about that.

HOW THINGS BECOME COLD

Do not
become cold.

Do not
become someone

who *used* to care.

Who used to show
love.

Do not
let them change

the way you are.

The way you feel
about yourself.

Do not
be that person

who follows
the trend.

Who will do anything
to fit in.

ROBERT M. DRAKE   77

Who will betray
their own heart

to be accepted.

Who will hurt
the people

who love them
in order

to please those
who do not.

Do not
become this person.

This is not you.

And their approval
isn't needed.
I hope
you remember this

when you
are vulnerable.

I hope
you stick with what

your heart
tells you

when presented
with these types

of people.

You do not
need them

in your life, baby.

You stay away
from them.

And do not
let them
attach themselves

to you.

They will kill you.
They will drain you

of your energy
and love.

And they will do it
every chance

they get.
Stay strong.

THE WINDOWS ARE OPEN

You are
what you choose

to share
with others.

Sometimes
that's what makes you

who you are.

THE TIMES YOU'VE LEARNED TO LET GO

No matter what
you're going through,

sometimes
you just have to

open your heart.
And feel.

I DO NOT MAKE THE RULES

People change.

And that's just
something

you need
to get used to.

THE SEARCH IS NEVER OVER

Find someone
who will help

relieve the anxiety,
not add to it.

Someone
who will help you

ease off
the stress

and depression,
not give you more of it.

Someone
who soothes the soul.

Who helps
soften up

the world a bit,
not add to its
hard edges.
Who will make
your problems

a little bit more
bearable.

More tolerable.

Someone
who makes

everything easier
on the heart.

On the mind.
On the soul.

Those are the kinds
of people

you need.

The ones who help you
when you need them

the most.
The ones who make
the sun

feel a little warmer
than it is.

The ones who give
love

without effort.

Find them.
Follow them.

Love them.

You need them
more

than you think.

THE LAST MESSAGE TO MY FRIEND

Remember.

Always follow
your heart

and not
the crowd.

THERE IS ALWAYS A LITTLE MORE TIME

You can still
make it work.

All you have to do
is make the time,

be patient,
and listen

to each other.

That should be
the first step

you take
in order to heal

your broken
relationship.

WHEN HOPE CLEARS YOUR HEART

You have to believe
that the good times

are still ahead.

That something positive
is about to happen.

That type
of hope

is priceless.

It can turn
a bad situation

into something good.

Remember this.

Sometimes hope
is all
we have.

WHEN A HELPING HAND
IS YOUR SAVIOR

Conversation
is everything.

Sometimes
that's all you need

to pull you
out of the darkness.

Someone
who's willing to listen.

Someone
who's willing to stay,

no matter how
late it gets.

Deep people
with deep hearts

and deep thoughts

can sometimes

save your life.

ROBERT M. DRAKE   90

They can sometimes
save you

from yourself.

WHEN YOU THOUGHT OTHERWISE

You're too real
for people.

And maybe
that's why

you haven't found
love.

Because everyone
you've met

is either fake
or full of shit.

Is either
looking out for themselves

or

just taking
advantage of people

for their own
personal gain.

So I get you
when you say

ROBERT M. DRAKE   92

you'd rather be single.

Because nowadays
it's hard to find

someone
to believe in.

It's hard to find
someone

to open up with.

To be yourself with.
To be soft

and vulnerable with.

I get you.
Because a lot of people
give you fake vibes.

And almost everyone
you've met

is only thinking
about themselves.

WHEN YOUR HOME DOESN'T FEEL LIKE HOME

It's hard
to trust anyone.

When even
your own parents

talk down to you.

When even
the people

you're supposed to be
the closest with

negatively criticize
you harder

than anyone else
you know.

WHEN YOUR MOUTH
DOESN'T MATTER

One day.

I will forget you.
And you will

regret
all the things

you did to me.

And all the things
you failed

to say.

HOW IT FEELS WHEN YOU FEEL
LIKE YOU CAN'T LET GO

It hurts
when you ignore me.

When you don't
reply

or call me back.

Because
I still remember

when you used to
be more attentive.

I still remember
what it felt like

when you cared.

I just hope
the real you

comes back soon.

Because I don't
think
I'm ready
to say good-bye.

Some things
are just too hard

to forget.

Some things
are just too hard

to ignore.

WHEN POEMS SPEAK MORE
THAN THE TRUTH

You can still
love them.

But that's not
going to change

anything.

An asshole
is an asshole.

And sometimes
you have to put

your feelings
and personal beliefs

aside
for your own
well-being.

Because, yes,
maybe in the beginning
you thought
they were *the one.*

Maybe at first
everything was too good

to be true.

But you must
understand.

People cannot live
with masks

forever.

They cannot hide
beneath lies.

They cannot hold
all that rage

and chaos
within.

Like I said,
an asshole
will always be

an asshole.

ROBERT M. DRAKE 99

And almost
always

does it begin
and end the same.

They make you
fall in love

with them,
and then,

with a little time given,
they tear you apart.

They take advantage
of you.

They get too comfortable
and begin

to treat you
like shit.

They begin
to care less.

ROBERT M. DRAKE   100

To not give
a fuck about you.

Until you reach
your last straw

and explode.

And then
they have the nerve

to say
they're the victim.

That you're too vicious.
Too aggressive.

Too out of control.

When, in reality,
you've just had
enough.

Your tired.
You're exhausted.

And you have
no other way

of expressing yourself.

So, yes,

you can still love them.
But, also,

you must understand
that it is time

to let them go.

UNTITLED THREE

I know
in your mind.

In your heart.

You have been programmed
to apologize

for everything.

If someone
let's *YOU* down,

you apologize.

If you can't remember
something,

you apologize.

If you're asking someone
for help,

you apologize, etc.

I can go on.
You have been stripped

of your right
to feel things.

And to feel them
in your own way.

We have been programmed
to apologize

for our scars.

For our flaws.
Our doubts.

Our fears.

For every
little thing

we don't like
about ourselves.
They want us
to hate

who we are.

They want us
to stay put.

To not grow.
To not fight for a chance

to be loved.

They want us caged.
Not free.

Lost.
Not found.

They want our hearts
confused.
Not clear.

We don't know
who we are.
We don't know
what to feel.

What to love.

And it is all
because we have never been taught

how not
to feel sorry

for ourselves.

How not
to apologize

for the way we love.

But we can't
blame them

for everything.

We can't
point a finger

at all the people
who've made us feel
broken.

Who've made us feel
as if

we hate ourselves.

No.

We have to be
better than that.

We have to know
that we are capable

of more.

But really know.

With all soul.
All heart.

We have to know
that our flaws.
Doubts.
Fears.

And scars.
are a crucial part

of who we are.

And that we
still have many more

of those
types of feelings

waiting for us.

We have to stop
apologizing

for everything.

Stop
hating ourselves.

Stop
being so nonchalant
about the things
we really feel.

The things
we *really*

want to say.

You can't let them
make these decisions

for you.

And you can't let them
tell you

how to feel
about yourself.

You just can't.

It's time
to break out of this state
of mind.

It's time
to free yourself
from their standards.

From their walls.
From their boundaries.

'Cause in reality,
they don't want you

to discover
your power.

They don't want you
to love yourself.

To know
and control

what you feel.

The moment you do,
they are powerless.

Because the moment
you stop apologizing

and start
loving who you are.

Is the moment
they lose.

And you win.

Amen.

WHY DO THEY LEAVE
AND NEVER RETURN?

Sometimes
I wish you

knew what I felt.

Maybe then
it would be enough
to make you

want to stay.

r.h. Sin

Where does it all go when lost? You know, those things you fail to appreciate, those moments you're never present for, and all those people you take for granted. And I wonder if you even notice them slowly fading from beside you, or is it that you're only aware when it's too late? There's a sorrow that resides in being ungrateful, a sadness that only reveals itself when you begin to search for what or whom you were too busy to acknowledge only to discover the absence of everything and everyone that deserved more of your time. I have witnessed people lose the **people who love them the most because they** failed to love them enough to say sorry, say thank you, and say anything worth being heard. I have often been on the receiving end of offerings that I no longer wanted, tired of waiting, searching for an exit, reaching for the door, and begged to stay where I could no longer consider home. And so maybe I do know where the things that aren't appreciated end up. For one, I have been lost only to find myself somewhere better, staying in hopes that my journey for a home will finally end.

Some endings are beautiful, the way the foundation crumbles beneath fearful feet, a heart afraid of leaving. You fall into a black hole of mourning, drowning beneath the sorrow of midnight, fighting back the tears, searching for reasons to run back, but the road behind you is a dead end. There's a storm ahead, and the rain strangely feels inviting as the dark clouds summon you in hopes of somehow getting you to understand that, beyond this chaos, something majestic awaits you on the other side. There's a type of love that can only be cultivated once you've had your heart broken, and there is a strength that can only be forged during the darkest of hours. In the end, the beauty is that somehow you figure out how to love yourself again, despite feeling broken.

_____

How lonely you must feel to love the way you
do, to fall into hands that will hurt you. You
are staring into the eyes of a mate who will
disappoint you—pointing you in the direction of
a sadness you never wanted. You build so much
of your hope on a foundation not strong enough
to hold you, holding on to someone who keeps
you from the peace you've always wanted.

_____

The darkness isn't all that bad. The absence of light can often provide you with an opportunity to see the bigger picture. The city can't see all the stars because of the buildings and streetlights, but the desert gets to witness the midnight sky and all of its glory. So, give me darkness, because I long to see the moon and the last bit of light from dying stars. Give me darkness, because it'll force me to become a torch to light my own way. Give me an evening alone so that I can prove once more that I deserve to see another sunrise. Some people see a blacked-out sky and fear that they won't be able to move freely, but in the depth of the night lives one more opportunity to shine.

When you're done getting angry, you're closer
to letting go. You see no need to fight with this
person because you realize that they are no longer
worth fighting for. You save your energy once
you know that sharing that energy with them is
a waste of time, and so when you're done getting
upset, you daydream about letting go. I speak
from experience, as I can still remember the
relationships of my past and how I left with a sort
of ease that would suggest that I didn't care in
the first place. But that's the thing. Sometimes
you care so much that being mistreated and
disrespected and unappreciated drives you up a
wall and sometimes closer to an exit.

Some of us are so used to being on the opposite
end of mistreatment, and so we deal with it over
an extended amount of time because we've grown
strong enough to tolerate it. And, often, we stay
with a person not out of love but simply because
we can bear the harm of loving the wrong person.
I've been guilty of trying harder when I should
have quit. I've had my share of disappointment
from investing hope in a hopeless situation. I've
even stayed in a relationship because I believed
that I was suitable for that person even knowing
they were wrong for me, but there comes a
moment in the matrix where you wake up and
realize that peace can be cultivated only in the
absence of the person you were trying to make
peace with.

When it's done, you'll know. You'll feel relieved
at the idea of walking away. You'll begin to
reason with yourself with a newfound clarity;
you'll stitch a silver lining as you figure out that,
all this time, you were just too good of a person
for someone who only intended to make you feel
bad. And the best thing about it is that you'll owe
them no explanation as you gather your things
to move forward with your life. Do not waste
another moment on people who drain you of your
peace of mind and distract you from the love you
deserve.

———————————————

I remember it like it was yesterday. The sky
transformed into a blue-gray hell as the sun got
lost behind the clouds, and the afternoon began
to swell with tears, raining without warning.
It was storming without consideration of those
deserving the sun. And the wind ripped through,
unraveling all sense of hope, destroying all the
plans we had made for the future. You stood
there, staring toward me with dead eyes, lost of
all feeling of the type of life that resides within
the chambers of love. I lost you to the temptations
of the world, and I was no longer yours due to
the realization that my moon was too bright for
the nights you'd rather sleep than stay up beside
me to dream the greatest dreams. Your mind
elsewhere and my heart fixated on places you'd
never go—a home, made of paper, torn by us
both.

Sometimes the sorrow is sweet, the way it arrives
at the end of something stale and sour. A toxic
love, with a lover who hated to see your heart
happy—and it'll hurt so good to leave behind
something not made to last.

I saw more stars that night; it was as if the night sky decided to show me more of its secrets the moment you left.

I figured you'd come back, singing that old song
of regret. Finally, taking ownership of the bullshit
you put me through. Here you are again, with
some empty apologies and more weak forms of
manipulation. Trying to reenter a door no longer
existing for you, with a knob you're no longer
strong enough to turn. I thought you'd learn the
first time or maybe the second; the third time is
deliverance, as I plan to free myself from your
hold. You see, I've grown cold to your advances,
not willing to provide more chances. It's like I
have all these questions, but you've run out of
answers.

I stopped wanting you the way I had; you lose
interest in the things and or people you no longer
feel you need. But I needed to be disappointed
by you to see a proper exit, one that would lead
me in an endless direction toward everything you
will never be and everywhere you'll never reside.

———————————

Nostalgia is a pretty lie, the past filtered in all the pretty colors you like. You admire what's behind you, moments no longer filled with life, while neglecting the present and anything that lives within it. You've been tending to dead flowers, unable to see that you've been killing the only garden you have left.

Toxic people will start fires in your heart, then complain about the temperature of the heat in your reaction. Stay away from toxic people.

———————

it wasn't beautiful

it wasn't the way the movies showed it

and it wasn't like the songs i'd heard

there was nothing special

about losing something of my own

to someone who i would have never fucked

if i were old enough to know better

Fumbling around in the dark with my innocence, searching for a place to put it. Kissing it goodbye before it would be gone. Lost in nostalgia, left behind somewhere I'll never return to with someone I'll never see again.

―――――――――――――

I live with your ghosts, the ones you write about
when you pour out the pain that lives within
you. I live with the understanding that you pay
tribute to your heartache instead of rejoicing in
the peace and love that I've provided. I live with
the realization that my passion and effort will
somehow never be significant enough for the pain
they've caused you.

—————————————

I feel like I'm screaming behind a steel wall, 100 miles in the depth of darkness. Too far to be heard, never seen. My existence has yet to be realized by someone willing to help. Who would be willing to lend a hand to a nonexistent figure, not yet a stranger but solely unknown? I've been drowning for years, struggling against the current, longing to breathe freely but denied moments of peace. I'm starting to forget the image that is my own as I sit in a room without mirrors and no one around to tell me what they see. I look down at my limbs in agony, knowing that I can't view myself entirely, only fragments, fragments without a face. Without a reflective surface, my eyes can't see my eyes, and so, at this moment, I'm a stranger to myself.

———————————

I felt sadness and hid behind a smile. I'd laugh so hard with hopes of drowning out the pain. I stood there beside you when it was best to walk away. I'd hear the words "I love you" and think of it as a translation for "I'll hurt you." And now, every time I think of forever, I remember that it ends.

―――――――――――

I think they tear you down to hold you back.
Every insult, all the criticism, you somehow
begin to believe it, and once you do, you're stuck.
Unable to move forward, fighting to let go.

I always found it strange that you decided to
try and punish me for every little thing but
somehow felt the need to reward all the people
who repeatedly made you feel like shit and never
apologized for it. I guess it's just harder to hold
a person accountable when you know they don't
give a fuck about you. Yeah, that has to be it.

We need cheaters. They're lessons; they're examples. It's nice to know what a piece of shit looks like so that we don't step in one.

Some people teach you how and what to fully love, while others teach you what to avoid and how to walk away. I have found that there are things to be learned from those who wish to cause you pain, and, often, the ones who hope to hurt you only inspire you to become stronger and wiser.

_____

after fall, i sit with winter

the rainstorms colder

the air a bit more stoic

there's an uneasiness in the air

but somehow, those frigid surroundings

feel like home

the chaos silenced, nearly frozen

the chill is maddening

but i find solace

despite being pricked

by the wind's teeth

Being good to someone who is afraid to be happy
is a terrible hell for a heart that deserves heaven.

I've learned to pay attention to the actions of those around me. Sure, anyone can say a nice thing, but what a person does is vital in knowing who they truly are. Some people will wait and watch you drown, and some people will be willing to jump into the deep end for you, even stay to lend a helping hand. Some people will stand beside you and your struggles, reminding you that anything is possible and that this too will pass, and there will be others who will pretend to have had faith in you when you've made it to the other end. Pay attention.

In this life, you will discover with time that a cheater is just a stepping-stone to a greater understanding of what you want from future relationships. Sometimes you have to get what you don't want to figure out what you truly deserve.

i'm tired of being treated like an airport

made to feel like a nonplace

something to pass through

something to leave

in the middle of nowhere

only useful to those

who don't intend to stay

———————————

I have endured the most uninteresting parts of
you for far too long. You initially promised love
but gave me shit, and now I must find a way to
move on with no idea of what or where I'm going.

So I'm writing this, and when I finish, I look
over to the winter sky to see little chunks of cold
drifting toward the city. (I forgot it was snowing.)
It was just cool . . . but this is what I was writing.

the roses are wilting

their stems bending

forcing them to bow

toward a wintry Queen

her breath a cold whisper

her stare, still and icy

with intentions of freezing

anything that drifts in her way

_____

where warmth once resided

the chill of winter lives

empty promises now frostbitten

lies frozen over like lakes

the cold air creating ghost towns

because the chill is too much to take

_____

there's a song that lives

in the pouring rain

a melancholy melody

a sound of pain

a frantic whisper

it fills the night

as it serenades

the midnight sky

Sometimes goodbye is the only response. You sit there quietly, taking it all in. Reflecting on what has happened, remembering all the moments of disappointment. It all comes rushing back through you like the blood in your veins. It hurts, even more so than the first time, because it is at this moment that you are faced with the decision to leave. That same heart that chose to love, despite often being broken, must now find the strength to detach itself from someone whom you believed to be the one. And this will be one of the most challenging things you'll ever have to do, but you'll do it because you love yourself that much.

It feels like returning home, that split-second decision to move on. You leave because it's not working anymore; you walk away, putting yourself in a better position to better secure everything you believed you had lost. You move forward while searching for some sort of meaning, clarity, a reason as to why you had to suffer. You let go to free your hands of anything that shouldn't be kept. You remove all the things that weighed you down, negative feelings caused by those who didn't know what to do with the endless amounts of love you gave.

_____

I think she has the power to divide the ocean; her
existence calls into question whether mythical
creatures can inhabit the earth or whether angels
can live among us. I see God's light in her eyes;
there are bits of heaven in her stare.

I believe that people spend more time saying instead of doing. How often is something expressed through words but falls short of materializing into something tangible? In your own life, you've witnessed this often, so much that you may not even realize that it's happening, or maybe you're guilty of it as well. "Love" has become a sort of buzzword, a default expression. A word rooted in manipulation or loneliness, something said to help fill a void. I know this because I've lived it. Someone says, "I love you," and that same love that isn't based upon something real or profound is then utilized to capture you in a selfish web. Soon enough, you see that when it comes time to display the true meaning of that love, the person who has proclaimed it takes issue with proving it to be a genuine feeling. People say anything and do nothing close to what has been promised. How is it that someone can love you so much and yet make you feel so hated? Promises of forever are omens of something ending far too soon, and this happens far too often.

It's crazy the way things work out, the way
things fall apart even when you hope that it all
remains in one piece. There's an air of chaos
that exists in spaces unexplored, and you often
find yourself in those spaces with no intention
of being there. You think that if the universe
is listening, then it must have misheard you or
misread the moment. You don't mean to offend,
but it's easier for people who are used to a certain
treatment to get offended by what you express,
and everything that comes after makes the hole
of misunderstanding deeper. You want to have
these healthy dialogues about the world, but you
realize that you're talking to people who aren't in
the proper space to understand what you mean.
Too much of that just forces you to fall silent. Too
much of that just makes you shut down. None of
what you said was wrong, but you feel that way
because you're not saying it to the right person,
and maybe that person is simply yourself. You
feel that most things should go unsaid and be
locked away from ears that will take issue with
you sharing knowledge too intricate for others to
comprehend

I think that's why I wake up with the desire
to search for my silence, as if saying nothing
will protect me from the static that lives within
moments of a misunderstanding. After all the
good I've done for people, I always wonder why
they find it difficult to give me the benefit of the
doubt. How is it that the people I love and who
claim to love me back are so quick to assume that
I'm attacking them when I'm just trying to share
what I know or exchange ideas in a world that
doesn't want us to think freely. Since childhood,
I've been forced into a corner of silence, leaving
it only when that other person questions why
I'm so quiet. Whenever I begin to speak or
give an answer, I'm faced with the realization
that I've said too much or not enough of what
the person deems acceptable for that particular
exchange. And experiencing that as a child well
into adulthood can fuck up a person and or make
it difficult to be open to self-expression. I think
that's why I leave it all on paper, in books, and
in digital recording. There's no judgment, or
maybe there is, but I'll never know. There's no
one to offend, just moments of self-reflection
and a better understanding of myself. I write to
help others and to better articulate what I may be
feeling at the moment. I could just so easily do
that with the spoken word, but it doesn't take long
to understand that sometimes people are just not
willing to listen.

I admit, there were times when I would get angry, but I don't anymore. And I can't say that I fully don't care, because I'm writing this now. But, at this very moment, there is an overwhelming calm that blankets me. I don't see the point in allowing something or anyone to disrupt my peace, especially when I had no intention of distracting them from theirs. I believe that instances like the ones I face when dialogues are tainted provide me with the understanding of how to handle things the next time. And sometimes the best action is no action. Sometimes the right thing to say is to say nothing at all. Isn't it difficult to speak when your words will be transformed into weapons of harm when you only intended to educate? And if what you express is turned against you in a way that fills you with regret, isn't it best to give silence to those who have often shown to be experts in misinterpreting you? Now, this is in no way to promote being silent, especially in moments of injustice and wrongdoing. These words are my subconscious truths spewed out in paragraph form to lend a helping hand to those who have experienced difficulty in speaking to people who are not ready to hear them. (You can't keep talking to people who are not prepared to hear you.) This is a hard lesson to learn for many, as we readily share information that can be weaponized and forged into something it was never meant to be. And it will always happen in exchanges with those we genuinely care about, but you can't explain your way out of it; the more you see, the greater the frustration. There is nothing to clarify to the person who is used to being attacked. There is nothing to say to a person who will hear things differently than how you said them.

All in all, there is something that needs to be understood. It is not your fault when your intentions are misread, and no matter how well you spell it out, there will always be people who fail to grasp the meat of what you're trying to express. Sometimes people digest information based on how they're feeling. If you're speaking to someone who doesn't respect you, chances are the things you say will come off differently depending on the particular subject. If the person you're attempting to have a dialogue with is used to emotionally harmful interactions with others, then that interaction will be plagued with noise. It is best to think about what you've said and reflect on the information you've given to others and not take offense to their being offended or lacking the ability to process that information. Not everything in this life is meant to hurt you, and I see no point in getting angry with people for being mad at you, but there lies something to be learned from these people. Say nothing when there is nothing you can say, and save your expressions for those who will take the moments needed to decipher what is being said. In simplest terms, stop speaking to people who do not wish to listen.

———————————————

You told me I'd never find someone like you, and I smiled, because that was my wish all along.

———————————

I wish I had your confidence, the way you
exaggerated your importance in my life to the
point of believing that I'd be lost without you,
and I am grateful for your absence, because you
helped prove yourself wrong.

––––––––––––––––––––

The days are longer when spent with the wrong
person. The minutes pull you into oblivion; the
hours drag you into hell.

What I love most about a breakup is that you no longer have to wait on the person who chose to waste your time. What I love about being left behind is the fact that you realize that what you had was never worth missing. What I love about the end is that it gives way to a better beginning. Breakups are beautiful in a way that allows you to come together with yourself and possibly someone worthy of your love and devotion. In the beginning, it hurts; that pain comes from the genuine belief that the person you were with was worth your love. But as time passes, you begin to see the beauty in being without the person who refused to love you properly.

You find ways to outrun your demons, no matter how dark and painful it gets. That alone speaks to the power that lives within your soul.

_____

Never forget the way it felt when he left you to
fuck someone else, and never let him return when
he pretends to miss you.

_____

Please write a "Dear Future" letter to yourself,
and tell her to say no to exes who want another
chance.

The problem with love is that it's initially taught
to us by people who do not know the correct
definition. The word "love" gets thrown around
like a weightless ball and lands into the hands
of those who want nothing more than to use it to
either fill a void and or to manipulate vulnerable
people. More times than not, the first person you
fall for is the first person who makes you fall for
lies disguised as love, and from there, you enter
a cycle of choosing doors labeled "love" that lead
to hell and heartache. I wish people were more
mindful of love and how it is to be used. I wish
more people took their time with it instead of
rushing themselves into a wall painted with their
blood due to the wounds of always having their
hearts broken. The problem with love is that,
before we practice it on ourselves, we feel rushed
into relationships in which love will never dwell.

I promised myself that if I were given a real
chance at genuine love, I'd be prepared to love
you back in ways that would calm the doubt that
has lived in your head ever since the ending of
your last relationship. I'd not only say the right
things but my actions would then add value to
those words spoken toward your heart. I'd go
on to redefine everything you'd come to believe
about love and remind you to smile with every
passing day. And this is the way it begins, nearly
hopeless, a rare dream, thought unbelievable
until it takes place. I've been staring out into the
darkness, hoping you'd emerge and that the life
I've longed for would begin to take shape. And
maybe you're reading this and thinking the same
thing.

You've willed yourself into staying because the thought of starting over puts a strain on your mind. Your heart is stuck between loving the wrong person and loving yourself enough to leave that person behind.

I think deeply of the heart that has been betrayed,
partly because I've known betrayal just as long
as I've known my own name. The lies began
at age three, my parents pretending to love one
another, and maybe this is why I've chosen to be
in relationships with those who have pretended
to love me. I think about you, the person who has
wounds similar to mine. I find that writing about
you allows me to work through my shit, those
troubling times. I recall and reclaim by urging
you to do the same and to forgive somehow those
who will never say sorry or accept any blame.
I think deeply of what you've been through,
people who love to use you then give you hell
for wanting to leave, as if you should settle for
someone who refuses to choose you.

———————————

cold air whispering

into hues of faded brown

dark greens nearly black

and lakes so close to frozen

the sun seems weak

you speak in a whisper

afraid that you'll hear yourself

because if you did

you'd finally know the truth

the summer keeps the lie alive

the heat distracts you so well

but the stillness of winter

forces you to remember

how many lies

too many lies

look what we tell ourselves

the shit is hopeless

we know this

and yet we choose hell

we make excuses

we create reason

there's no logic

to this shit

we see fire

we don't run

we endure

and decide to sit

how many lies

so many lies

we've chosen

to betray ourselves

staring into the eyes

of those who hurt us

expecting them to help

_____

winter came, and the days

mirrored the walls of your heart

months removed from summer

a few days after the fall

thinking back to when you fell

and in moments, you lost it all

_____

you may look upon a storm

and be threatened by its powerful winds

and its lack of concern for those

searching for the sun

you may look toward the sky

and feel indifference toward its rage

struck with fear by its desire for chaos

but you can also look inward

for the strength to overcome

to stand still and firm

refusing to be moved

by all things that provoke fear

and a feeling of uncertainty

this stormy season will pass

it's never fair

the way life drifts to an end

without compassion

without warning

and so we fight for tomorrow

forcefully pushing forward

out of breath as we attempt

to outrun death

I think the heart hears what it wants, lost in translation. Afraid of the truth because it hurts, accepting whatever lies it can tolerate. You've done this so often that it feels customary to settle. You then tell yourself that it's easier said than done—the act of leaving is too difficult—but you fail to realize that the most challenging part is not leaving. The hardest thing you're facing is the action of staying with someone who will keep you from finding the one who will love you without filling your heart with pain. And I'm writing this with the hope that you'll move on with your life.

relationships are gardens

be with someone

who will do anything

to extend the life of a rose

---

hell happens

so that heaven

can be realized

_____

look into the mirror

lead yourself back to you

back to home

———————

some of us have to suffer

in an attempt to grow

———————————

i buried the empty promises

with the rest of our past

so that flowers could grow

into gardens that last

if you're tired of the hurt, leave

if where you are is absent of peace

take all your things and leave behind

anything that was never yours

do not stay where your heart

is refused the chance to grow

do not lie in a bed that is placed

in a space that never feels like home

_____

you know it's over

when you look toward

the person you love

and see many things

you want to leave behind

_____

it's not that you don't love them anymore

it's more of a realization that staying

will never satisfy this need for love

that lives within your heart

————

the roads

leading to your ex

are dead ends

old roads won't point you

in the direction of places

worth visiting

I knew we'd eventually burn out, like a candle
lit for way too long, plenty of nights of waiting
up when neither one of us came home. Thinking
back to those times, I heard you whispering
on the phone. Telling me the love was real, but
oftentimes I felt alone.

(to be continued . . .)

_____

too much of the heart

given to someone

who does too little

and never enough

_____

sometimes the heart breaks

in an attempt to drain itself

of the person who broke it

_____

I'm tired of being the person they fall in love with
until they find someone "better."

—————————————

you were never listening

i could have yelled

maybe screaming would suffice

but i chose to say nothing

because that's what you gave me

_____

you were absent

always somewhere else

silent in my life

distracting me from love

and i was loyal to a fault

a daily devotion toward heartache

———————

quiet people

say things to themselves

that others don't deserve to hear

————————————

stop prioritizing people

who put you in second place

---

all that matters now

is that you be good enough

for yourself

———————

bring your fire

there are things

to be burned

———————————

trust the timing of a lie

a denied truth is a message

a sign that it is time

to move forward, to let go

you didn't know

you could swim

until you felt as if

you were drowning

the unnerving silence

helped you find your voice

the wounds won't heal

if you pretend they're not there

don't let your past

interrupt your destiny

---

maybe in order to grow

you need to be rooted somewhere else

your ex has

nothing new

to show you

_____

my past is a version of hell

that houses all the people

who did not deserve

to be a part of my future

You don't have to explain why you said no.

So many people apologize without accepting the wrong they've done. Those apologies are almost always from a place of guilt, a way to make themselves feel better without actually having to do better.

———————————

pick a road that doesn't lead you back

to where you've struggled to leave behind

_____

being with you felt like a battle

and i was tired of going to war

when all i wanted was peace

—————————————

One day, I'll find the right words and the right person to say them to.

---

someone who genuinely loves you

is a wool coat for the coldest days of winter

_____

so often you believe

you've fallen behind

comparing yourself with others

without realizing

that maybe your journey

is just different

and maybe your path

is uniquely yours

leading to a destination

tailor made just for you

_____

the scars are poems

they tell an epic story

of pain and how you overcame it

_____

you're single because

you're a better companion

to yourself

———————

being single

is the perfect place

to be found

by the right person

being single

is the beginning

not the end

———————————————

change is made impossible

by those who cling to the past

———————————————

the fear of starting over

is never worse

than continuing to remain

in an unhealthy relationship

The people who choose time with you over time
spent on social media are so fucking important.

Choose to walk away from anyone who makes
you compete with others in order to be chosen.

—————————————

When your desire for peace of mind is stronger
than the feelings you have for a person, moving
on from a toxic relationship is easier to do.

As much as I wanted to get angry, that part of me
no longer existed, killed off by constant doubt,
neglect, and humiliation. We'd been here before,
and so none of this was new. And the eventual
end was everything I expected. After some
time of getting hurt, and after the many second
chances given to you, you see someone who
never deserved it. I became numb to the bullshit,
and with each transgression, my resolve to move
on grew stronger. Trust me, letting go wasn't the
easiest thing, but I knew staying with you would
only make life more difficult.

You deserve love and compassion that exists all year round. And I know you're tired of feeling like you have to provide an incentive for people to be kind to you. It's exhausting to know what you deserve and not being able to find it.

This life has given you scars; the people in it have broken your heart. And, despite this feeling of pain living within you, you're reading this now, and that just means you've found a way to survive. I'm proud of you. I may not know you, but I know your pain.

I hope something beautiful finds you, even if that means finding more of yourself.

I sit here at year-end, with hours left before sunset, overtaken by regret, overthinking myself into hell-like scenarios. A song of what-ifs playing in the background of my mind while remembering the pain of what happened. It isn't raining; well, it is somewhere you can't see. There's a storm growing within the depths of my heart, flooding my soul, spilling out of my eyes. It hurts, but I'll tell no one, because I've yet to meet a person who knows what to do with my vulnerability. But this isn't me missing you; this is me mourning myself. This is the song I'm singing to the person staring back at me from a broken mirror—the one who damned themselves by trying to love you.

I think there was always a part of you that hated me, no matter how many times you claimed to love me. Your actions didn't always match your words. Those inconsistencies drove me mad, and the insane part was that I believed that staying longer would somehow encourage some behavior change. But how can someone be better without being held accountable?

How much time are you willing to lose? Moments
spent on people who drain you of whatever peace
you have left. The energy that gets invested
in things that distract you from cultivating
happiness. You know that detaching from those
who hurt you would promote some growth, but
you struggle with leaving because you don't
want to be a bad person but imagine trying to
be good to people who mistreat you. Imagine
the type of life you'd have continually making
space for people who shouldn't be allowed to
hurt you. Those friendships and relationships
that fail can be built into the foundation beneath
your feet. You can turn those moments of pain
and disappointment into stepping-stones toward
something beautiful. Consider this a sign, maybe
a warning. This idea of staying where you're
unhappy has to end if you ever truly want a
chance at peace.

There's a harshness in the air; the season is
changing its colors. The rain is chilled, icy to
the touch, and the sky filled with melancholy.
Your search for warmth has brought you here;
you starve for something profound. You require
something that will resonate with your soul.
Despite how cold, you're determined to grow.
And with these words, you bloom, a winter rose.

_____

i just sat there, nothing more to say

the silence eating me up from within

i thought nothing of your apology

i lost everything because of you

and so when i find the courage

to flourish without you

there will be nothing left

for you to return to

absolutely nothing left

in the wake of this betrayal

for i will have discovered the peace

in letting go of a lover who tainted

my belief in love

there are prisons

made to look like love

made to resemble home

designed to fool you

into believing in a lie

i've seen angels love demons

dark flames disguised as warmth

soles of feet burning

while trying to escape hell

i've seen summer fall into a pit of winter

then spring back to life like flowers

beneath a July sun

and i want to see you survive this

There are all types of love in this world, and I hope you find the one that lasts.

Changing is a part of survival. You had to transform into everything you thought impossible so that you could outlast the struggles of loving the wrong person.

What is meant for you will find its way to your heart's door. And when it arrives, you'll be ready, because the heartbreak is just preparation for something better.

The silence that follows the pain you feel is the heart's way of saying goodbye without words. And even though it didn't feel like it at the time, you were preparing to leave, to move forward without even realizing it. You took all you had left, and along the way, you found out that it was everything you needed to set yourself free, and that's what I admire about you. The ground beneath your feet can begin crumbling into dust, and at that moment, you figure out how to fly.

Sometimes we find ourselves rooted in the wrong spaces. We long for nourishment, hoping to be cared for in a way that helps us grow. Those seeds of hope are often planted in the wrong places. It's like we've been planting gardens in graves this entire time, but the beautiful thing about this realization is that we discover that, despite the cold and the winter-like feeling that can plague the soul, there is still an opportunity to grow.

---

come winter, despite the cold

from the root of heartache

roses will still find a way to grow

r.h. Sin index

after fall, i sit with winter   136

all that matters now   190

As much as I wanted to get angry, that part of
    me no longer existed, killed off by constant
    doubt, neglect, and humiliation.   214

Being good to someone who is afraid to be happy is a
    terrible hell for a heart that deserves heaven.   137

being single   208

being with you felt like a battle   202

bring your fire   191

change is made impossible   209

Changing is a part of survival.   224

Choose to walk away from anyone who makes you
    compete with others in order to be chosen.   212

cold air whispering   165

come winter, despite the cold   228

don't let your past   195

Fumbling around in the dark with my innocence,
    searching for a place to put it.   128

hell happens   173

How lonely you must feel to love the way you do,
    to fall into hands that will hurt you.   116

how many lies   166

How much time are you willing to lose?   218

I always found it strange that you decided to try and
    punish me for every little thing but somehow felt the
    need to reward all the people who repeatedly made
    you feel like shit and never apologized for it.   133

I believe that people spend more time
    saying instead of doing.   149

i buried the empty promises   176

I feel like I'm screaming behind a steel wall,
    100 miles in the depth of darkness.   130

I felt sadness and hid behind a smile.   131

I figured you'd come back, singing that
    old song of regret.   123

if you're tired of the hurt, leave   177

I have endured the most uninteresting parts
    of you for far too long.   141

i just sat there, nothing more to say   220

I knew we'd eventually burn out, like a candle lit
    for way too long, plenty of nights of waiting up
    when neither one of us came home.   182

I live with your ghosts, the ones you write about when
    you pour out the pain that lives within you.   129

I'm tired of being the person they fall in love with
    until they find someone "better."   185

i'm tired of being treated like an airport   140

In this life, you will discover with time that a cheater
    is just a stepping-stone to a greater understanding
    of what you want from future relationships.   139

I promised myself that if I were given a real chance at
    genuine love, I'd be prepared to love you back in ways
    that would calm the doubt that has lived in your head
    ever since the ending of your last relationship.   162

I remember it like it was yesterday.   120

I saw more stars that night; it was as if the
    night sky decided to show me more of its
    secrets the moment you left.   122

I sit here at year-end, with hours left before
    sunset, overtaken by regret, overthinking
    myself into hell-like scenarios.   216

I stopped wanting you the way I had; you
    lose interest in the things and or people
    you no longer feel you need.   124

It feels like returning home, that split-second
    decision to move on.   147

I think deeply of the heart that has been betrayed,
    partly because I've known betrayal just as
    long as I've known my own name.   164

I think she has the power to divide the ocean;
  her existence calls into question whether
  mythical creatures can inhabit the earth or
  whether angels can live among us.   148

I think the heart hears what it wants,
  lost in translation.   171

I think there was always a part of you that hated me, no
  matter how many times you claimed to love me.   217

I think they tear you down to hold you back.   132

it's never fair   170

it's not that you don't love them anymore   179

it wasn't beautiful   127

I've learned to pay attention to the actions
  of those around me.   138

i've seen angels love demons   222

I wish I had your confidence, the way you
  exaggerated your importance in my life to the
  point of believing that I'd be lost without you,
  and I am grateful for your absence, because
  you helped prove yourself wrong.   155

look into the mirror   174

maybe in order to grow   196

my past is a version of hell   198

Never forget the way it felt when he left you to
  fuck someone else, and never let him return
  when he pretends to miss you.   159

Nostalgia is a pretty lie, the past filtered in
  all the pretty colors you like.   125

old roads won't point you   181

One day, I'll find the right words and the
  right person to say them to.   203

pick a road that doesn't lead you back   201

Please write a "Dear Future" letter to yourself, and tell
  her to say no to exes who want another chance.   160

quiet people   188

relationships are gardens   172

So I'm writing this, and when I finish, I look
  over to the winter sky to see little chunks
  of cold drifting toward the city.   142

So many people apologize without accepting
    the wrong they've done.   200

Some endings are beautiful, the way the
    foundation crumbles beneath fearful feet,
    a heart afraid of leaving.   115

some of us have to suffer   175

someone who genuinely loves you   204

Some people teach you how and what to
    fully love, while others teach you what to
    avoid and how to walk away.   135

Sometimes goodbye is the only response.   146

sometimes the heart breaks   184

Sometimes the sorrow is sweet, the way it arrives
    at the end of something stale and sour.   121

Sometimes we find ourselves rooted
    in the wrong spaces.   227

so often you believe   205

stop prioritizing people   189

The darkness isn't all that bad.   117

The days are longer when spent with
    the wrong person.   156

the fear of starting over   210

The people who choose time with you over time spent
    on social media are so fucking important.   211

The problem with love is that it's initially taught to us by
    people who do not know the correct definition.   161

There are all types of love in this world, and I
    hope you find the one that lasts.   223

there are prisons   221

There's a harshness in the air; the season
    is changing its colors.   219

there's a song that lives   145

the roads   180

the scars are poems   206

The silence that follows the pain you feel is the heart's
    way of saying goodbye without words.   226

the wounds won't heal   194

too much of the heart   183

Toxic people will start fires in your heart,
    then complain about the temperature of
    the heat in your reaction.   126

trust the timing of a lie   192

We need cheaters.   134

What I love most about a breakup is that you
    no longer have to wait on the person who
    chose to waste your time.   157

What is meant for you will find its way
    to your heart's door.   225

When your desire for peace of mind is stronger than
    the feelings you have for a person, moving on
    from a toxic relationship is easier to do.   213

When you're done getting angry, you're
    closer to letting go.   118

Where does it all go when lost?   114

where warmth once resided   144

winter came, and the days   168

You deserve love and compassion that
    exists all year round.   215

you didn't know   193

You don't have to explain why you said no.   199

You find ways to outrun your demons, no matter
    how dark and painful it gets.   158

you know it's over   178

you may look upon a storm   169

you're single because   207

your ex has   197

You told me I'd never find someone like you, and I
    smiled, because that was my wish all along.   154

You've willed yourself into staying because the thought
    of starting over puts a strain on your mind.   163

you were absent   187

you were never listening   186

Andrews McMeel Publishing
a division of Andrews McMeel Universal
1130 Walnut Street, Kansas City, Missouri 64106

www.andrewsmcmeel.com

21 22 23 24 25 RR2 10 9 8 7 6 5 4 3 2 1

ISBN: 978-1-5248-6789-8

Library of Congress Control Number: 2021940984

Editor: Patty Rice
Art Director/Designer: Diane Marsh
Production Editor: Elizabeth A. Garcia
Production Manager: Cliff Koehler

Cover illustration by Hannah Olson

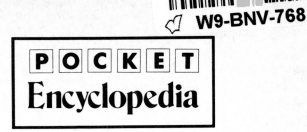

POCKET
Encyclopedia

Adrienne Jack

RANDOM HOUSE   NEW YORK

First American edition 1989

Copyright © 1989 by Grisewood &
Dempsey Ltd. All rights reserved under
International and Pan-American
Copyright Conventions. Published in
the United States by Random House.
Inc., New York, and simultaneously in
Canada by Random House of Canada
Limited, Toronto. This edition first
published in Great Britain by Kingfisher
Books Ltd., a Grisewood & Dempsey
Company, in 1983; revised 1987;
copyright ©, 1983, 1987 by Kingfisher
Books Ltd.

*Library of Congress Cataloging in
Publication Data:*
Jack, Adrienne.
    Pocket encyclopedia.
    Includes index.
    Summary: An illustrated encyclopedia
with over 600 entries on topics
including the universe, countries of the
world, plants and animals, and science
technology. 1. Children's encyclopedias
and dictionaries. [1. Encyclopedias and
dictionaries.] I.Title. AG5.J23 1988 031
88-4462
ISBN: 0.394-89993-8
Manufactured in Spain
1 2 3 4 5 6 7 8 9 0

Introduction

This pocket encyclopedia contains over 600 separate entries. They are arranged in alphabetical order. The information they contain is both interesting and useful.

The encyclopedia can be used in lots of ways. You can look up information on a particular subject for a special project, or you can use it to answer questions that you have been puzzling over, or you can enjoy just browsing through this encyclopedia, stopping when a picture or entry catches your eye.

This is how to look things up:

1. The entries are arranged in *alphabetical order*. Flick through the book until you come to the correct letter for the entry you want to look up. To make this easier, each letter of the alphabet has a thumbprint, which is repeated on the side of each page.

2. Use the *cross-reference*. "See also" followed by a word or words in capital letters appear at the end of many articles. These words are separate alphabetical entries that will give you more information about your subject.

3. Use the *index*. Sometimes the subject you are looking for may not have a main entry. Look up your subject in the index at the end of the book. The information you need may be contained in an entry with a different title. For instance, information on the Amazon River appears in the articles on Brazil and South America.

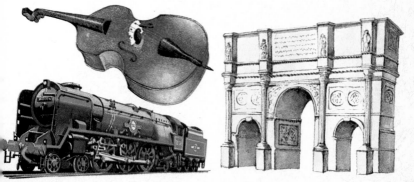

AARDVARK
The aardvark of Africa is a curious animal. It has no close relatives, although its way of life is like that of the anteater. Aardvarks have strong claws which they use to break open termites' nests.

ABORIGINE
Aborigines are the native people of Australia. They came to Australia thousands of years ago from southeastern Asia. Aborigines are hunters and food-gatherers. The men hunt emus, kangaroos, and game with boomerangs and throwing spears. The women gather nuts, berries, roots, and fruits.

But this semi-nomadic way of life has changed for many aborigines. Today many live and

◀ **Different kinds of** African animals gather to drink at a water hole.

work in the cities or on large farms.

ACID
Acids are sour-tasting chemicals. The sour taste of a lemon is caused by *citric* acid. Sour milk contains *lactic* acid. Vinegar contains *acetic* acid. These are weak acids and are harmless. Strong acids, such as *sulfuric* acid, *nitric* acid, and *hydrochloric* acid, are poisonous.

AFRICA
Africa is the world's second largest continent. Most of the land is a great plateau or table-land, surrounded by a narrow coastal plain. In the east are volcanic mountains such as Mount Kilimanjaro (19,340 feet high) and Mount Kenya (17,060 feet high).

Some of the longest rivers in the world flow through Africa. They include the Nile (4,145

5

miles), the Zaire, once called the Congo (2,720 miles), and the Niger (2,585 miles).

The equator falls near the middle of Africa. The climate near the equator is hot and wet.

AFRICA

Great rain forests grow here. On either side of the equator there are vast savannas. These grasslands are dry for most of the year. Traveling away from the savannas you will find areas of scrub, then semi-desert, and finally desert. The Sahara is in the north and the Kalahari is in the south.

A great variety of wild animals lives on the high plains of Africa. In game reserves, visitors can see antelopes, elephants, zebras, giraffes, lions, and many others.

Much of Africa is thinly populated. In the north the people are mainly Arabs or Berbers. They follow the Muslim religion. South of the Sahara most of the people are black Africans.

Most Africans are farmers, growing crops of corn, yams, sweet potatoes, beans, and fruit to feed themselves. Cocoa, coffee, oil palm, tea, tobacco, cotton, and sugar are grown to sell to countries all over the world. The continent is rich in minerals.

See also COUNTRIES OF THE WORLD; EGYPT; NIGERIA; SOUTH AFRICA.

AIDS
AIDS stands for *acquired immune deficiency syndrome*, a deadly disease caused by a virus. The virus itself is called the *human immunodeficiency virus*, or HIV-1 for short. The disease cripples the body's immune system, leaving the victim with no defense at all against infection. AIDS spread from developing countries and rapidly through the Western world in the early 1980s. It is spread chiefly through sexual contact and exchanges of blood. A cure is still not in sight.

AIR
Air is the substance that fills the "empty" space around us. Air is a mixture of gases. Its main gases are nitrogen and oxygen. Oxygen is the gas animals must breathe to live. Air is invisible and has no taste. But when air moves we can feel it as wind. Water vapor, an invisible substance, is also present in air.

A layer of air, the atmosphere, surrounds the earth. The air in the atmosphere presses down upon us. This is called atmospheric pressure.

See also GAS.

AIR-CUSHION VEHICLE
These vehicles ride on a cushion of air not more than a few feet

▼ **The hovercraft** was invented in 1955 by Christopher Cockerell.

7

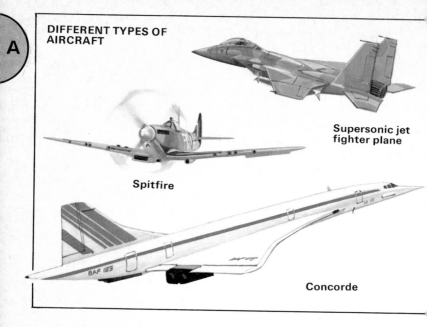

DIFFERENT TYPES OF AIRCRAFT

Supersonic jet fighter plane

Spitfire

BAF 123

Concorde

thick. They move best over water, but can travel over beaches and flat land. Because they do not have to push against water as ships do, they can manage greater speeds, and easily reach 75 miles per hour. Their advantage over planes is that they can carry large loads — dozens of cars and up to 400 passengers at a time. The hovercraft, an air-cushion vehicle, was invented in 1955 by British engineer Christopher Cockerell. Today, fleets of hovercrafts provide a smooth, speedy shuttle service across the English Channel.

AIRCRAFT

Two American brothers built and flew the first airplane in 1903. They were Wilbur and Orville Wright from Dayton, Ohio. Their first flimsy flying

Boeing 747 passenger airplane

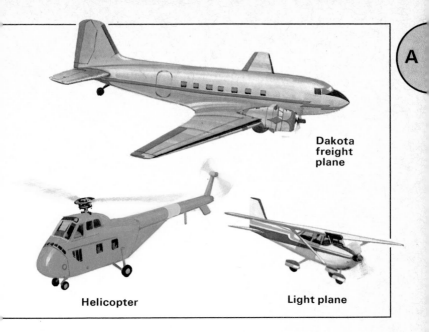

Dakota
freight
plane

Helicopter

Light plane

machine was made of wood, cloth, and wire. It could fly only a few yards at a time and could not travel much faster than a bicycle.

Modern planes are very different from the Wright Brothers' flying machine. They are sleek and streamlined and made of aluminum. With their powerful jet engines they can travel at fantastic speeds.

There are many different types of planes. Whatever they are like, all planes have certain things in common. They all have wings that enable them to fly. A wing has a special shape, called an *airfoil*. Its front edge is rounded but it tapers to a point at the rear. All planes have a *tail*. The tail helps to keep the plane traveling along a straight flight path.

To guide a plane through the air, a pilot moves hinged panels, called control surfaces, at the rear of the wings and the tail. Moving these surfaces makes the plane's nose go up or down or to left or right. Many planes are flown with the help of electronics.

Planes are thrust through the air either by a stream, or jet, of gases or by propellers. In a jet engine fuel is burned to make hot gases. As these gases shoot backward, they cause the plane to shoot forward. Propellers have a twisted, curved shape and "screw" themselves through the air when they spin.

See also BLERIOT; JET ENGINE; LINDBERGH; WRIGHT.

ALABAMA

Alabama is a southern state bordering the Gulf of Mexico. Cotton was once the source of Alabama's wealth, but today it is a major industrial state because of its rich resources of iron ore and coal. The capital is Montgomery; Mobile is a busy seaport. Cotton is still produced, along with soybeans, corn, and peanuts.

See also page 263.

ALASKA

About a third of the state of Alaska lies north of the Arctic Circle. This makes it the most northerly state in the United States. Its capital is Juneau. Until recently, lumbering and fishing were Alaska's chief industries. In 1969, huge deposits of oil were discovered, and today oil is the state's largest industry.

See also page 263.

ALEXANDER THE GREAT
(356–323 B.C.)

Alexander was king of Macedonia in Greece and a mighty conqueror. His great dream was to conquer the whole world. He subdued his Greek neighbors in 336 B.C. By 327 B.C. he had conquered the huge Persian Empire to the east. He then led his men into India, but they were exhausted and he turned back. When he reached Babylon he died of a fever. He was buried in Alexandria, the great Egyptian city he had founded.

10

THREE TYPES OF ALGAE

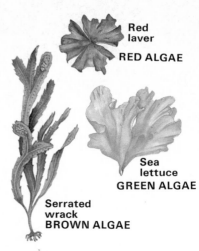

Red laver
RED ALGAE

Sea lettuce
GREEN ALGAE

Serrated wrack
BROWN ALGAE

ALGAE

Algae are the simplest plants. Seaweeds are common algae. Another is the green slime that covers the sides of an aquarium. Algae live where there is moisture.

Like all plants, algae use the energy in sunlight to make their food. In turn, they are food for many water animals, including shellfish and even whales.

There are four kinds of algae. Green algae live near the surface of the water. Lower down live blue-green, brown, and red algae.

See also PLANT; SEAWEED.

ALLOY

When one metal is mixed with another, the result is an alloy. If copper and zinc are mixed, they form the alloy brass. Copper and tin make the alloy bronze. The most common alloy is steel, which is a mixture of iron and carbon, and often other substances. We use most metals in the form of alloys. They are usually stronger and harder than pure metals.

ALPHABET
An alphabet is a group of letters or signs that stand for sounds. It is used to write a language.

The English alphabet comes from the Roman alphabet. It has twenty-six letters. Many other languages use the same letters but pronounce them differently. The letters of the Greek alphabet are used as signs by scientists. The first two Greek letters, *alpha* (A) and *beta* (B), give us our word "alphabet."

▲ **From top to bottom:** letters from our alphabet; the Russian, the Japanese phonetic, the Greek and Arabic alphabets.

ALUMINUM
Aluminum is our most important metal, after iron. It is light, does not rust, and can be made into strong alloys, so is used in the building of aircraft and ships. It conducts heat well and it is often used to make pots and pans. It is also made into thin sheets for bottle tops and aluminum foil.

See also ALLOY; METAL.

▼ **An open-pit bauxite** mine. Bauxite is an ore from which aluminum is extracted.

ALZHEIMER'S DISEASE
Alzheimer's disease mostly affects older people. People who have the disease begin to suffer severe loss of memory, and this gets worse over the years. It is known that Alzheimer's disease results from abnormalities in the brain, but the cause remains a mystery.

AMERICAN HISTORY
Spain was the first European country to establish a colony in North America (1565), but after 1600 most of the Atlantic coast came under the control of Britain. English settlers came to colonies from New England to

11

▲ **British "redcoats"** fire on the colonial militia at the Battle of Lexington in 1775.

Georgia, an area that was to become the original 13 states. By 1763, after the French and Indian Wars, Britain had won the former French territories in northern and central North America.

Though loyal to the British king, the American colonists began to resent British rule. Without their consent, Britain decided to keep a standing army in America. Unfair taxes and the refusal to allow the colonies to be represented in the British parliament worsened relations. In 1775 the Revolutionary War broke out, and in 1776 the colonies declared their independence from Britain. They finally achieved it in 1781, and in 1787 drew up a constitution that is still the basis of American government today.

George Washington became the first U.S. president in 1789.

The new nation rapidly expanded westward after the Louisiana

George Washington

Territory was purchased from France in 1803. Conflict with Britain once again resulted in war, this time in the War of 1812. Conflict within the nation over slavery and states' rights built up and finally exploded in the Civil War (1861–65). The period of prosperity that followed the war saw the building of railroads right across the continent and the rapid development of the West. When Europe went to war in 1914 the United States at first did not become involved, but was drawn into the war in 1917, joining forces with Britain and France against Germany. The pattern was repeated during World War II, when the United States joined the Allies in their fight against Hitler's Germany, Italy, and Japan. Since then, the United States has been involved in the Korean War and the Vietnam War. Today there is an uneasy balance of power between the United States (and its allies) and the Eastern bloc, headed by the Soviet Union.

AMPHIBIAN
Amphibians are cold-blooded animals such as frogs, toads, newts, and salamanders. They were the first prehistoric animals to adapt to life on dry land and they still spend part of their lives in water and part on dry land.

All amphibians have backbones and nearly all lay their eggs in water. The young breathe through gills. Later most develop

AMPHIBIANS

A

Edible frog

Smooth newt

Fire salamander

lungs and can leave the water. Amphibians drink by absorbing water through their skin, so they must keep themselves moist.

See also FROG AND TOAD.

ANGLO-SAXON
Anglo-Saxons — the Angles, Saxons, and Jutes — were people from Germany who invaded and settled in Britain in the A.D. 400s and 500s. They drove the original Celtic people into Wales and Cornwall. The Anglo-Saxons ruled in Britain until the Norman Conquest in 1066.

ANIMAL

There are two great groups of living things on earth — animals and plants.

Unlike most plants, most animals can move about. Many have senses with a nervous system and a brain. Senses help their owner to find food and escape enemies. Animals use the oxygen they breathe to burn food, which gives them the energy they need. All animal life developed, or evolved, from simple plantlike creatures. The lowest animals, such as the ameba, consist of one cell. Higher animals are made up of many cells joined together.

The animal kingdom is divided into two groups. The larger is the *invertebrate* group. It includes insects, worms, crabs, spiders, snails, and starfish.

Animals with backbones are called *vertebrates*. The lowest vertebrates are fishes. Then come amphibians, reptiles, birds, and mammals. Most mammals give birth to live young. Almost all others lay eggs.

All animals behave in certain ways at certain times. This automatic behavior, such as nest-building, migrating, or attacking prey, is called *instinct*. Invertebrates almost always act instinctively. Vertebrates have more complex brains and so they can also learn. Most animals can send each other simple signals through sounds or gestures.

See also BRAIN; CAMOUFLAGE; CELL; EVOLUTION; MIGRATION; PARASITE; REPRODUCTION; SENSES.

Use the Index to find the different animals and animal groups.

ANT

Ants are called social insects because they live in large colonies. There may be as many as a million ants in one nest.

There are three kinds of ant in a colony — a queen, workers, and males. The queen mates with a winged male and spends her whole life laying eggs. The female workers cannot lay eggs. They look after the nest, collect food, and care for the young. The

INVERTEBRATES

Sea cucumber
(echinoderm)

Butterfly (insect)

14

VERTEBRATES

Eel (fish)

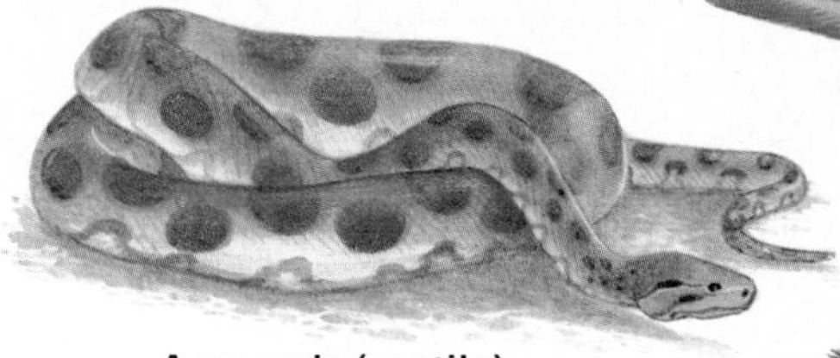

Anaconda (reptile)

Chimpanzee (mammal)

Seal (mammal)

Rhinoceros (mammal)

Flamingo (bird)

A

15

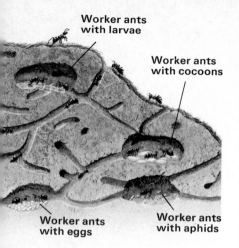

Worker ants with larvae

Worker ants with cocoons

Worker ants with eggs

Worker ants with aphids

▲ **A section** through a wood ants' nest, showing different chambers.

males do not work beyond mating with the queen.

There are ants in all parts of the world but the coldest. Some have unusual habits. The umbrella ants chew up leaves and use them for growing food. Legionary or army ants march in vast columns and eat any living thing in their path.

ANTARCTICA

The Antarctic continent is covered with a sheet of ice thousands of feet thick. Its long coastline is a wall of capes and cliffs. There are mountains and volcanoes. The South Pole is near the center of a high, windswept plain.

The Antarctic is colder than the Arctic. Even in summer, the temperature rarely rises above freezing point. Algae, mosses, and lichens are the only plants.

There are no land animals, apart from some tiny insects. But the sea is rich in plankton, fish, seals, and whales, and there are penguins and other birds.

ANTELOPE

The graceful antelopes are related to cattle. They run swiftly on two-hoofed toes and, like cows, chew the cud. Unlike deer, antelopes never shed their horns.

There are antelopes in Africa and Asia. Most live in herds on grassy plains. But some kinds prefer forests or marshes.

APE

Apes are the animals most like human beings. They have the same number of teeth and the same kind of skeleton. They also have the same kind of blood and catch many similar diseases.

After human beings, apes are

▲ **The only people** in Antarctica are scientists. This man is measuring the movement of a glacier.

the most intelligent of all animals. Even so, an ape's brain is only half the size of a human's. Young apes are playful and are easily tamed. Apes use their hands and feet skillfully and can solve simple problems.

Unlike monkeys, apes have no tails. Sometimes they stand erect, but usually they move about on all fours, walking on the knuckles of their hands. Apes include the gorilla, chimpanzee, gibbon, and orangutan.

ARCHAEOLOGY

Archaeology is the study of how people lived long ago through the clues they left behind — their buildings, weapons, ornaments, coins, bones, and tools.

Archaeologists excavate, or dig out, buried finds. The deeper they dig, the older the objects they find. From human bones, broken pots, kitchen trash, and other remains they can learn how the people lived, what foods they ate, and what skills they had developed. As a site is excavated, each fragile find is carefully cleaned and labeled.

Archaeologists tell the age of an object in several ways. They study the soil and other remains found near it. They can date a find by measuring the amount of natural radioactivity left in certain objects — the carbon-14 method — or by counting the

17

▲ **Archaeologists** mark out the site with a grid to make an accurate plan. Then they carefully remove soil or rubble to uncover the historic remains beneath.

number of tree rings, called dendrochronology.

Archaeologists are not only interested in ancient civilizations and buried sites. Industrial archaeology is the study of old factories and machinery.

ARCHERY

The use of bows and arrows is called archery. Prehistoric people used bows for hunting and in battle. In the Middle Ages, English archers were famous for their skill with the longbow, which had a longer range than the more complicated crossbow. Bows and arrows became out of date when guns were invented. Today archery is a sport.

ARCHIMEDES (287–212 B.C.)

Archimedes, a Greek mathematician and philosopher, lived in Sicily. He discovered that if an object is weighed first in air and then in liquid it will lose weight equal to the weight of liquid it displaces.

ARCHITECTURE

Architecture is the art and science of designing buildings. The architect draws the plans that the builders follow. Many differ-

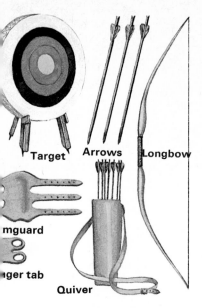

Target   Arrows   Longbow

mguard

ger tab

Quiver

ARCHERY EQUIPMENT

ent styles of architecture have been used through the ages. Architecture tells the story of how civilizations grow.

The Greeks tried to be perfect in everything they did. Their system of building was quite simple. Rows of tall marble columns supported heavy stone beams, on which the roof was placed.

Greek architecture was later copied by the Romans. But the Roman architects added two important developments: the arch and the vault, a roof supported by arches. The arch was a good way of spanning a wide distance quickly. Small stones and cement could be used instead of heavy marble beams.

In Europe during the Middle Ages stone was the natural building material for building strong castles and long-lasting cathedrals. At first architects followed Roman styles. This is called *Romanesque* architecture. But from around 1150 they began building tall, slender churches and cathedrals. Pointed arches were used instead of round ones. This is called the *Gothic* style.

During the Renaissance architects returned to the Greek and Roman styles. They liked the simple and regular "classical" designs. But gradually more decoration was added until, by the 1600s, the *Baroque* style was

A

PERIODS OF ARCHITECTURE

B.C.	
3200s	Ancient Egyptian begins
600s	Classical Greek begins
100s	Classical Roman begins
A.D.	
400s	Byzantine period begins
950s	Romanesque period in Northern Europe
1000s	Norman period begins in England
1150s	Gothic period begins in France
1400s	Renaissance period begins in Italy
1600s	Baroque period begins in Italy
1720s	Georgian style begins in England
1750s	Rococo style begins in Italy
1890s	Art Nouveau in Europe
1920s	Modern architecture begins with Functionalism and the International Style

fashionable. It was very ornate. Even straight stone columns were twisted into spiral shapes.

An important development in the 1900s was the introduction of steel and reinforced concrete. These materials allowed architects to build more quickly and much higher than before. The first very tall buildings, called "skyscrapers," were built in the United States. Now they are built all over the world.

Today's architects use simple shapes. The architect tries to design a new building so that it will fit in well with other buildings near it.

See also CASTLE; CHURCH; EGYPT, ANCIENT; GREECE, ANCIENT; ROME, ANCIENT.

ARCTIC

The Arctic is the cold frozen zone around the North Pole. Most of it is frozen sea surrounded by land. At the North Pole the sun never rises in winter. In summer the sun never sets.

During the short Arctic summer, grass, flowers, and moss grow on the tundra plains. Arctic animals include seals, walruses, whales, polar bears, foxes, owls, weasels, musk oxen, and reindeer. The only people native to the Arctic are Eskimos. Arctic minerals include coal and oil.

ARGENTINA

Argentina is the second largest country in South America. It is a land of farms and ranches. From them come many different products. Rice, sugar cane, and other tropical crops are grown in the north. Cattle and grain come from the central plains, or *pampas*. Grapes and fruit are farmed

Argentina was ruled by Spain from 1516 to 1810. In 1966, military leaders took control of the government. In 1982, Argentina and Britain fought a war over the ownership of the Falkland Islands.

See also page 79.

ARISTOTLE (384–322 B.C.)

Aristotle was a Greek philosopher who invented the method of thinking called *logic*. A student of Plato, Aristotle became tutor to Alexander the Great. His writings cover many subjects, including politics and nature.

ARIZONA

One of the southwestern states, Arizona attracts many tourists

▼ **Hoover Dam,** on the Arizona border, is one of the highest in the world.

ARCHITECTURE THROUGH THE AGES

Greek Doric: Temple of Neptune, Greece

Roman: Arch of Constantine, Rome, Italy

Byzantine: Santa Sophia, Istanbul, Turkey

Renaissance: Florence Cathedral, Italy

Gothic: Bourges Cathedral, France

Modern:
◀ Empire State Building, New York City (1930s)
Sydney Opera House, Sydney, Australia (1960s) ▶

21

who come to see the Grand Canyon and other natural wonders in the state's varied landscape. Arizona is an agricultural state, but manufacturing industries are expanding. Once Spanish territory, Arizona was taken over by the United States after the Mexican War in 1848.

See also page 263.

ARKANSAS
The territory that became the state of Arkansas was part of the Louisiana Purchase of 1803. It lies along the Mississippi River in the south-central United States. Arkansas produces most of the nation's bauxite, the ore from which aluminum is made. There are also important oil and natural gas wells. Little Rock, the capital and largest city, is an industrial and commercial center.

See also page 263.

ARMADILLO
This South American mammal looks like a small pig, but it is armored like a tank. It is a timid animal and rolls itself into a ball when frightened. Armadillos eat worms, insects, and roots. They dig burrows with their strong claws.

ARMOR
Before gunpowder was invented, soldiers fought in hand-to-hand combat. To protect their bodies, they wore armor. Leather made good, light armor and could be made stronger by adding plates of bronze or iron. The Greeks and Romans wore helmets, leg armor, and breastplates.

Later armorers learned to link together tiny iron rings to produce coats of mail. Mail gave good protection against swords and spears, but steel plate was even stronger. Plate armor covered the whole of a man's body. But even steel armor was no defense against the cannon. By the 1600s soldiers needed to move more quickly, so they began wearing less armor.

ART
Art is as old as humankind. We can still marvel at cave paintings made over 20,000 years ago. Some of the world's most beautiful sculpture was done in ancient

▼ **A detail** from *Virgin and St. Anne* by Leonardo da Vinci.

Greece and Rome. During the Middle Ages, the Christian religion influenced art, and many religious paintings were made.

At first, figures were stiff and unlifelike. During the Renaissance, however, painters such as Leonardo da Vinci and Michelangelo created much more lifelike people in their paintings. Dutch artists such as Rembrandt painted ordinary indoor scenes as well as religious paintings. In the 1700s and early 1800s there was a revival of classic art forms — that is, the art of ancient Greece and Rome. Greek and Roman styles were copied in painting, sculpture, and architecture.

Later in the 1800s art became more realistic again. One group of painters, called Impressionists, rejected realism. Impressionists such as Renoir and Cézanne began to paint with little dabs of color, creating pictures that gave an impression of a scene rather than a photographic copy. This new freedom was taken even further in the 1900s with Abstract art and Cubism. Paintings became an arrangement of shapes and colors rather than portraits or landscapes. The Spanish artist Pablo Picasso was perhaps the greatest of many modern painters and sculptors to pioneer the new techniques.

▲ *Lady with Umbrella* by French Impressionist Claude Monet.

▶ **A modern** *Madonna and Child* by the British sculptor Henry Moore (Tate Gallery, London).

23

Sculpture, too, became freer — often just dramatic or pleasing shapes, or abstract outlines of the human form. *Kinetic* art included mobiles and sculptures that moved in some way.

ARTIFICIAL INTELLIGENCE

Artificial intelligence is a branch of science that studies ways of making machines, especially computers, intelligent. It first emerged in the 1950s from another field of study called cybernetics, an attempt to build artificial "brains" by creating models of neurons. In the 1970s, rather than re-creating general intelligence, scientists concentrated on expertise in a specific subject. In the 1980s they moved on to machines that learn and acquire knowledge by their own efforts, such as the learning system called EURISKO.

ASIA

Asia is the largest continent (17,139,445 square miles). It stretches from the Arctic to the equator and from Japan in the east to the Middle East and Russia in the west. It contains 42 separate countries and its population of over 3,000 million is more than half the world's total population.

There are many different types of land and climate in Asia. In the north are evergreen forests, flat grasslands called *steppes*, and cold tundra plains. In central Asia are the world's highest

▲ **Asia has many** differences of climate, wildlife, and ways of life. The main regions are the hot, wet monsoon lands of the southeast, the central high-lying deserts and snowcapped mountains, and the great plains and forests to the north.

24

Arctic Ocean

A

U.S.S.R.

JAPAN

KOREA

Gobi
Desert

Tibetan
Plateau

CHINA

Pacific
Ocean

Himalayas

SOUTHEAST
ASIA

INDIA

Indian
Ocean

MALAYSIA

INDONESIA

25

mountains, including the mighty Himalaya mountains. Some of the world's longest rivers flow across the continent.

Almost all Asia's people live either in the fertile river valleys or on the coastal plains. Most of them are farmers, scraping a living out of a small patch of land. But more and more people are going to live in the cities.

Rice is the chief crop of the warm, wet monsoon lands of southern Asia. Rice and fish are the main foods of many Asians. Other crops are tea, sugar, cotton, coffee, and spices.

Asia has many valuable raw materials. The forests provide timber and rubber. There are minerals such as coal, iron, copper, and tin. In the Middle East there is oil beneath the desert. The most important industrial country in Asia is Japan, which manufactures many products to sell in other countries. China, Korea, and India are rapidly developing as industrial nations.

Asia has a long history of rich and powerful civilizations. The great religions of Christianity, Islam, Hinduism, and Buddhism all began in Asia. Asian peoples reached high levels of progress in the arts and sciences long before the rest of the world.

European explorers came to Asia in the 1400s in search of riches and spices. They set up trading stations and later founded colonies. Today all the countries of Asia are independent and run their own affairs.

See also CHINA; COUNTRIES OF THE WORLD; INDIA; JAPAN; MIDDLE EAST.

ASTRONAUT

An astronaut is a person who travels in space. People have been dreaming of doing this for thousands of years but it was

only in April 1961 that the first person in space orbited the earth. This was the Russian cosmonaut Yuri Gagarin. A few years later, in July 1969, the American astronaut Neil Armstrong became the first person to set foot on the moon.

Traveling in space is one of the most exciting and dangerous things people have ever done. The astronauts have to be well trained before they can go. For example, they must learn to withstand the great force caused by the rocket thrust, and to eat, move, and sleep without the aid of gravity.

In space there is no air to breathe, so astronauts must take air with them in their spacecraft. When they leave their spacecraft, they must put on a spacesuit. This supplies them with air and

▲ **Astronauts** exploring the moon. The first astronauts on the moon were Neil Armstrong and Edwin Aldrin in 1969.

keeps their bodies at the right temperature.

See also GRAVITY; SPACE FLIGHT; SPACE SHUTTLE.

ASTRONOMY

Astronomy is the study of heavenly bodies and their motion.

▲ **Astronomers** in Istanbul in the Middle Ages.

People first began to record what they observed in the heavens in ancient times. They used these records to predict things such as eclipses and comets. Later records of this sort were used to work out, check, and correct calendars.

Astronomers now work with a variety of instruments in well-equipped observatories. Their most useful instrument is the telescope, which gathers and strengthens the feeble light from the stars. Radio telescopes collect radio waves sent out by objects such as quasars and pulsars. In recent years astronomers have learned much from information collected by spacecraft on their journeys.

See also COMET; CONSTELLATION; COPERNICUS; GALILEO; METEOR; STAR; TELESCOPE; UNIVERSE.

ATHLETICS

The sport of athletics began with the exercises used to train men for battle. The ancient Greeks loved athletics, and at the Olympic Games young men competed with each other at running, wrestling, and throwing.

The modern athlete must train hard to do well. In an athletics match today there are running (track) events and jumping and throwing (field) events.

ATLANTIC OCEAN

Second only in size to the Pacific, the Atlantic Ocean covers an area of more than 31,000,000 square miles and includes many gulfs and seas. Islands include Greenland, Iceland, the British Isles, the West Indies, the Azores, and the Falkland Islands. On the ocean floor are tall underwater mountains, including the Mid-Atlantic Ridge, a mountain chain running from Iceland almost to the tip of South America. Atlantic currents include the Gulf Stream, which warms northern Europe, and the Brazil Current.

ATOM

Every substance is made up of one or more chemical elements. Iron is an element. If you could cut a piece of iron into smaller and smaller pieces, eventually you would be left with tiny particles called atoms. They are the smallest particles of an element that can exist. They are so small that the period that ends

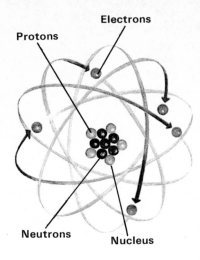

▲ **An atom** of boron. The nucleus, made up of protons and neutrons, is surrounded by whizzing electrons.

this sentence has about 200 billion atoms in it!

At the center of the atom is a solid *nucleus*. This contains two kinds of particles called *protons* and *neutrons*. The protons have an electric charge. At the outside of the atom are tiny particles called *electrons*, which circle the nucleus. They also have an electric charge, which keeps them attracted to the nucleus.

Every element has a different kind of atom. Atoms of different elements combine to form molecules of a new substance. Two atoms of hydrogen (H) combine with one atom of oxygen (O) to form one molecule of water. We can therefore represent water like this: H_2O.

AUSTRALIA

Australia is the largest island in the world and the smallest continent. Low mountains run all the way down the east coast. Most of the center is grassy plain, and the western part consists of flat scrubland, barren, rolling hills, and desert. About four-fifths of the continent is hot desert.

Along the northeastern coast is a chain of beautifully colored coral reefs, islands, and sandbanks called the Great Barrier Reef. Most people have settled in the southeast where there is enough water.

The seasons are the exact opposite of those in the northern hemisphere. When it is spring in the United States it is fall in Australia. Winters are mild and there is plenty of sunshine.

The Dutch discovered Australia in 1606, but they did not settle it. Captain James Cook claimed eastern Australia for Britain in 1770. In 1788, 800 convicts were landed in Botany Bay. These convicts became Australia's earliest colonists.

▼ **Australia** is a huge island. Most of the center is hot and dry. All the fertile, well-watered lands are near the coasts. Australia's plants and animals are unlike any others in the world.

AUSTRALIA

Coral Sea

Great Barrier Reef

Timor Sea

Great Sandy Desert

Ayer's Rock

Great Dividing Range

Gibson Desert

Great Victoria Desert

Nullarbor Plain

Indian Ocean

Tasmania

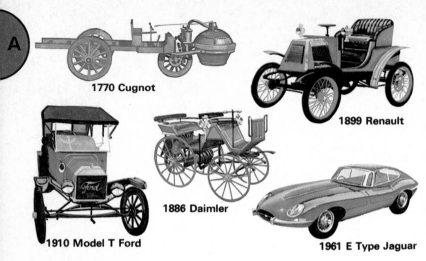

1770 Cugnot

1899 Renault

1886 Daimler

1910 Model T Ford

1961 E Type Jaguar

Australia is a farming country. It produces wool, dairy foods, meat, fruit, and wheat to sell to the rest of the world. Australia mines valuable minerals, too. They include gold, silver, coal, lead, copper, tin, and uranium.

The country is also the home of many strange animals, such as the platypus and emu, which are found nowhere else in the world. Many of the native animals are marsupials, or animals that carry their young in pouches until they are old enough to look after themselves. These include the kangaroo, koala, and wombat.

See also KANGAROO; KOALA; MARSUPIAL; PLATYPUS; and page 79.

AUSTRIA

The independent republic of Austria is a land of tall mountains, thick forests, quiet meadowland and farms, and beautiful lakes.

The forests are Austria's greatest wealth. They provide timber for the saw mills and factories, and for export. Iron ore, lead, zinc, and copper are mined, and steel and paper are manufactured.

See also page 78.

AUTOMOBILE

Two German engineers, Karl Benz and Gottlieb Daimler, built the first automobiles in 1885 and 1886. These had a gasoline engine, like most modern cars. Later, some cars were built with steam engines; others were driven by electricity from batteries. But in the end the gasoline engine proved to be the most successful.

At first, cars were handmade and expensive. It was not until 1908 that they began to be made cheaply. In that year Henry Ford started to mass produce his Model T, called the Tin Lizzie. It marked the beginning of the modern automobile industry.

A modern car is a collection of 10,000 or more separate parts. These parts make up several basic units: the body, the engine, and the transmission are the main units. The transmission carries power from the engine to the driving wheels. The other units are the steering, the braking, and the suspension.

See also FORD.

AZTEC
The Aztecs were an ancient people who lived in Mexico. Their great city, Tenochtitlán, was built on a lake and had huge temple pyramids. When the Spanish explorer Cortés entered Mexico in 1519, he was astonished to find such an advanced civilization.

The Spaniards wanted the Aztecs' gold. Although their army was small, they had guns and horses and were able to conquer the Aztecs.

▲ **The ruins** of an Aztec pyramid.

B

BACH, Johann Sebastian
(1685–1750)
J. S. Bach is the most famous of a great family of German composers and musicians. He was master of the organ and composed hundreds of pieces of music, including many choral works.

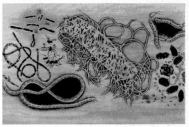

▲ **Bacteria** have tiny hairs or whiplike tails to help them move around.

BACTERIA
Bacteria are among the smallest living things. Each one is made up of just a single cell and can be seen only under a microscope. There are millions of bacteria all around us.

Some bacteria feed on dead creatures, causing them to decay. They make the soil rich and help plants grow. Bacteria also turn meat rotten and milk sour. Some bacteria cause disease.

31

Badger

BADGER

The badger is a relative of the weasel. It is a powerfully built animal with short legs and a black and white striped head.

Badgers dig deep burrows called sets, from which they emerge after dark to find food. They will fight fiercely if attacked, but if left alone they are peaceful animals.

BALLET

Ballet is a classic form of dance performed on the stage. It may tell a story or act out an idea or feeling. Classical ballet is based on a number of set positions and movements which are arranged by a choreographer in various ways. Ballet originated in Italy, but was first recognized in France where the Royal Academy of Dancing was founded in 1661. Modern ballet allows dancers a great deal more freedom of movement.

Ballet is recorded in a special way and can be danced over and over again. Some of the ballets performed today were first presented 140 years ago.

BALLOON AND AIRSHIP

Balloons and airships use gases such as helium, hydrogen, and hot air to fly. These gases are lighter than air. Balloons can only drift in the wind; airships can be flown.

The first balloon to carry people was built by the Montgol-

Giffard's airship, 1852

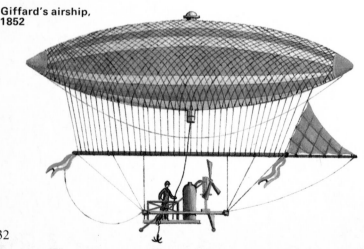

fier brothers in 1783. A fire was built beneath an open-ended bag, filling it with hot air.

Today balloons are used mostly by weathermen. Those called radiosondes carry instruments into the air to measure such things as temperature and atmospheric pressure. Balloons are also used for sport.

Airships are usually bigger than balloons and are cigar-shaped. They have enclosed cabins and engines.

The first airship flew in 1852. Airships were later used for travel and in war. But they proved to be unsafe and so were not built for these purposes after the 1930s. Airships are used today for advertising and for moving heavy, awkwardly placed goods.

BAROMETER

A barometer is an instrument used to measure air pressure. It can help forecast the weather and measure height above sea level.

There are two major types of barometer: the mercury and the aneroid. The aneroid barometer is the more commonly used. It consists of a drum from which most of the air has been removed. When the pressure of the air outside the drum changes, the size of the drum changes. This change in size is recorded by a pointer on a scale.

Generally speaking, if a barometer shows high pressure, it means good weather.

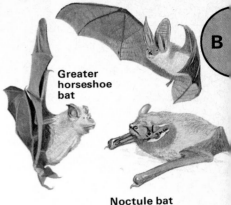

Long-eared bat

Greater horseshoe bat

Noctule bat

B

BASEBALL

Baseball is the American national sport. It may have come from an English game called rounders. Two teams of nine players each take turns to bat the ball and score runs around the baseball diamond. The national championships are decided in the World Series, held each October.

BASKETBALL

Basketball is played on a court by two teams of five players each. Points are made by throwing a ball through a basket. Each basket made counts as two points. Free throws, for fouls, count as one. It helps to be tall in this game.

BAT

Bats are the only mammals that can fly. Their wings are covered with thin, elastic skin. They sleep by day, hanging upside down in caves or other dark places.

Insect-eating bats cannot see well. Yet they can fly in the dark without bumping into obstacles. They send out very high-pitched squeaks and listen for the echo as it bounces off nearby objects.

The vampire bat of South America feeds on the blood of other animals. The largest bats are fruit eaters.

BEAR

Bears may look cuddly and playful, but they are dangerous animals. They are very strong and have sharp claws. Although some bears can be tamed, they may still attack without warning.

Bears live mainly in forests and mountains. They are meat-eating mammals. But they will also eat almost any kind of plant or insect. Some bears hibernate (sleep) during the winter, living on fat stored in their bodies.

There are several different kinds of bears. The largest—the grizzly, the Kodiak, and the polar bear—are from North America. The polar bear also lives in northern Europe. The sun bear, from Asia, is the smallest.

BEAVER

These rodents have stout bodies and short legs. Their webbed feet and paddle-like tails make them good swimmers. They can stay underwater for several minutes.

Beavers live in family groups. They make a home safe from enemies by damming streams and small rivers with branches, stones, and mud. In the pool formed behind the dam, the beavers build their lodge, a dome-shaped den of mud and sticks with an underwater entrance.

▼ **A polar bear** waits by a hole in the ice, hoping to catch a seal.

BEE

Bees are very useful insects. They make honey and wax. More important, bees help plants to make seeds by pollinating flowers.

Some bees are solitary. Others, such as the bumblebee and the honeybee, are social insects and live in large colonies.

Social insects build a nest or hive. In every hive there are many worker bees, a few male drones, and a queen.

After mating with a drone, the queen bee begins to lay thousands of eggs. The workers are small female bees. They build the wax cells of the comb and gather nectar and pollen from flowers to store inside. Workers also feed the queen and the larvae and guard the hive. Drones do no work, and in the autumn they are driven from the hive to die.

See also INSECT.

▲ **A beavers' lodge.** The beavers go in and out under water but sleep in a dry chamber inside.

▼ **A queen bee** circled by workers. She lays eggs in wax cells.

BEETHOVEN, Ludwig van
(1770–1827)
Beethoven was a great German composer who wrote nine wonderful symphonies and many works for individual or groups of instruments. In later life he became deaf but still continued to write music.

See also MUSIC.

BEETLE
Beetles are one of the largest groups of insects. Beetles have two pairs of wings, but only the back pair are used for flying. The front pair have become hard wing covers.

Beetles and their larvae can be harmful. The Colorado beetle attacks potato crops. Grain weevils damage corn. Wood-worms, larvae of the furniture beetle, bore tunnels in timber.

Other beetles are useful. Ladybugs eat aphids, and burying beetles clear dead animals away.

See also INSECT.

BELGIUM
Belgium is a small country wedged between France, Germany, Luxembourg, and the Netherlands. Its population of 9,941,000 makes it one of the most densely populated countries in Europe. It has many industries and great quantities of coal. Belgium has three languages —Flemish, French, and German. Its capital, Brussels, is the headquarters for the European Economic Community.

See also page 78.

BELL, Alexander Graham
(1847–1922)
This Scottish-born teacher of the deaf is best remembered as the inventor of the telephone. On March 10, 1876, Bell spoke the historic first message over the telephone to his assistant: "Mr. Watson, come here; I want you."

BIBLE
The Bible is in two parts—the Old and New Testaments. It was written at different times and by different people, but most of it is thousands of years old.

The Old Testament is held sacred by Jews and Christians. It tells the stories of the Jewish people, their kings, and prophets.

COMMON BEETLES

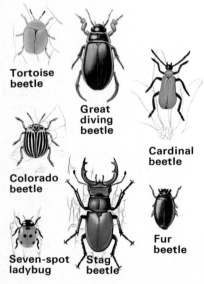

Tortoise beetle

Great diving beetle

Cardinal beetle

Colorado beetle

Fur beetle

Seven-spot ladybug

Stag beetle

▲ **Alexander Graham Bell,** teacher of the deaf and inventor of the telephone.

The New Testament is sacred only to Christians. It contains the four gospels of Matthew, Mark, Luke, and John. Gospel means "good news." Each of these "evangelists" tells the stories of Jesus's life: his birth in Bethlehem, his teaching, his death on the cross, and his resurrection.

See also CHRISTIANITY; JESUS CHRIST.

BICYCLE

The first bicycle was built in about 1790 by a Frenchman named De Sivrac. Early bicycles were steered by the front wheel and propelled by the rider pushing his feet on the ground. Later bicycles had pedals to propel them. The famous high-wheeler bicycle had the pedals attached to its huge front wheel. More and more improvements were made until, by the end of the 1800s, bicycles resembled today's models.

The modern bicycle is propelled by pedals attached to cranks. The cranks turn a toothed chain which is attached to a cog on the rear wheel.

BILL OF RIGHTS

The Bill of Rights is the name given to the first ten amendments to the U.S. Constitution. These contain rights of the people against the powers of the government. They include such things as freedom of speech, freedom of the press, and fair treatment in the courts of law. The rights were added to the Constitution soon after it was adopted in 1789. Some of them were already in the charters of a number of the colonies.

◄ **A high-wheeler** from the 1880s.
▼ **A racing bicycle** used today.

BIOLOGY

Biology is the study of living things—their structure, their development, and their relationship to other living things. Within the wide field of biology are many more specialized sciences, such as *botany* (the study of plants), *zoology* (the study of animals), *cytology* (the study of cells), *genetics* (the study of heredity), *anatomy* (the study of the structures of plants and animals), *bacteriology* (the study of bacteria), and *paleontology* (the study of fossils). *Ecologists* study the relationship of plants and animals and their environments and how to preserve them for future generations.

In recent years, *space biology* has been added to the list. Scientists in this field study what happens to living things when they are taken into space, where there is no atmosphere and astronauts face extreme temperatures and weightlessness.

▲ **Biologists** study relationships between animals. This hermit crab provides food for the anemones it carries on its whelk-shell home.

BIRD

All birds have wings, though some cannot fly. They have feathers, and beaks instead of jaws.

Most birds are perfectly built for flying. Their bones are hollow, light but strong. Their wing muscles are powerful. Their feathers help them fly and also keep them warm and dry.

Flying is hard work and birds use up a lot of energy, so they spend a lot of time eating. Birds rely mostly on eyesight to find food, but their taste and hearing are also good. Their sense of smell is poor. Birds are born with all the skills they will need. Much of their behavior is not learned but comes from instinct.

Birds reproduce by laying eggs. In order to hatch, the eggs

Crowned cranes

Toucan

Hummingbird

Spoonbill

Blue jay

Bird of paradise

Crossbill

Blackbird

Pheasant

▲ **Birds** from different parts of the world. Their beaks are different shapes to suit the kinds of food they eat.

39

must be kept warm, so parent birds sit on them. When the young hatch, they are helpless and must be fed.

See also DUCK AND GOOSE; EAGLE; HUMMINGBIRD; KIWI; OWL; PENGUIN; SWAN.

BISON

Bison are wild cattle. They are large, powerful animals with humped shoulders, thick fur, and short horns.

The North American bison is sometimes called the buffalo. Vast herds of bison provided food for the American Indians. But white men killed so many that the bison nearly died out. Now it is a protected animal. The European bison, or wisent, is also rare.

BLACK HOLE

When a star begins to lose its ability to produce energy, it begins a slow process of collapsing onto itself. The atoms that make up the star get closer and closer together and the star forms a ball about as big as the earth. This star is called a *white dwarf*.

If the collapsing star is very big or explodes powerfully, its atoms may become even more densely packed. The electrons and protons combine to become neutrons. This is called a *neutron star*.

When even the neutrons are crushed by gravity, the entire star disappears into a *black hole*. It is called a black hole because the pull of gravity is so great that not even light can escape from it.

See also STAR.

BLERIOT, Louis (1872–1936)

Blériot, a Frenchman, was one of the great pilots in the history of flying. He designed and built many early airplanes. In 1909 the London *Daily Mail* offered a

▼ **The American bison,** or buffalo, is a protected species.

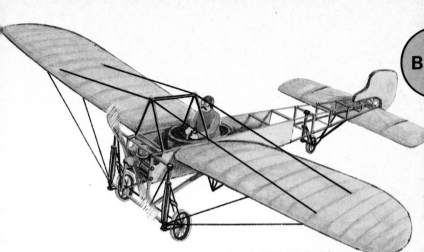

prize to the first person to fly the English Channel. Blériot accepted this challenge and flew the 25 miles from Calais, France, to Dover, England, in 37 minutes. He continued to design and later to manufacture planes.

BLOOD

Blood is made up of red and white cells that float in a liquid called plasma. It is pumped around the body by the heart. There are about five quarts in an average adult.

Blood serves several very important functions. Its main purpose is to carry substances around the body. It takes oxygen from the lungs and nutrients from the intestines and distributes them to body cells. It takes waste products from the cells to the lungs and kidneys. Blood also carries heat to all parts of the body from the muscles, where most body heat is produced.

▲ **Louis Blériot** in his monoplane.

▼ **The network of arteries** that circulate the blood around the body.

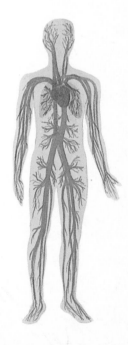

Finally, blood protects the body. It is able to clot when the skin is wounded and it fights infection. The white cells can attack germs and can produce substances to counteract poisons produced by the germs.

See also HEART.

BONE

Bones make up the framework or skeleton of all vertebrates (animals with backbones). They are very strong. Two-thirds of a bone is mineral, which makes it hard. One third is animal matter, which makes it difficult to break.

Bones have several functions. They protect important organs such as the brain, heart, and lungs, and support the limbs. Some bones are hollow and filled with a red substance called marrow. Marrow makes the red and white cells of the blood.

All bones have names of their own such as scapula (shoulder blade), patella (kneecap), and skull. There are 206 bones in the human body.

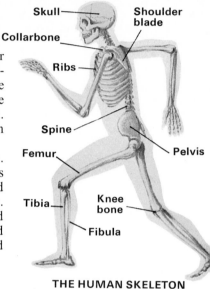

THE HUMAN SKELETON

Skull — Shoulder blade
Collarbone
Ribs
Spine
Femur
Tibia — Knee bone
Fibula
Pelvis

▼ **The Gutenberg** printing press.

BOOK

Books are one of the most important inventions. All that we know, all the ideas, thoughts, beliefs, and literature of the past, can be found in books. We use them for learning, for amusement, and for inspiration.

The earliest known books were written by the Egyptians about 2500 B.C. They were written on paper made from reeds and were rolled up to form a scroll. The Romans were the first to make modern-looking books.

They were inscribed by hand on parchment or vellum made from animal skin.

It was not until about 1439, when Johannes Gutenberg invented his printing machine, that movable type was used. More than one book could then be printed at a time. Today hundreds of thousands of books are printed every year.

See also GUTENBERG; PAPER.

BOSTON TEA PARTY
In 1773 Britain decided to send more tea to her American colonies and levied a tax on it. A group of colonists, dressed as Indians, dumped 340 chests of

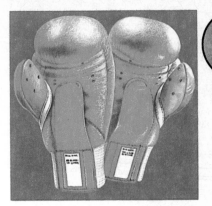

▲ **Early boxers** fought barehanded. Today boxers wear heavily padded protective gloves.

▼ **The Boston Tea Party** was one of many acts of protest that led to the Revolutionary War.

tea into Boston harbor in a defiant act that fanned the flames of revolution.

BOW
The bow has been a weapon for over ten thousand years. The first bow was wood, with arrows of reed tipped with stone, then iron or bronze. In the Middle Ages a bow was set into a gunlike stock to make a powerful weapon, the *crossbow*, but the *longbow* became the most accurate long-range weapon.

BOXING
Boxing is the ancient sport of fighting with the fists. Today the fists are gloved, and the matches are divided into three-minute rounds. Boxers are classed by weight. They follow rules set out by the English Marquis of Queensberry in 1872.

BRAHMS, Johannes
(1833–1897)

This great German composer wrote songs, dances, concertos, and symphonies. His *German Requiem* is one of the world's great works for chorus and orchestra. Brahms was a lifelong friend of Robert Schumann, the Romantic composer, who first realized Brahms's genius.

BRAILLE

Braille is a form of writing used by blind people. A braille book has raised dots on its pages instead of printed letters. The dots are arranged in patterns that represent letters or words. By touching the dots with their fingertips, blind people can read. They can also type in braille, using a machine which stamps out the dots through the paper.

The braille alphabet was invented by a Frenchman named Louis Braille. He lived from 1809 to 1852, and was blind from the age of three.

BRAIN

The brain and its extension, the spinal cord, are called the central nervous system.

The brain is divided into several different parts, each with its own job. One part, the *medulla*, controls breathing, heart rate, and digestion, all of which you do without thinking. The *hypothalmus* controls the body's temperature and the amount of salt and water in the blood.

The largest part of the brain is the *cerebral cortex*. Different parts of the body are linked to different areas of the cortex. Sight, hearing, and speech have their own areas, as do memory, thought, and movement.

The spinal cord receives mes-

▼ **The raised dots** that make up braille words can be seen in this photograph.

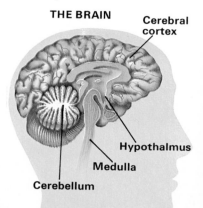

THE BRAIN

Cerebral cortex

Hypothalmus

Medulla

Cerebellum

sages from the nerves and carries them to the brain. It also carries messages from the brain to the nerves. These connect with the muscles to make them work.

BRAZIL

This is the largest country in South America. It covers 3,286,000 square miles. The equator crosses the north of Brazil. Just south of the equator the mighty Amazon River flows from the Andes to the Atlantic.

The Amazon valley is a vast area of tropical plants and animals. Today many of the trees are being cut down, destroying this important natural area.

Most of Brazil's 143,300,000 people live in cities. Brazil is the world's largest producer of coffee. Beef, cocoa, corn, sugarcane, and tobacco are also produced. Oil has been discovered and there are many industries.

The Portuguese ruled Brazil from 1500 to 1825. It became a republic in 1889.

See also page 79.

BREATHING

All animals breathe. They need oxygen from the air to burn the food they eat and make energy.

Humans breathe through lungs. Lungs are spongy bags inside the body which fill with air when we inhale. Oxygen from the air enters the blood, and we breathe out carbon dioxide.

Fishes breathe through gills, which trap the oxygen dissolved in water. Insects breathe through tiny holes on the outside of their bodies. Plants take in oxygen through their leaves.

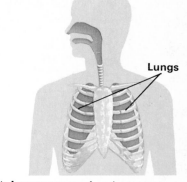

B

Lungs

▲ **Lungs expand** and contract as we breathe in and out.

BRIDGE

There are three basic types of bridge—*girder, arch,* and *suspension.* These types can be combined in many ways and can be made of wood, stone, brick, iron, concrete, or steel.

The kind of bridge used for a site depends upon three factors: the hardness of the ground, the width and depth of the valley or

Girder bridge: Winninger, Germany

45

Arch bridge: Coalbrookdale, Britain

Suspension bridge: Golden Gate, San Francisco, California

river to be spanned, and the weight to be carried.

The Romans built marvelous arch bridges, some of which still stand. Coalbrookdale, the first iron bridge, is an arch bridge. It was built in Britain in 1779.

The longest suspension bridge in North America is the Verrazano-Narrows bridge in New York City, completed in 1964. It is 4,260 feet long. The Golden Gate Bridge in San Francisco, another well known suspension bridge, is 4,200 feet long.

BRONZE AGE

The Bronze Age followed the Stone Age. During this time, people used bronze instead of stone, flint, wood, and bone for their weapons and tools.

Bronze is a mixture of copper and tin which can be hammered into many shapes to make weapons, tools, and jewelry. It was used by the great early civiliza-

tions in the Middle East and Egypt.

BUDDHA

Buddhism is one of the world's great religions. Its founder was Gautama, who lived from 563 to 483 B.C. He was rich, yet he was sad, for he knew the world was full of suffering. So he gave away his riches and spent many years

▼ **A statue of Buddha** in a Bangkok temple.

trying to find the answer to the world's unhappiness.

He taught that there are eight "paths" to *nirvana*, or perfect peace. For this he was called Buddha, meaning "enlightened one," and today millions of Buddhists follow his teachings.

BUFFALO
Buffalo are wild cattle of Africa and Asia. There are several kinds. The Indian water buffalo likes muddy swamps. It is a useful working animal and also gives meat and milk. The African, or Cape, buffalo cannot be tamed. It has massive horns and can be very dangerous.

BULB
Plants make their own food, and some are able to store this food in special leaves called bulbs.

An onion is a bulb. When it is cut, you can see the closely

▼ **The scaly skin** of a bulb protects the fleshy leaves inside.

packed layers of leaves. Daffodils, tulips, and hyacinths also have bulbs. In spring they use food from the bulb to make new leaves.

BULGARIA
Bulgaria is a communist country in Eastern Europe. It covers 42,823 square miles, and its capital is Sofia. In the north are the Balkan Mountains; to the east is the Black Sea. Farmers in Bulgaria grow fruit, vegetables, and tobacco.

Bulgaria has always had close ties with the Russians, who drove the Turks out of Bulgaria in the 1800s.

See also page 78.

BUTTERFLY AND MOTH
Butterflies are some of the most beautiful insects. They fly by day and their scaly wings are often brilliantly colored. Most moths are less colorful. Moths usually fly at dusk. Butterflies and moths belong to the same family. Moths have hairier bodies, and they fold their wings flat when resting. Most butterflies hold their wings upright.

Female butterflies and moths lay eggs which hatch into larvae called caterpillars. Caterpillars eat almost nonstop and grow by shedding their skins. Some, such as that of the cabbage butterfly, are harmful to crops. Others, such as the silkworm, are useful.

When the caterpillar is fully grown, it stops eating. It fastens

47

SOME BUTTERFLIES AND MOTHS

Peacock butterfly

Swallowtail butterfly

Small copper butterfly

Meadow brown butterfly

Common blue butterfly

Clouded yellow butterfly

Large white butterfly

Puss moth

Death's head hawkmoth

itself to a leaf or twig and becomes a chrysalis. Inside the hard case of the chrysalis the caterpillar changes its shape. Soon the chrysalis splits and out crawls the adult insect.

BYZANTINE EMPIRE

In A.D. 330 the Roman emperor Constantine made the city of Byzantium the capital of the eastern half of the Roman Empire. He renamed it Constantinople. It became the center of the powerful Byzantine Empire.

This empire became the storehouse of Greek learning and Roman law because it was not plundered by barbarians as Rome was after A.D. 500. It was here that the Greek Orthodox Church was formed.

The empire finally fell to the Turks in 1453.

▼ A mosaic of the emperor Constantine IX, who ruled the Byzantine Empire from 1042 to 1055.

CAESAR, Julius (100–44 B.C.)

Julius Caesar was a Roman soldier, writer, and statesman. He was a brilliant general. He conquered Gaul—today France, the Netherlands, and Germany —and in 55 B.C. he invaded Britain. He wrote a book about his military experiences.

He disobeyed the Roman senate and brought his army back into Rome. He captured Rome and became dictator in 49 B.C. Caesar had many enemies. They thought that he would make himself emperor, so they assassinated him on the Ides of March (the 15th) in 44 B.C.

See also ROME, ANCIENT.

CALCULATOR

Calculators are machines that help you to solve mathematical problems. One of the first calculators was the abacus, which was used in the Middle East over 5,000 years ago. Today most calculators are electronic and work very fast.

See also COMPUTER.

CALENDAR

A calendar is a way of dividing up the year into months, weeks,

and days. Practically everyone in the world uses the same kind of calendar. The Romans worked out our present calendar nearly 2,000 years ago. They based it on the movements of the earth around the sun and the moon around the earth. In 1582, Pope Gregory XIII made some minor changes to the Roman calendar. This calendar, called the Gregorian calendar, is used today.

CALIFORNIA

The third largest state, California has more people than any other. Gold first brought settlers from the east to California; today it is the warm climate and the electronics and aircraft industries. Los Angeles, San Diego, and San Francisco are the largest cities. The state's varied landscape includes beautiful sandy beaches, the Sierra Nevada range, and Death Valley.

See also page 263.

▶ **Disneyland,** near Los Angeles.

▲ **Camels** are a useful means of transport in North African countries.

CAMEL

For thousands of years this strange-looking animal has been used to carry people and their goods. The camel is well adapted

50

to desert life. It stores fat in its hump and can go for days without water. Its wide, padded feet do not sink into the sand.

The Bactrian camel from Asia has two humps. It can live in very cold regions. The Arabian camel has only one hump.

CAMERA

A camera is a lightproof box with a window, or lens, on one side. When you take a picture, a shutter moves aside and lets light from the object you are photographing pass through the lens. The light falls onto a strip of light-sensitive film, forming an image of the object.

When the film is treated with certain chemicals, or *developed*, the image shows up. The developed film is called a *negative*. The process of printing changes the negative image into a *positive* picture on specially coated paper. The result is a photograph. It may be in black and white or in color depending on the type of film used.

To take a clear photo, the right amount of light must hit the film, and the lens must be focused to

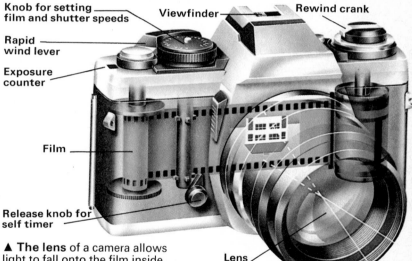

Knob for setting film and shutter speeds
Viewfinder
Rewind crank
Rapid wind lever
Exposure counter
Film
Release knob for self timer
Lens
A CAMERA

▲ **The lens** of a camera allows light to fall onto the film inside. When this happens, an upside-down image of the scene in front of the lens (in this case a house) is formed on the film.

the distance from the object. Some cameras make these adjustments automatically. Others have controls to allow you to do it more accurately yourself.

CAMOUFLAGE

Many animals are colored or shaped to match their back-

51

ground. We call this camouflage. Camouflage makes an animal difficult to see, and so protects it from enemies.

Spots or stripes help to hide an animal by breaking up the outline of its body. The zebra's stripes blend with the long grass on which it grazes. The leopard's spots conceal it among the sun-dappled leaves of a tree.

Most fishes have dark backs and light undersides. This makes them harder to see from above and from below. Many insects and reptiles are so well camouflaged that it is hard to spot them until they move.

Some animals trick their enemies by looking like something else. This is called *mimicry*. Leaf insects look like leaves, stick insects look like dead twigs. Some flies look like stinging wasps. Some harmless insects look like others which are poisonous or bad-tasting.

CANADA

Canada is the second largest country in the world. Only the Soviet Union is bigger. Yet Canada has only about 25 million people. It covers the northern part of North America, stretching from the Atlantic Ocean in the east to the Pacific in the west, and north to the Arctic Ocean. Canada's southern neighbor is the United States.

Canada is a land of high mountains, thick forests, and vast plains. It has so many lakes and rivers that more than seven percent of its area is made up of fresh water.

Because of its size Canada has a variety of climates. The west coast has cool summers and mild, wet winters. On the plains and in the east the summers are hot and the winters cold. The north has short, cool summers and cold winters.

The land is very rich. The plains produce wheat and dairy products, and timber comes from the forests. There are many minerals such as coal, oil, natural gas, gold, and uranium. Fast-running rivers provide hydro-electric power.

Canada is divided into ten

▲ **Camouflage** is a useful means of protection for some animals. These insects use several techniques: the stick insect (4) and thorn tree hoppers (3) imitate pieces of twig. The leaf butterfly (2) and leaf insect (6) mimic leaves. The color of the red underwing moth (1) and the bush cricket (7) matches their background, and the pink orchard mantis (5) disguises itself as a flower.

provinces and two territories. Each has its own government. But the federal (central) government in the capital, Ottawa, makes laws for all Canada. Canada is a parliamentary democracy, and is a member of the British Commonwealth.

See also page 79.

CANAL

Canals are man-made rivers. They are built to carry cargo boats, barges, and ships. Canals have many other uses. They provide water for irrigating the land. In some low-lying countries they drain the land. And in Venice, Italy, canals form the "roads" of the city.

Some canals have been in use for a very long time. Parts of the Grand Canal in China are over 2,000 years old. Today, the most important canals are the ship canals of Suez, Panama, and the St. Lawrence.

▲ **Mount Robson Park** in the Canadian Rockies.

CANCER

Cancer is a dangerous disease spread by the uncontrolled growth of body cells. After heart disease, it is the leading cause of death in the world today.

Scientists everywhere are trying to find a cure for cancer. Simply educating people to spot cancer symptoms at an early stage has saved many lives, as has treatment by surgery, radiation, and drugs.

CAPE CANAVERAL
A narrow strip of land along Florida's east coast, Cape Canaveral became world famous as the launching site for the U.S. space program. Today the Kennedy Manned Space Flight Center builds and tests spacecraft and rockets. The Apollo mission that put the first man on the moon was launched from the Cape in 1969.

CARBON
Carbon is one of the chemical elements. All living things contain carbon. If you hold a plate above a candle flame, a black deposit of carbon forms on it. Both charcoal and coke are forms of carbon. The "lead" in pencils and diamonds are natural forms of carbon.

CARTOON
Today cartoons are usually amusing films with animated talking animals, or strips in newspapers and comics. Originally, though, they were full-scale, detailed drawings made by artists as a kind of pattern for painting a picture or making a tapestry.

Besides being amusing, modern cartoons can also be comments upon an important event or personality of the day.

See also DISNEY.

CASSETTE AND CARTRIDGE
Cassettes and cartridges are used in recording. Cassettes carry reels of tape and can be record-

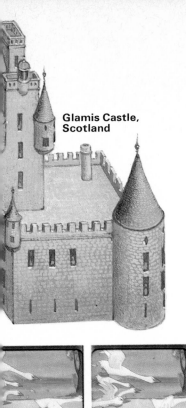

Glamis Castle, Scotland

▲ **Cartoon films** are made up of a series of still drawings.

ings of sound for playing on a home or car cassette player, or of sound and pictures, such as a videocassette. A film cartridge is similar to a cassette but contains photographic film. The cartridge simply slots into a camera and, when exposed, is removed to be developed, without any manual winding.

CASTLE

Hundreds of years ago a castle was the safest place in time of war. The earliest castles were wooden forts. They were built on hilltops and surrounded by banks of earth and ditches. Inside there was room for the local people and their animals.

In the Middle Ages castles were built of stone. The outer walls were high and thick. There were towers along the walls, with slits through which archers could fire arrows. Around the walls was a ditch, or moat, filled with water. In the center of the castle was a massive tower called a keep. Inside the keep, or in a separate building, was a great hall, where the nobleman and his family lived, and a chapel. Elsewhere in the castle were kitchens, storerooms, barracks for soldiers, stables for animals, and a well.

It was difficult to capture a castle once the defenders had pulled up the drawbridge over the moat. Inside they had enough food and water to last for weeks. From the shelter of the castle walls they could shoot at the attackers or drop boulders and boiling oil on top of them.

When an army laid siege to a castle, they surrounded the castle walls. If they failed to force their way in, they would try to starve the occupants out.

Although they must have been cold and damp to live in, castles were good strongholds until cannons were invented. Stone walls did not stand up to being bombarded by cannonballs.

C

FIVE CAT BREEDS

Tortoiseshell shorthair

Russian blue

Seal-point Siamese

White longhair

Red longhair

CAT

A fluffy, playful kitten does not look very fierce. But it is a close relative of the mighty tiger. All cats are flesh-eating mammals. They hunt by stealth, usually alone. They move soundlessly because their claws retract into soft pads on their feet. They can see well, even at night, and they have a keen sense of smell.

Domestic cats are descended from the African wildcat. The cat was sacred to the ancient Egyptians. In Europe cats did not become common mouse hunters until the 1700s.

Cats make good pets. There are many kinds. But they are independent animals and go back to living in the wild quite easily. The European wildcat looks like a large tabby, but it is very fierce.

Cats can breed twice a year. The female gives birth to five or six kittens. The young of the big cats, such as lions and tigers, are called cubs. All cats, even well-fed pets, are hunters, and the big cats are the fiercest hunters of all.

and yaks, and bulls, oxen, and cows.

Cattle are kept to supply milk, meat, and hides. In many parts of Asia and Africa that are used to carry loads.

People have kept cattle since ancient times. Pictures of them appear in Egyptian tomb drawings and reliefs.

▼ **Four wildcats,** from left to right: a caracal, lynx, tiger, and black panther.

▲ **The magnificent Gothic cathedral** at Chartres, in France, was built between 1194 and 1225. It is famous for its beautiful stained glass.

CATHEDRAL
A cathedral is the most important Christian church in an area called a *diocese*, headed by a bishop. The cathedral contains the bishop's *cathedra* (seat), or throne. Many magnificent cathedrals were built in Europe in the Middle Ages. Most have beautiful carvings, statues, and stained glass windows. Built to glorify God, they demanded the best engineering skills of their time.

CATTLE
Cattle is the term applied to animals such as buffalo, bison,

CAVE

Caves are found in the sides of hills and cliffs. They are hollowed out of the rock by the sea or by underground streams.

Some caves were used by early people as dwelling places and are very interesting to archaeologists. They often contain relics and fossils.

See also STALACTITE AND STALAGMITE.

CELL

All living things are made up of cells. Most cells can only be seen under a microscope.

The animal called an ameba has only a single cell. But the human body has millions of cells, each with a job to do.

The center of a cell is the nucleus; around the nucleus is a blob of jelly called protoplasm. Cells join together to make tissues—the materials of which our bodies are built. Different cells build skin, bone, blood, nerves, muscles, and glands. Cells reproduce by dividing. In this way worn-out cells are replaced by new cells as we grow.

Plants are also made up of cells. They have a thick cell wall, which gives them their stiffness.

CENTIPEDE & MILLIPEDE

Centipedes have long, segmented bodies with one pair of legs on each segment. They hide under logs and stones and come out at night to hunt. These creatures run quickly and seize insect prey

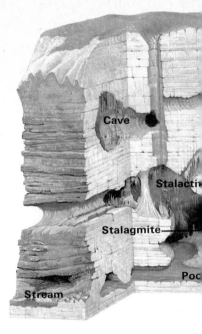

▲ **A section** through limestone showing caves hollowed out by streams. Notice the stalagmites and stalactites.

in their poisonous claws.

Millipedes have two pairs of legs on each segment of their bodies, but move more slowly than centipedes. They burrow into loose soil and eat rotting plants.

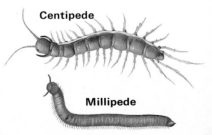

58

CEREAL

Cereals are important food crops. They belong to the grass family. The fruit or seed of the plant is called a grain.

In tropical lands the most important cereals are rice, corn, and millet. In cooler climates the chief cereals are wheat, oats, barley, and rye.

Rice is the main food for over half the people in the world. It grows in warm and wet climates and needs plenty of water.

Much of the world's wheat is grown on the plains of Canada, the United States, Australia, and empire in Europe. This Christian empire was the greatest since the time of Rome, and became known as the Holy Roman Empire.

Charlemagne and his warriors fought against many enemies, including the Moors in Spain. As well as being a great soldier, Charlemagne also built schools and libraries. Scholars from all over Europe came to his court.

CHAUCER, Geoffrey (1341–1400)

Chaucer was a great English poet whose most famous work is *The*

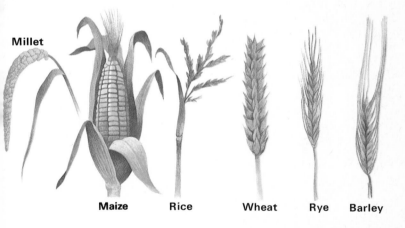

Millet   Maize   Rice   Wheat   Rye   Barley

the Soviet Union. The grain is ground into flour and used to make bread, pasta, and breakfast foods.

CHARLEMAGNE (742–814)

The name Charlemagne means Charles the Great. He was king of a people called the Franks and he conquered and ruled a huge *Canterbury Tales.* He was the first important author to write in English rather than Latin. *The Canterbury Tales* describes a group of people on a pilgrimage to the tomb of St. Thomas à Becket at Canterbury. They entertain themselves by telling tales that give a vivid picture of life in Chaucer's time.

CHEESE

Cheese is made from the solid part, or curd, of sour milk. Bacteria are added to milk to make it sour. The curd is then separated from the watery part, or whey. It is heated, pressed, cooled, and stored until the cheese is ready.

There are many different kinds of cheese. Some famous English cheeses are Cheddar, Gouda, and Swiss. Cheeses such as Roquefort (France) and Gorgonzola (Italy) have blue veins in them. These are caused by special molds.

CHEMISTRY

Chemistry is one of the main branches of science. The people who practice chemistry are called chemists. They look into the properties and makeup of matter. They try to find out what substances are made of, how they are put together, and how they react with other substances.

CHESS

This is a game which has been played for hundreds of years. It

▲ **The Atacama Desert** in Chile is the driest place on earth.

probably came from India, where it was known in the 600s. It spread from the East and had reached Europe by the 1000s.

Chess is played by two players on a board with 64 squares. Each player has 16 pieces which can only be moved in special ways. They attack, defend, and can be captured and taken out of play. The king is the most important piece and the game is won when it is taken.

CHILE

Chile is a long, narrow country that lies along the west coast of South America. The Andes Mountains run down its eastern border. Chile's people speak Spanish and are mostly Roman Catholics. The country contains over one-fourth of the world's copper resources. The capital is Santiago.

See also page 79.

◄ **An international** chess tournament.

CHINA

China is the world's third largest country. About a fifth of the world's people are Chinese. For much of its history, China has been cut off from the rest of the world.

China became a united empire more than 2,000 years ago. The land was ruled by royal families called dynasties. To keep out nomadic enemies, the emperor Shih Huang Ti built the Great Wall of China. Writing, music, and painting flourished. Wise men studied the works of such teachers as Confucius and Lao Tse.

Cities and roads were built and merchants sailed as far as Africa and India. The Chinese invented paper and printing and discovered how to make silk and gunpowder. Their fine pottery, or porcelain, was so famous that we still call all crockery "china."

For centuries the Chinese did not want anything to do with the outside world. But gradually China was made weak by civil wars and bad government. Europeans started trading in China in the 1800s and tried to run things for their own advantage. At first the Chinese were unable to stop them. Then, in the early 1900s, they overthrew the last of the emperors and set up a republic.

Later China was split by fighting between Communists and Nationalists. During World War II Japan invaded China. By 1949, the Communists had won the civil war, and China, led by Mao Zedong, became a Communist state.

See also page 79.

C

▼ **Part of the Great Wall of China** built by the emperor Shih Huang Ti about 2,000 years ago to keep out invaders from the north. It stretches for 2,100 miles.

61

◀ **St. Luke** and St. Matthew writing their gospels, which became part of the New Testament in the Bible.

CHLOROPHYLL

Chlorophyll is the substance in plants that makes their leaves green. It plays an important part in the process of *photosynthesis*, by which plants make food. Chlorophyll must be present before water from the soil and carbon dioxide from the air can combine, with the help of energy from sunlight, to form sugars.

CHRISTIANITY

Christianity is one of the world's great religions. Christians follow the teachings of Jesus Christ, whom they believe is the son of God who came to live on earth in human form.

There are over a billion people on earth who call themselves Christians. They belong to many different sects, or groups. But all accept the Bible as their holy book. The most important Christian festivals are Christmas, which celebrates Christ's birth, and Easter, which marks his death and resurrection. Christian worship takes place on Sunday, a holy day and day of rest.

Christianity is almost 2,000 years old. We date our calendar from the year in which it is thought Jesus was born.

See also JESUS CHRIST.

CHURCH

Christians began to build churches in the A.D. 300s when the Roman emperor Constantine was converted and they no longer had to worship in secret. These early buildings were patterned after the Roman basilica—an oblong hall with aisles and an apse, or rounded part, at the end. Later a transept, or two wings, was often added to make the shape of a cross.

From the 400s to the 1100s many churches adopted the Romanesque style, which had round arches and thick walls. In the Middle Ages the Gothic style appeared. This featured pointed spires, tall, narrow arches, richly stained glass windows, and lots of stone carvings. Such churches were meant to inspire awe and wonder in the worshiper.

CHURCHILL, Winston Leonard Spencer (1874–1965)

Churchill was Prime Minister of Britain during World War II.

One of Churchill's ancestors was a great English general, the Duke of Marlborough (1650–

1722). Churchill led an adventurous life as a soldier and newspaper reporter before becoming a politician. But his greatest years were from 1940 to 1945 when his stirring speeches and strong leadership encouraged people during the war against Hitler's Germany.

CIRCUS
The circus is a popular entertainment, often held inside a large tent. The circus show features clowns, acrobats, jugglers, trick riders, and performing animals. There may be daring high-wire walkers and trapeze fliers, as well as elephants, lions, sea lions, dogs, and chimpanzees trained to do tricks.

In ancient Rome the circus was a huge race track. Thousands of people came to watch chariot races. The charioteers had to be strong and skillful to

▲ **Tokyo,** the capital of Japan, is also its largest city.

drive the horses around the tight bends of the track.

CITY
In prehistoric times people lived in groups for protection. They built a village with a wall or ditch

▼ **A performing horse** in the circus ring.

63

around it. Gradually, some villages grew into towns. The most important towns or trade centers became the first cities.

Thousands of years ago the Egyptians built great cities. The ancient Greeks built Athens, with its beautiful temples. The city of Rome was the center of the Roman Empire.

In the Middle Ages, European cities such as London, Antwerp, and Venice became rich through trade. But they were still small compared with cities today.

When the Industrial Revolution began in the 1700s, cities grew rapidly as people left the countryside to work in the new factories. Today cities are still growing as people arrive in search of jobs and better lives, and the largest cities have more people than many countries.

CIVIL RIGHTS MOVEMENT
The most recent civil rights movement in the United States began in the 1950s when black

▼ **Dr. Martin Luther King**
preached nonviolence in the fight for civil rights.

Americans fought for equal treatment as American citizens. Schools were desegregated in many parts of the country. Other forms of discrimination were soon eliminated. The outstanding black leader of the movement was Dr. Martin Luther King, Jr. Today blacks and other minority groups are still working to win civil rights.

CIVIL WAR
A war fought between citizens of the same country is called a civil war. Sometimes a civil war marks a great change in a country's history.

The American Civil War (1861–65) was fought between the government (the Union), backed by the northern states, and the southern states (the Confederacy). The war was fought over the rights of each state to make its own laws, in particular, the laws regarding slavery. In 1860 the southern states thought that the new Republican president, Abraham Lincoln, would abolish slavery. The large farms, or plantations, of the South depended upon slave labor, and the abolition of slavery would ruin them.

In 1861 eleven southern states decided to break away, or *secede*, and form a separate nation, the Confederate States of America. War broke out in April, when the Confederates fired on Fort Sumter in Charleston harbor, South Carolina. At first the war went

64

▲ **The Battle of Williamsburg,** May 5, 1862. The Confederate forces withdraw after heavy fighting. The opposing armies still faced each other in the traditional fashion, but improved firepower caused horrific casualties.

well for the South. Under their brilliant commander, Robert E. Lee, the South won a victory at the Battle of Bull Run in July 1861. But in 1863 the tide turned after the Battle of Gettysburg, in Pennsylvania. In 1864 General Ulysses S. Grant took command of the Union armies, and in April 1865 Lee surrendered. Both sides had suffered tremendous losses.

The slaves were freed (in 1863) and the southern states rejoined the Union. But it took many years to repair the damage the war had done to the nation, and many more years for the slaves to gain their rights as American citizens.

▼ **President Lincoln** at Sharpsburg, Maryland, in October 1862.

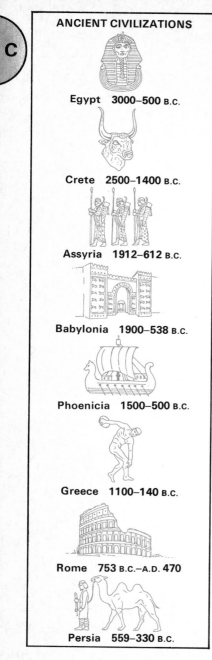

ANCIENT CIVILIZATIONS

Egypt 3000–500 B.C.

Crete 2500–1400 B.C.

Assyria 1912–612 B.C.

Babylonia 1900–538 B.C.

Phoenicia 1500–500 B.C.

Greece 1100–140 B.C.

Rome 753 B.C.–A.D. 470

Persia 559–330 B.C.

CIVILIZATION

Civilized people are able to develop arts, skills, trade, and learning. Civilization began when people no longer had to spend all their time searching for food. Farming and trade developed as people settled in one area. As they grew more prosperous, they built cities, temples, and roads. Most civilizations in ancient times had strong armies. Mighty empires spread their way of life by conquest.

Only the ruins of these great civilizations of the past now remain. But they have left their mark on our lives. Western civilization today, for example, owes a great deal to the ideas of the Greeks and Romans. The modern world is a mixture of civilizations.

CLEOPATRA (69–30 B.C.)

Cleopatra, Queen of Egypt, was one of the most fascinating women in history. Two famous Roman rulers, Julius Caesar and Mark Antony, fell in love with her. Antony even gave parts of the Roman Empire to Cleopatra. The angry Romans made war on Antony and defeated him. Antony killed himself, and Cleopatra also took her own life.

CLIMATE

Climate means the typical weather of a place over a long period of time.

Several factors affect climate. One is latitude—that is, how far a place is from the equator. The sun's rays are most direct at the equator, so it is hotter there. At the poles the rays spread over a large land area and it is cool. A second factor is how close a place is to the sea. Water heats and cools more slowly than land. Away from the sea, land becomes much hotter in the summer and colder in winter.

The chief elements of climate are *temperature* and *rainfall*. The world's main climatic regions are based on average temperatures and rainfall figures measured over many years.

CLOCK AND WATCH

A clock is an instrument for measuring the time. A watch is a clock that is small enough to carry around.

Although the Chinese probably had clocks as early as A.D. 600, the earliest European clocks were made about 1200. They were made by blacksmiths and were often crude and clumsy. They used the force of gravity and were not very accurate.

A more accurate clock was developed when Galileo discovered that the pendulum could be used to measure time. From this time clocks have been improved and ordinary clocks are accurate to within a few minutes a year.

Today, two very precise clocks are used. One is the quartz crystal clock. The second is the cesium atomic clock, which keeps time

to within one second in 300 years.

See also GALILEO.

CLOTHING

People discovered thousands of years ago that wearing the skins of animals kept them warm. Later they learned how to make cloth from plant fibers. They realized that they did not need to kill a sheep to keep warm, but could clip its wool for weaving. Dyes were made from plants.

Factory-made cloth appeared during the Industrial Revolution. In the late 1800s the first *synthetic*, or man-made, fibers were invented. Today a wide variety of clothes are available, and the selection of colors and materials is larger than ever.

CLOUD

When it rains, the puddles soon dry. The water has turned into

▼ **Different types** of clouds bring different weather: cumulus clouds mean fine weather; low stratus clouds, rain.

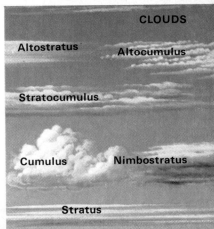

CLOUDS

Altostratus

Altocumulus

Stratocumulus

Cumulus

Nimbostratus

Stratus

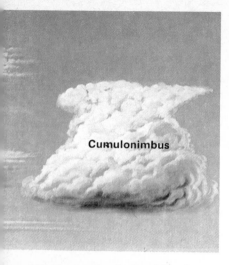

▲ A cumulonimbus cloud
brings thunder and heavy rain.

invisible water vapor.

The vapor rises into the air, and the higher it rises, the cooler it becomes. As it cools, the vapor turns back into water. Millions of tiny drops of water, so light they float in the air, make clouds.

When the air can hold the water droplets no longer, they fall as rain. When the air is very cold, they turn to ice and fall as hail or snow.

By studying the different kinds of clouds, scientists can tell what sort of weather to expect.

See also FOG; RAIN; WATER.

COAL

Coal is one of our most important fuels. It can be burned to heat buildings. At power stations it is burned to make electricity. Coal is also made into coal gas and coke, which are both good fuels. A lot of coke is used in the steel industry. Many chemicals can be produced from coal to make dyes, plastics, medicines, and explosives.

Coal is mined from the ground. It is formed from the remains of forests of huge ferns and trees which grew millions of years ago. When these died, they became covered by mud and sand. In time the mud and sand changed into rocks. The dead plants were squeezed until they changed into coal. Most coal is deep underground and mining it is expensive and dangerous.

See also MINING.

▼ In some coal mines, shafts are dug down to the seams, or workings. Miners travel down in a cage, and fresh air is pumped down ventilation shafts.

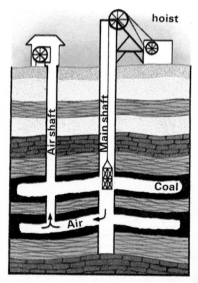

COFFEE

Coffee is made from the roasted and ground beans of the coffee plant. Coffee bushes grow best in warm, wet, highland areas, such as in Brazil and Kenya. Inside each red berry are one or two beans. At harvest time, the beans are removed and dried in the sun. Then they are roasted until they are brown, and sold either ground or whole.

COIN

Coins are small pieces of metal that have been issued by a government for use as money. Gold, silver, bronze, copper, and various other alloys are used to make coins. They are made in a place called a mint. The first coins were made just before 600 B.C. in Asia Minor.

See also MONEY.

COLD WAR

This is the name given to the conflict between the Western nations, headed by the United States, and the communist countries of the Eastern bloc, headed by the Soviet Union. War has never actually broken out, and an uneasy peace based on military might has been maintained ever since the end of World War II. Tensions between East and West eased slightly in the mid-1980s after Mikhail Gorbachev became Soviet premier. Both sides worked to agree on a reduction in the number of nuclear weapons they held.

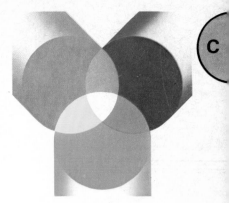

C

▲ **The three primary** light colors are red, green, and blue. Other colors are made by mixing them.

COLOMBIA

Colombia is a country in northern South America that covers 439,620 square miles and has its coastline on two oceans—the Atlantic and Pacific. Bogotá, the capital, is a center of art, learning, business, and government. Coffee, grown on the fertile highlands, is Colombia's chief crop.

See also page 79.

COLOR

White light is actually a mixture of all colors. It is only when white light is split up, as it is in a rainbow, that we see its different colors.

The first person to understand light and color was Sir Isaac Newton. In 1666, by passing light through a glass prism (a triangular solid block of glass), he obtained all the colors in a rainbow. This band of color is

C

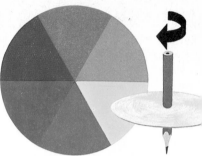

▲ **Mixing paints** is different from mixing lights. You cannot make white by mixing colored paints.

▲ **White light** is made up of a mixture of colors. You can see this if you spin a colored top – the colors merge into white.

called the spectrum. Newton then combined the colors again by passing them through a second prism to form white light.

The colors of the spectrum are always in the same order—red, orange, yellow, green, blue, indigo, and violet.

We see the color of a thing, such as a yellow flower, because all the other colors are taken in and only the yellow is reflected. A white flower gives back all the colors of light.

COLORADO

Colorado is a Rocky Mountain state. It has been important as a mining region since the Gold Rush of 1858, which brought settlers to the territory. Today it produces molybdenum, a metal

used to make rockets and harden steel. The state's dry climate and good skiing bring many tourists. Colorado also has aerospace and electronics industries.

See also page 263.

▶ **Cliff dwellings** built by Indians in the 1100s can be seen at Mesa Verde in southwestern Colorado.

COLUMBUS, Christopher
(1451–1506)
This Italian explorer discovered America by accident. He believed he could reach the Indies (Asia) by sailing west, instead of east, for he was sure the earth was round. He persuaded the king and queen of Spain to let him try, and in 1492 he set out with three ships, the *Santa Maria, Pinta,* and *Niña,* across the Atlantic Ocean. When he reached the Caribbean islands, Columbus was convinced he had reached Asia. So he called them the Indies.

▲ **Comet Kohoutek,** first seen in 1973.

COMET
Comets are heavenly bodies. They are glowing balls of gas and dust which travel in an orbit, or path, around the sun. Some of them have long tails. But they only start to glow when they get near the sun. Some comets take only a few years to circle the sun; others take thousands of years. The most famous comet is Halley's Comet, which orbits the sun every 76 years.

COMMONWEALTH
Most of the countries which were once part of the British Empire now belong to the Commonwealth of Nations. It includes huge countries, such as Australia, Canada, and India, and tiny islands. Nearly all the members are self-governing, but their laws, schools, and way of life are often similar. Some still trade mainly with Britain. The richer members try to help the poorer countries, and Commonwealth leaders meet regularly to discuss their economic and financial problems.

COMMUNICATION
The exchange of information, ideas, or feelings is communication. Animals communicate with one another, but people have the most complicated forms of communication.

Speech was the earliest means of communicating. The Sumerians were the first to invent writing, and the Phoenicians developed the first alphabet sometime before 1000 B.C.

Until the 1400s, all books in Europe were handwritten. Then Johannes Gutenberg invented a system of printing from movable type. Communication took a giant step forward, with the

C

printing of many copies of books, newspapers, and eventually magazines. The invention of photography brought about visual communication through pictures and films, and electricity made communication over huge distances possible, by means of the telegraph, telephone, and television. Computers have revolutionized modern communications because they can store, sort, and provide information at amazing speed.

COMMUNISM

In a "commune" people share everything they have. The main idea behind communism is that wealth should be shared. So communist governments control almost all factories, mines, farms, and shops.

Karl Marx and Friedrich Engels put forward communist ideas in the 1800s, after the Industrial Revolution. The first country to have a communist government was Russia, after the 1917

▲ A mainframe computer consists of several large units – the input station, central processor, memory stores, and output units such as printers.

revolution. Later, much of eastern Europe and Cuba also became communist. So did China, although its ideas about communism are different from those of the Soviet Union.

COMPUTER

Computers are electronic machines like calculators. But computers do more than work out mathematical problems. They can *process* information. This means that they can be given information, store it, and sort through it in order to carry out a task. What is more, they can work at incredible speeds.

Computers cannot think. They have to have instructions called *programs* to tell them what to do with the information they are given. These programs can be changed so that computers can

72

do an enormous number of different things. Today they are found in offices, hospitals, factories, and schools. They can send spacecraft to outer planets, help forecast the weather, run machines, and play games.

Every computer has four main parts. The *input* is where the computer receives instructions and information; the *central processing unit* (CPU) is where calculations are carried out; the *memory* is where information and instructions are stored, and the *output* is where the result is displayed.

The first electronic digital computer, ENIAC, was built in 1946. It filled a whole room. Today the programs to run a computer can be held electronically on tiny silicon chips and computers are much smaller. The largest are called mainframes and the smallest are called micros. In between come the minicomputers.

See also CALCULATOR; COMMUNICATION; ELECTRONICS; SILICON CHIP.

CONCRETE

Concrete is a mixture of stones, gravel, cement, and water that hardens when it dries. It is used for building and for paving. Liquid concrete is poured into molds to give it shape. Reinforced concrete is concrete poured around metal rods that give it extra strength.

CONGRESS

Congress is the legislative branch of the United States government. It has two parts: the House of Representatives and the Senate. Each state elects two senators; the number of representatives it elects depends on the population of the state.

HOW A BILL BECOMES A LAW

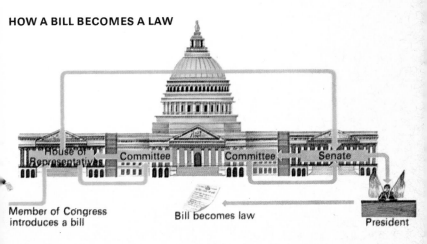

House of Representatives   Committee   Committee   Senate

Member of Congress introduces a bill   Bill becomes law   President

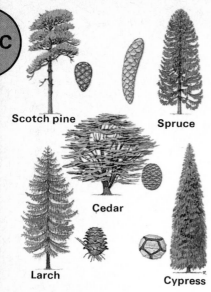

Scotch pine

Spruce

Cedar

Larch

Cypress

CONIFER

Conifers are plants that have cones instead of flowers for making pollen and seeds. They are all trees or shrubs, and are mostly found in the cool parts of the world. Conifers include cedars, larches, pines, firs, and spruces. Most of them have needlelike leaves, which they do not shed in winter.

CONNECTICUT

Connecticut is tucked into the southwestern corner of New England. One of the most prosperous states, its industries make helicopters, aircraft parts, submarines, and electrical equipment. Busy cities include New Haven, Bridgeport, Waterbury, and Hartford, the capital. The region that is now Connecticut was first visited by the Dutch explorer Adriaen Block in 1614.

See also page 263.

CONSERVATION

Conservation is the protection of nature, including natural resources such as water, soil, minerals, forests, and wildlife.

For centuries people have made use of these resources without any thought of preserving them. Conservationists work to prevent the pollution of our earth, air, and water and the destruction of rare animals.

CONSTELLATION

From earliest times people have studied the night sky. It did not

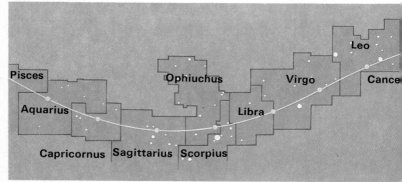

Leo

Pisces

Ophiuchus

Virgo

Cance

Aquarius

Libra

Capricornus   Sagittarius   Scorpius

take them long to realize that the sky had a systematic pattern. The stars were in fixed groups, or constellations. People saw the shapes of animals and the heroes of their myths and named groups of stars after them.

Some constellations always come up in the east in a certain order just before sunrise and seem to travel in the same path as the sun. These are the twelve figures or signs of the zodiac.

There are 88 constellations. The Greeks identified and named 48 of them. Some can be seen only in the Northern Hemisphere and some only in the Southern Hemisphere.

See also ASTRONOMY; STAR; UNIVERSE.

CONSTITUTION OF THE UNITED STATES

The United States Constitution went into effect in 1789 and is the document on which the United States government is based. It is divided into three sections: the *preamble*, seven *articles*, and 26 *amendments*, or additions, to the document. The preamble states why the Constitution was written; the articles set out how the government should be organized and how state and federal governments relate to one another. The first ten amendments are often called the Bill of Rights. Any amendment must be proposed by a two-thirds majority of each house of Congress and approved by three-fourths of the states.

COOK, Captain James
(1728–1779)
James Cook made three voyages of discovery to the Pacific and Antarctic oceans.

The first was an expedition to the South Seas in 1768. He sailed to Tahiti and then to New Zealand. In 1770 he reached Botany Bay in Australia and claimed it for Britain.

On his second voyage (1772–75), he sailed 75,000 miles, going right around the world. On his third expedition he discovered the Hawaiian Islands. He was killed there by natives.

See also EXPLORER.

COPERNICUS, Nicolaus
(1473–1543)
Copernicus was a Polish astronomer. He showed that the earth was not the center of the universe. He stated that the earth

▼ **This map** traces the sun's path against the constellations of the zodiac. The yellow circles mark its position on the first of each month.

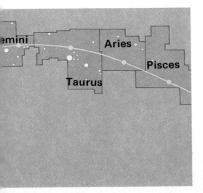

75

revolves once every 24 hours, that it travels around the sun once a year, and that it and the other planets form the solar system.

See also ASTRONOMY.

COPPER

Copper was one of the first metals to be used. At first people used pure copper, which they found on the ground. But they later learned how to extract it from ore by smelting.

Pure copper is very soft. It is often mixed with other metals to make a harder alloy like brass.

See also METAL.

CORAL

Coral is a kind of limestone made by tiny animals, called *polyps*, that live in warm seas. Groups, or colonies, of these creatures make limestone shells around themselves, gradually building up lacy fans, stubby branches, or rounded lumps of coral. Some colonies form thick underwater walls known as reefs.

▼ **Corals live** in tropical seas. They use their tentacles to trap small swimming animals and other food particles in the water. Corals can retract, or pull back, their tentacles into their shells for protection.

CORN

Corn is a kind of grass that was originally native to the Americas. Today it is grown all over the world, mainly as a feed crop. Corn is the most important farm crop in the United States: Iowa, Nebraska, Illinois, Minnesota, and Indiana produce the most.

CORTES, Hernando
(1485–1547)
Cortés was a Spanish soldier who conquered the Aztec empire in Mexico between 1519 and 1521 with fewer than 600 men. Cortés also had guns and therefore great power over the people, as they thought he was a god. He ruled as governor until 1530.

COSTA RICA
Costa Rica ("rich coast") is a country in Central America, smaller than New England. It was named by Christopher Columbus. Costa Rican farmers raise coffee, the country's most

▲ **These fluffy** bolls of cotton will be cleaned by a machine called a gin and pressed into bales.

valuable crop; cacao; sugarcane; bananas; and beans. The country has been a stable democracy for many years.

See also page 79.

COTTON
Cotton is a very useful plant. Inside its round fruits, called bolls, are masses of white fibers. When the fruits ripen, they split and the fibers are blown away, spreading the seeds. But in the cotton fields, the bolls are picked before this can happen.

Cotton grows best in warm, wet lands. It is grown in the Soviet Union, the United States, India, China, Egypt, and Brazil.

See also SPINNING AND WEAVING.

COUNTRIES OF THE WORLD

There are over 160 independent countries in the world. They vary enormously in size, from the Vatican City (the world's smallest country) to the world's largest country—the U.S.S.R.

The table on these pages shows all of the independent countries of the world with their capital cities and population.

EUROPE

Country	Population	Capital
Albania	3,000,000	Tirana
Andorra	47,000	Andorra la Vella
Austria	7,500,000	Vienna
Belgium	9,900,000	Brussels
Bulgaria	8,900,000	Sofia
Cyprus	700,000	Nicosia
Czechoslovakia	15,500,000	Prague
Denmark	5,100,000	Copenhagen
Finland	4,900,000	Helsinki
France	55,400,000	Paris
Germany, East	16,700,000	East Berlin
Germany, West	61,700,000	Bonn
Greece	10,100,000	Athens
Hungary	10,800,000	Budapest
Iceland	200,000	Reykjavik
Ireland	3,600,000	Dublin
Italy	57,400,000	Rome
Liechtenstein	28,000	Vaduz
Luxembourg	400,000	Luxembourg
Malta	400,000	Valletta
Monaco	28,000	Monaco
Netherlands	14,500,000	Amsterdam
Norway	4,200,000	Oslo
Poland	37,300,000	Warsaw
Portugal	10,400,000	Lisbon
Romania	22,800,000	Bucharest
San Marino	23,000	San Marino
Spain	38,600,000	Madrid
Sweden	8,300,000	Stockholm
Switzerland	6,500,000	Bern
Turkey	52,100,000	Ankara
United Kingdom	56,400,000	London
U.S.S.R.	280,000,000	Moscow
Vatican City	1,000	Vatican City
Yugoslavia	23,100,000	Belgrade

AFRICA

Country	Population	Capital
Algeria	22,800,000	Algiers
Angola	8,200,000	Luanda
Benin	4,000,000	Porto-Novo
Botswana	1,100,000	Gaborone
Burkina Faso	7,100,000	Ouagadougou
Burundi	4,900,000	Bujumbura
Cameroon	10,000,000	Yaoundé
Cape Verde	300,000	Praia
Central African Republic	2,700,000	Bangui
Chad	5,200,000	N'Djamena
Comoros	469,000	Moroni
Congo	1,700,000	Brazzaville
Djibouti	300,000	Djibouti
Egypt	50,000,000	Cairo
Equatorial Guinea	400,000	Malabo
Ethiopia	43,800,000	Addis Ababa
Gabon	1,000,000	Libreville
Gambia	800,000	Banjul
Ghana	13,600,000	Accra
Guinea	6,100,000	Conakry
Guinea-Bissau	900,000	Bissau
Ivory Coast	10,100,000	Abidjan
Kenya	21,000,000	Nairobi
Lesotho	1,500,000	Maseru
Liberia	2,200,000	Monrovia
Libya	4,000,000	Tripoli
Madagascar	10,300,000	Antananarivo
Malawi	7,300,000	Lilongwe
Mali	7,900,000	Bamako
Mauritania	1,900,000	Nouakchott
Mauritius	1,000,000	Port Louis
Morocco	23,700,000	Rabat
Mozambique	13,900,000	Maputo
Namibia	1,100,000	Windhoek
Niger	6,500,000	Niamey
Nigeria	105,400,000	Lagos
Rwanda	6,300,000	Kigali
São Tomé & Príncipe	100,000	São Tomé

AFRICA

Country	Population	Capital
Senegal	6,700,000	Dakar
Seychelles	100,000	Victoria
Sierra Leone	3,600,000	Freetown
Somalia	7,800,000	Mogadisho
South Africa	33,200,000	Pretoria
Sudan	22,900,000	Khartoum
Swaziland	600,000	Mbabane
Tanzania	22,400,000	Dodoma
Togo	3,000,000	Lomé
Tunisia	7,200,000	Tunis
Uganda	15,200,000	Kampala
Zaire	31,300,000	Kinshasa
Zambia	7,100,000	Lusaka
Zimbabwe	9,000,000	Harare

ASIA

Country	Population	Capital
Afghanistan	15,400,000	Kabul
Bahrain	400,000	Manama
Bangladesh	104,100,000	Dacca
Bhutan	1,400,000	Thimbu
Brunei	200,000	Bandar Seri Begawan
Burma	37,700,000	Rangoon
Cambodia	6,200,000	Phnom Penh
China	1,042,000,000	Beijing (Peking)
Hong Kong	5,500,000	Victoria
India	785,000,000	New Delhi
Indonesia	168,400,000	Djakarta
Iran	46,600,000	Tehran
Iraq	16,000,000	Baghdad
Israel	4,200,000	Jerusalem
Japan	121,500,000	Tokyo
Jordan	3,600,000	Amman
Korea (N.)	20,100,000	Pyongyang
Korea (S.)	43,300,000	Seoul
Kuwait	1,900,000	Kuwait
Laos	3,800,000	Vientiane
Lebanon	2,600,000	Beirut
Malaysia	15,700,000	Kuala Lumpur
Maldives	200,000	Malé
Mongolia	1,900,000	Ulan Bator

Country	Population	Capital
Nepal	17,000,000	Katmandu
Oman	1,200,000	Muscat
Pakistan	101,900,000	Islamabad
Philippines	58,100,000	Manila
Qatar	300,000	Doha
Saudi Arabia	11,200,000	Riyadh
Singapore	2,600,000	Singapore
Sri Lanka	16,400,000	Colombo
Syria	10,600,000	Damascus
Taiwan	19,200,000	Taipei
Thailand	52,700,000	Bangkok
Turkey	52,100,000	Ankara
United Arab Emirates	1,300,000	Abu Dhabi
U.S.S.R.	280,000,000	Moscow
Vietnam	62,000,000	Hanoi
North Yemen A.R.	6,100,000	San'a
South Yemen P.D.R.	2,100,000	Aden

SOUTH AMERICA

Country	Population	Capital
Argentina	31,200,000	Buenos Aires
Bolivia	6,200,000	La Paz
Brazil	143,300,000	Brasilia
Chile	12,000,000	Santiago
Colombia	30,000,000	Bogotá
Ecuador	9,600,000	Quito
French Guiana	78,000	Cayenne
Guyana	800,000	Georgetown
Paraguay	4,100,000	Asunción
Peru	20,200,000	Lima
Surinam	400,000	Paramaribo
Uruguay	3,000,000	Montevideo
Venezuela	17,300,000	Caracas

NORTH AND CENTRAL AMERICA THE WEST INDIES

Country	Population	Capital
Anguilla (Br.)	7,000	The Valley
Antigua and Barbuda	100,000	St. John's
Bahamas	200,000	Nassau
Barbados	300,000	Bridgetown
Belize	200,000	Belmopan
Bermuda	62,000	Hamilton
Canada	25,400,000	Ottawa
Costa Rica	2,600,000	San José
Cuba	10,100,000	Havana
Dominica	100,000	Roseau
Dominican Republic	6,200,000	Santo Domingo
El Salvador	5,100,000	San Salvador
Greenland (Dan.)	50,000	Godthaab
Grenada	100,000	St. George's
Guadeloupe (Fr.)	332,000	Basse-Terre
Guatemala	8,600,000	Guatemala City
Haiti	5,800,000	Port-au-Prince
Honduras	4,400,000	Tegucigalpa
Jamaica	2,300,000	Kingston
Martinique (Fr.)	328,000	Fort-de-France
Mexico	81,700,000	Mexico City
Nicaragua	3,000,000	Managua
Panama	2,200,000	Panama City
Puerto Rico (U.S.)	3,600,000	San Juan
St. Kitts-Nevis	51,000	Basseterre
St. Lucia	100,000	Castries
St. Vincent and the Grenadines	100,000	Kingstown
Trinidad & Tobago	1,200,000	Port-of-Spain
United States of America	238,900,000	Washington, D.C.

AUSTRALASIA

Country	Population	Capital
Australia	15,800,000	Canberra
Fiji	700,000	Suva
Kiribati	60,000	Bairiki
Nauru	8,000	Yaren
New Caledonia	170,000	Nouméa
New Zealand	3,400,000	Wellington
Niue	4,000	Alofi
Papua New Guinea	3,400,000	Port Moresby
Solomon Islands	300,000	Honiara
Tonga	100,000	Nuku'alofa
Tuvalu	8,000	Funafuti
Vanuatu	100,000	Vila
Western Samoa	200,000	Apia

C

Greenland

ICELAND

Alaska
(USA)

IRELAND

CANADA

PORTUGAL

UNITED STATES
OF AMERICA

TROPIC OF CANCER

MEXICO

BAHAMAS

CUBA

MORO

MAURITANIA

PUERTO RICO
DOMINICA
ST LUCIA

46

53

54 55

56

CAPE
VERDE
ISLANDS

26

48
50

47

52

57

27

28

VENEZUELA

29

49

51

58

5960

30

EQUATOR

COLOMBIA

31

ECUADOR

PERU

BRAZIL

BOLIVIA

TROPIC OF CAPRICORN

PARAGUAY

URUGUAY

ARGENTINA

Falkland Islands

1 DENMARK	11 YUGOSLAVIA	21 NORTH YEMEN A.R.
2 NETHERLANDS	12 ALBANIA	22 BHUTAN
3 BELGIUM	13 CYPRUS	23 BANGLADESH
4 LUXEMBOURG	14 LEBANON	24 CAMBODIA
5 W. GERMANY	15 ISRAEL	25 TUNISIA
6 E. GERMAN	16 SYRIA	26 SENEGAL
7 SWITZERLAND	17 JORDAN	27 GAMBIA
8 AUSTRIA	18 KUWAIT	28 GUINEA BISSAU
9 CZECHOSLOVAKIA	19 BAHRAIN	29 GUINEA
10 HUNGARY	20 UNITED ARAB EMIRATES	30 SIERRA LEONE

C

31 LIBERIA	41 DJIBOUTI	51 COSTA RICA
32 BURKINA FASO	42 MALAWI	52 PANAMA
33 TOGO	43 ZIMBABWE	53 JAMAICA
34 CENTRAL AFRICAN REPUBLIC	44 SWAZILAND	54 HAITI
35 EQUATORIAL GUINEA	45 LESOTHO	55 DOMINICAN REPUBLIC
36 GABON	46 BELIZE	56 BARBADOS
37 CAMEROON	47 GUATEMALA	57 TRINIDAD AND TOBAGO
38 UGANDA	48 HONDURAS	58 GUYANA
39 RWANDA	49 EL SALVADOR	59 SURINAM
40 BURUNDI	50 NICARAGUA	60 FRENCH GUIANA

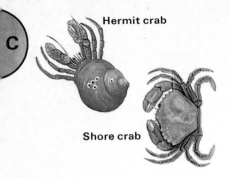

Hermit crab

Shore crab

CRAB

Along with shrimps, crayfish, and lobsters, crabs belong to the group of animals called crustaceans.

Most crabs live in the sea. They have jointed legs, like insects, and walk sideways. They seize food in their strong pincers, or claws.

There are about 5,000 kinds of crabs. They vary in size from tiny pea crabs less than half an inch across to giant spider crabs measuring three feet or more.

CROCODILE & ALLIGATOR

These reptiles are related. They both have tough, armored skin and their ears, eyes, and nostrils are located at the top of their heads. Unlike most reptiles, crocodiles and alligators lay their eggs in a nest or heap of dead leaves and plants. As the plants rot they provide heat which helps to hatch the eggs.

Crocodiles live in Africa, Asia, and Australia. They eat mostly fish, turtles, birds, and water mammals. They vary in size from 5 to 20 feet and have narrow, pointed heads.

Alligators live in America and China, where they can grow as large as crocodiles. They eat mostly fish.

CROMWELL, Oliver
(1599–1658)
Cromwell was one of the most famous men in English history. He helped to lead Parliament's army to victory over the Royalists in the Civil War and later became Lord Protector from 1653 to 1658. He was one of those who signed the warrant for the execution of Charles I.

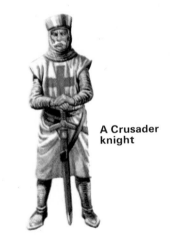

A Crusader knight

CRUSADES

The Crusades were wars in which Christian armies fought to win back the Holy Land of Palestine from the Muslims.

The First Crusade began in 1096 after Pope Urban II had

▲ **The Nile crocodile** lives in Africa. The bird on its back is looking for parasites to eat.

called on the Christians of Europe to capture Jerusalem, which was a sacred city to the Muslims, too. Many knights answered the call, and the First Crusade was a great success. The crusaders captured Jerusalem in 1099. But the Muslims were not beaten. In 1187, led by the great sultan Saladin, they recaptured Jerusalem.

There were eight Crusades in all. Thousands of crusaders went to the Holy Land. Before the Muslims finally defeated them in 1303, many crusaders had died of sickness or in battle.

The Crusades brought Europeans into contact with the way of life of the East. They learned Eastern medicine and science, and were encouraged to trade for the riches of the East.

CRYSTAL

If you look closely at sugar, you will see that it is made up of thousands of tiny glassy pieces with flat sides. These are sugar crystals.

All crystals have a definite shape. They have smooth, flat sides that meet in sharp corners. There are many different varieties of crystal shapes and sizes. Many crystals are so beautiful they are used as gems in jewelry.

CUBA

Cuba is a communist island nation in the West Indies. Part of the island is mountainous, and there are cedar and mahogany forests in the center. Sugarcane and tobacco are two valuable crops. Cuba was ruled by Spain until 1898. It became a communist country in 1959 under Fidel Castro.

See also page 79.

▲ **Pierre and Marie Curie** in their laboratory.

CURIE, Marie (1867–1934) **and Pierre** (1859–1906)

The Curies were among the earliest workers in the science of radioactivity. Radioactivity has to do with the powerful rays given off by some rare materials.

In 1898 the Curies discovered and worked on both polonium and radium. They shared a Nobel prize in physics in 1903 with Henri Becquerel for their work on radioactivity.

After Pierre Curie was killed in 1906, Marie took over his job as professor at the Sorbonne University in Paris. She was awarded a second Nobel prize, this time in chemistry, in 1911 for her further work on radium.

See also RADIOACTIVITY.

CUSTER, George (1839–1876)

George Armstrong Custer was an army officer and Indian fighter who died at the Battle of the Little Big Horn. A graduate of West Point (1861), he became the youngest general in the Union army during the Civil War. Custer later commanded the Seventh Cavalry in many attacks on the Sioux and Cheyenne tribes before the famous battle in which he and all his men were killed.

CYCLONE

A cyclone is a storm in which the wind circles or spirals inward around a low-pressure area. The winds can be very strong—up to 150 miles an hour—and there is often torrential rain, causing floods. Yet the center or "eye" of the storm is quite calm.

Cyclones often begin over water. When they hit the land they cause great damage. Houses may be blown down, trees uprooted, and crops damaged. People may be killed or injured.

CZECHOSLOVAKIA

Czechoslovakia is a landlocked country in Eastern Europe, covered with hills and mountains. Most of its people speak either Czech or Slovak, and the government has been communist since 1948. Czechoslovakia has coal and iron and an important steel industry. The capital, Prague, is a medieval town, filled with beautiful churches and handsome old buildings.

See also page 78.

DAM

A dam is a barrier built across a river or lake. Some dams are built to create a reservoir for storing water, others to control flooding or to produce water power for making electricity.

The New Cornelia Tailings Dam in Arizona is the world's biggest dam. It contains nearly 275 million cubic yards of earth and rock. Other dams are giant slabs of concrete. The Grand Coulee Dam in the state of Washington is the biggest concrete dam. It holds back the water by its sheer weight. Other concrete dams are strong because of their shape, which is arched toward the flow of water.

DARWIN, Charles Robert
(1809–1882)

Darwin was a great naturalist whose theory of evolution sought to explain why there are so many different kinds of plants and animals. Darwin said that those animals and plants whose slight differences made them better able to live in their environment would survive and pass on their differences to their offspring.

Darwin put forward this idea of natural selection in his *Origin of Species* in 1859.

DECLARATION OF INDEPENDENCE

The Declaration of Independence is one of the most important documents in American history. It is the document in which the original 13 colonies declared themselves free of Great Britain. The first draft of the document

▼ **The signing** of the Declaration of Independence took place in Independence Hall, Philadelphia.

▼ **Two red deer** stags fighting over a herd of females.

was written by Thomas Jefferson, and the final version was approved by the Continental Congress on July 4, 1776, now remembered as the birthday of the United States of America.

DEER

Deer are hoofed mammals, which run swiftly to escape their enemies. Like antelope and cattle, deer chew the cud. Usually only the stags (males) have horns, or antlers. Females are called does.

Deer live in cooler climates than antelopes. Most deer live in woodland, feeding on grass and leaves. The reindeer, or caribou, lives on the cold northern tundra. The largest deer is the moose of North America.

DELAWARE

Delaware, on the East Coast, is the second smallest state, after Rhode Island. It stretches over a peninsula between Chesapeake Bay and the Atlantic Ocean. Delaware is a manufacturing state and an important producer of chemicals. Delaware was originally settled by the Dutch and

then by Swedes, who founded present-day Wilmington in 1638.

See also page 263.

DEMOCRACY

The word *democracy* comes from two Greek words and means "government by the people." In ancient times emperors and kings had great power to make laws and collect taxes. In a democracy a group of men and women elected by the people make the laws.

Some democracies are republics. The head of state is an elected president. But some still have a king or queen, although the country is governed by a parliament.

If the people living in a democracy do not like the government, they vote against it at an election. The political parties put forward their ideas.

DENMARK
Denmark, in northern Europe, is in the region known as Scandinavia. It lies on the Jutland Peninsula and is surrounded by about 600 islands. Denmark is one of the few monarchies left in Europe. It exports butter and bacon and high-quality goods such as china and furniture.

See also page 78.

DESERT
Not all deserts are hot and sandy. Some are cold. Many are rocky. But all get very little rain and snow. About a fifth of the earth's land surface is desert.

Most deserts are in the middle of continents. There is little rain, because the moist winds from the sea are dry by the time they reach these deserts. Because there are no clouds, a desert may get very hot during the day. But at night, the dry soil quickly loses its heat and the desert becomes cold.

Strong winds blow away the soil, leaving bare rock, or sweep the sand into great waves called dunes. It is difficult for plants to live in such conditions. Many desert animals shelter from the sun by day and some come out only at night. Some never drink, but get all the moisture they need from their food.

The world's largest desert is the Sahara in Africa. There are other huge deserts in central Asia (the Gobi), in southern Africa, Australia, India, and North and South America.

DIAMOND
Diamonds are our most precious gems. They are cut from crystals that are found in rocks. Diamonds are a form of carbon. If

▼ **In the deserts** of the Middle East, nomads pass by on camels. In the distance is an oasis where there is water.

87

expertly cut, they sparkle with reflected light. Diamonds are expensive because they are rare and difficult to cut. They are the hardest of all the minerals. Some diamonds are made into cutting tools for industry.

DICKENS, Charles John Huffam (1812–1870)

Dickens is one of the greatest English novelists. He created many famous characters, such as the miser Scrooge in *A Christmas Carol*, and often wrote about children. In *David Copperfield* he described his own boyhood. Though his books contain many humorous characters, they also tell of the poverty, crime, and cruelty of his day. Dickens' writing encouraged people to do something about these problems.

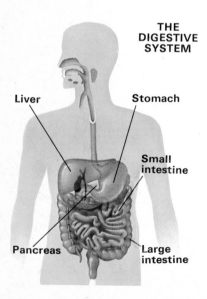

THE DIGESTIVE SYSTEM

Liver

Stomach

Small intestine

Pancreas

Large intestine

DIESEL ENGINE

The diesel engine is a kind of internal combustion engine, in which fuel is burned inside the engine. It uses a heavier, cruder fuel than gasoline and is more often used to drive heavy machines such as trains, ships, buses, and trucks. An efficiently run diesel causes less pollution than a gasoline engine. A diesel engine is similar to a gasoline engine, but does not use a spark to ignite the fuel. The diesel engine is named after its inventor, Rudolf Diesel, who built the first successful engine in 1897.

DIGESTION

The food we eat must be changed by the body before it can be absorbed by the blood and used to nourish the cells of the body. Food is changed into nourishment by the digestive system.

Digestion begins in the mouth where food is chewed into small pieces and mixed with saliva before being pushed down into the stomach. The stomach churns the food, mixing it with gastric juice, and turns it into a soft paste which passes slowly into the small intestine.

Inside the small intestine it is further broken down by being mixed with bile from the liver and juice from the pancreas. Much of this fluid passes through the wall of the small intestine into the blood. The waste passes into the large intestine and leaves the body as feces.

DINOSAUR

Millions of years ago, long before people lived on earth, the mighty dinosaurs ruled the animal kingdom.

The word *dinosaur* means "terrible lizard." The dinosaurs were reptiles, and some of them were the largest land animals that have ever lived. The first dinosaur appeared about 200 million years ago; the last dinosaurs died out about 65 million years ago. We know something of what they looked like from their fossil remains in the rocks. Some were quite small, but others were huge. There were plant-eating and flesh-eating dinosaurs.

Among the plant-eaters were the biggest dinosaurs, such as *Brachiosaurus* and *Diplodocus*. They walked on four thick legs,

▲ **A scene** from over 100 million years ago. The *Tyrannosaurus* attacks its plant-eating prey, the *Corythosaurus.* Behind them an armored *Ankylosaurus* grazes.

and had long necks and tails. Some giant dinosaurs were over 100 feet long. Others weighed 50 tons or more.

Flesh-eating dinosaurs were smaller and most of them ran on their hind legs. The largest and fiercest was *Tyrannosaurus,* the "tyrant lizard." It stood 18 feet high and weighed $5\frac{1}{2}$ tons. It had huge, sharp claws and long, sharp teeth.

Despite their great size and strength, dinosaurs had tiny brains. When they died out, mammals, which until then had been unimportant little animals, took their place. Scientists are not sure why dinosaurs became extinct. Perhaps the climate became cooler and the vegetation changed, so that the dinosaurs could not keep warm or get enough food.

See also FOSSIL; PREHISTORIC ANIMALS.

DISEASE

When something goes wrong with part of your body, you may have a disease.

Many diseases are *infectious*. They are caused by attacks on the body by tiny living things. Bacteria cause diseases such as typhoid fever and tuberculosis. Viruses give us influenza, measles, and the common cold.

Diseases can also be caused by poor diet and lack of vitamins. Sometimes glands can go wrong and upset the body. Some diseases are *hereditary*. This means they can be passed on from parents to children.

Drugs can cure many diseases. Vaccination and good health can protect us from others.

See also BACTERIA; DRUG; MEDICINE; VITAMIN.

DISNEY, Walt (1901–1966)

Walt Disney opened a motion picture animation studio in 1923 and by 1928 he had made his first short talking film which starred Mickey Mouse.

Disney's first full-length cartoon film was *Snow White and the Seven Dwarfs*. Other cartoon films included *Bambi, Pinocchio, Dumbo,* and *Cinderella*. He also made real-life films.

See also CARTOON.

DISTRICT OF COLUMBIA

The District of Columbia is the federal district that includes Washington, the U.S. capital. It covers 69 square miles between Maryland and Virginia on the north bank of the Potomac River. Local government consists of a mayor and a city council. Until the 1980s, residents were not allowed to vote in federal elections. The district was named after Christopher Columbus.

See also WASHINGTON, D.C.

DIVING

To remain underwater for more than a few minutes, divers must wear breathing apparatus. In

◄ **A diver** preparing to launch a diving bell, a special diving vessel for exploring below 650 feet.

90

SIX DOG BREEDS

Springer spaniel

Bulldog

Toy poodle

Greyhound

Scottish terrier

Pekingese

fairly shallow waters divers use a device called an aqualung. It supplies them with compressed air through a mouthpiece. Deep-sea divers wear a special pressure suit pumped up with air.

DNA and RNA

DNA and RNA are two kinds of *nucleic acid*—special molecules in cells that play an important part in growth and reproduction. RNA (ribonucleic acid) is found throughout the cell, where it controls protein-making. DNA (de-

oxyribonucleic acid) is found only in the nucleus of the cell. It carries a kind of "blueprint," or plan, that makes each living creature an individual.

DOG

The dog was the first animal to be tamed by human beings. Cave men probably reared wild dog pups and trained them to hunt.

Today, there are many different breeds, or kinds, of dog. Dogs used for hunting are called *sporting dogs*. Terriers, hounds,

▲ **Dolphins** are playful, intelligent marine mammals.

spaniels, setters, pointers, and retrievers are sporting dogs.

Working dogs do many useful jobs. Huskies, sheepdogs, German shepherds, and St. Bernards do a variety of jobs for people.

Even though the dog has lived close to people for so long, it still has the instincts of a wild animal. Before going to sleep, a dog will turn around and around—as if making a bed in dry leaves. Because wild dogs live in packs, or groups, the dog's instinct is to follow and obey the pack leader. This makes it easy to train. Its master becomes "pack leader."

The wild members of the dog family include coyotes, foxes, jackals, and hunting dogs.

DOLPHIN
Dolphins are small whales. They live in the sea or in big rivers, and they eat fish. Dolphins are mammals, so they have to come to the surface to breathe. They are marvelous swimmers and often play by leaping right out of the water and twisting in the air.

DRAGON
A dragon is a fabulous monster. It is represented as a gigantic reptile having a lion's claws, the tail of a serpent, wings, and a scaly skin. It often breathes fire.

We often think of dragons as being evil, fearful creatures, but this is not always so. The Chinese think the sign of a dragon can protect them from evil or injury.

DRUG
Herbs and chemicals that are used to cure diseases are called drugs. Some mosses and herbs contain healing substances that have been known to people since earliest times. By the 1600s nearly every town had an apothecary, or chemist, who made up pills and mixtures. Many of these did no good at all.

In the 1800s the first man-made drugs, produced from chemicals, were used. A great step forward was the discovery of penicillin in 1928. This was the first *antibiotic* drug, which could kill harmful bacteria.

Drugs can be dangerous if they are not used properly. People can become addicted to certain drugs; this means they cannot function without them.

See also DISEASE.

Shelduck

Canada goose

Mallards

DUCK AND GOOSE
Ducks are swimming birds, with short legs and webbed feet. They live on lakes and rivers, or on marshes or the sea. Male ducks are called drakes. They are often more colorful than females. There are many different kinds of duck.

Geese look rather like large ducks with long necks. They spend much of their time on land, nibbling grass or other plant food. The male goose is called a gander. Wild ducks and geese often migrate for long distances.

DYE
Dyes are substances used to color fabrics and other materials. Some dyes come from plants and animals. A red dye called madder comes from the roots of the mad-der plant. Cochineal is a scarlet dye obtained from the cochineal insect. But most of the dyes used these days are made from chemicals. Many of these man-made dyes have brilliant colors.

DYNAMITE
In 1866 Alfred Nobel, a Swedish chemist, accidentally made an important discovery. He mixed a very dangerous explosive called nitroglycerin with a kind of sandy earth called kieselguhr. It became a solid cheesy substance which could be handled safely but was still a powerful explosive. He called it dynamite.

Nobel made a fortune from explosives. With some of his wealth he set up a fund to give yearly prizes to scientists and writers whose work has helped humankind. These are known as Nobel Prizes.

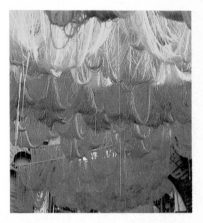

▲ **Dyed wool** hanging in a Moroccan market.

◄ **The golden eagle** has a wingspan of 7½ feet. It lives in mountainous areas.

EAGLE

These fierce birds of prey are the kings of the bird world. Some types have a wingspan of more than six feet. Eagles can fly to great heights. The largest eagles can carry off lambs and even young deer in their strong claws.

Today, eagles are protected by law. Eagles are becoming rare because people have shot and poisoned many of them.

EAR

Any sound causes vibrations which are passed by the *outer ear* down to the eardrum. The eardrum then vibrates, just like the skin of a musical drum. Three tiny bones in the *middle ear* pick up and pass on the vibrations. Inside the *inner ear* is a shell-like tube full of fluid. The vibrating

air makes the fluid vibrate too. Nerves send messages about the vibrations to the brain. And when the brain has worked out what the messages mean, we "hear" the sounds.

The inner ear also helps us keep our balance by means of the fluid-filled tubes.

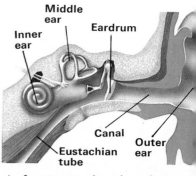

▲ **A cutaway drawing** of an ear.

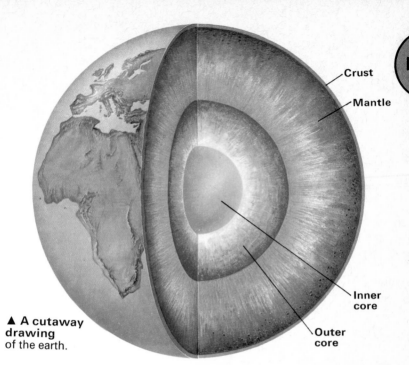

Crust

Mantle

Inner core

Outer core

▲ A cutaway drawing of the earth.

EARTH

The earth we live on is one of nine known planets that orbit the sun. Scientists think the earth was probably formed from a spinning cloud of gas and dust. From the age of the oldest rocks we know that the earth is more than four billion years old.

The earth has an invisible outer covering called the atmosphere. The atmosphere lies in several layers. The outer edge is about 1,000 miles from the earth. The lowest layer, the *troposphere,* is where life exists.

The earth is the only planet with large amounts of surface water. Oceans and seas cover 70 percent of its surface. The water was formed by chemical reactions after the earth had become a solid ball of rock.

The earth is rocky, and very rugged in places. It is made up of igneous rocks (produced by heat) and sedimentary, or deposited rocks. The surface is called the crust. Below the crust is the mantle. This is a thick layer of heavier rocks, up to 1,800 miles deep. Below this the rocks are molten (melted) because it is so hot. At the center of the earth is a core of solid rock, probably made of nickel and iron. The core acts as a giant magnet.

See also CALENDAR; FOSSIL; MOUNTAIN; OCEAN; PLANET; RIVER; ROCK; VOLCANO.

EARTHQUAKE

The earth's crust is made up of plates of rock, which can move and break. When they do, the ground shakes, or "quakes."

Not all earthquakes are major, destructive movements. About twenty severe earthquakes occur each year. But there are about a million minor tremors as well. Earthquakes are detected by instruments called seismometers.

See also VOLCANO.

EARTHWORM

Earthworms live in moist soil in gardens or lawns. They are made up of many segments. Tiny bristles on the segments help them to

East Germans mine more soft brown coal than any other nation. Until 1945, East and West Germany were one nation.

See also GERMANY and page 78.

ECHO

Sometimes when we shout, the sound of our voice comes back again a few seconds later. This is an echo. It happens when the sound is reflected by an object some distance away. Bats use sound echoes to find the insects they eat. Ships and submarines use sound echoes (sonar) to detect objects under water. Airports use echoes of radio waves (radar) to track aircraft.

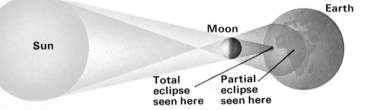

Sun

Moon

Earth

Total eclipse seen here

Partial eclipse seen here

move along in the ground. Earthworms eat little bits of leaves and decayed plant matter in the soil. They come to the surface to feed or after heavy rain. Earthworms help the garden by turning over the soil and breaking it up.

EAST GERMANY

East Germany is a communist country in Eastern Europe. It has low, flat land in the north and forests and mountains in the south. The Elbe and Oder rivers flow north toward the Baltic Sea.

ECLIPSE

When one heavenly body passes in front of another and blots out its light, we say an eclipse is taking place. The moon can cause an eclipse of the sun. This happens when the moon passes in front of the sun and blots out the sun's light. The moon's shadow falls on the earth and the sky goes dark. Then, as the moon's shadow passes by, daylight returns. An eclipse of the moon occurs when it moves into the shadow of the earth.

ECOLOGY

Ecology is the study of plants and animals and how they live in their natural communities. This science shows how living things make use of their surroundings, or environment, and studies the relationships between the plants and animals there.

Most plants and animals can live only in a particular kind of environment such as a desert, a pond, a marsh, or a forest. Each plant is suited to the temperature, soil, and water supply of the ground it grows in. Animals eat the plants or other animals. This link between plants and animals is called a food web.

ECUADOR

Ecuador is a country on the west coast of South America. Most of its people are Indian or part Indian, and speak Spanish or Quechua, an Indian language. Farmers in Ecuador raise cattle, llamas, and sheep. The capital, Quito, lies near the equator, but at 9,250 feet above sea level.

See also page 79.

EDISON, Thomas Alva
(1847–1931)

Edison was one of the world's greatest inventors. He patented nearly 1,300 inventions. Among these were the phonograph, the electric light, and an electric generating station. He said he owed his success not to genius but to hard work.

See also INVENTION.

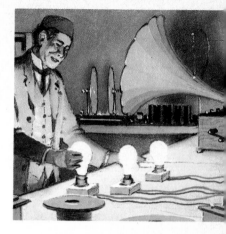

▲ **Edison** is shown with two of his inventions: the electric light bulb and the phonograph.

EGG

All animal life comes from some sort of egg. Some are laid by the female and develop outside her body before they hatch. Most mammals develop inside the mother's body. The egg, or ovum, must be joined with a sperm cell before it can develop.

EGYPT

Modern Egypt is a country of over 48 million people. Nearly all of them live on only four percent of the country's total area (386,900 square miles). This is the land irrigated by the Nile. The rest is desert.

Most Egyptians work on the land. They produce cotton, rice, fruits, grain, and vegetables. In some areas modern irrigation has been so successful that two or three crops are grown a year.

Egypt is an independent Arab republic. The major religion is Islam and the language is Arabic.

See also page 78.

EGYPT, ANCIENT

The civilization of ancient Egypt was centered on the river Nile. The Nile valley is hot and dry, but each year the river floods and spreads a rich silt over the land, making it fertile. The ancient Egyptians worshiped the Nile as a god.

The pharaohs (kings) of Egypt were very powerful. The people thought the pharaoh was a god. He owned everything and everyone had to obey his commands. The great pharaohs built huge tombs, often in the form of pyramids. The dead pharaoh was buried inside, surrounded by treasure and by all the things he would need in the next world, such as food, clothes, furniture, and weapons. The dead body was preserved, or *mummified,* before being buried. Archaeologists have learned much about ancient Egypt from tombs.

Rich Egyptians enjoyed lives of luxury. They had servants, slaves, dancers, and musicians. Ancient Egyptian civilization began around 3200 B.C. and lasted until 30 B.C., when Egypt was finally conquered by the Romans.

EINSTEIN, Albert (1879–1955)

Einstein was one of the most brilliant thinkers of modern times. He completely changed our ideas about space, time, and motion and about matter and energy. Einstein said that nothing can travel faster than light, and that mass and energy were different forms of the same thing. His ideas were set out in his famous theory of relativity.

EL SALVADOR

This country is the smallest in Central America. It has a mild climate and beautiful lakes and beaches. Many Salvadorians are farmers who raise cotton, sugarcane, and henequen, a plant used for making rope. In recent years conflicts between leftist and rightist guerrillas have disrupted the country.

See also page 79.

ELECTRICITY

Electricity is a form of energy. The electricity we use in our

▼ **A wealthy household** of ancient Egypt.

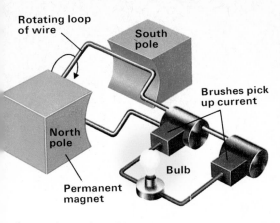

Rotating loop of wire

South pole

North pole

Permanent magnet

Brushes pick up current

Bulb

◀ A simple generator. An electric current can be made to flow when a loop of wire is rotated in the magnetic field between the poles of a magnet. Generators in power stations follow the same principles to make electricity for homes and factories.

E

homes is produced by generators in power stations. A battery is a portable supply of electricity.

Electricity flows through wires as electric current. It is actually a flow of electrons, the tiny particles present in all atoms. They flow easily in metals, which are called good conductors of electricity. Current can only flow if a wire makes a complete loop or circuit. Switches operate gaps in the circuit to start or stop the flow of electricity.

ELECTRONICS

Electronics is the study of the way electrons act as they flow through certain crystals, gases, or a vacuum. Electrons are tiny particles found in all atoms. Electronics explains how radar and television work. Electronic devices such as transistors and silicon chips are used in radios, calculators, and computers.

See also COMPUTER; RADAR; RADIO; SILICON CHIP; TELEVISION; TRANSISTOR.

▲ **Today African elephants** are closely guarded against poachers, who kill them for their valuable ivory tusks.

ELEMENT & COMPOUND

Elements are the building blocks from which all substances are formed. When a chemist splits up salt, he finds that it is made up of two substances called sodium and chlorine. No matter how hard he tries, he cannot split sodium and chlorine any further. They are chemical elements. In nature there are 92 elements, and scientists have made another 14.

Elements are made up of atoms. Groups of atoms joined together are called molecules. For example, a molecule of oxygen consists of two oxygen atoms. A substance whose molecules contain more than one kind of atom is called a compound.

Most elements are found as chemical compounds.

ELEPHANT

The elephant is the largest living land animal. A big male, or bull, may weigh 6 tons. Elephants live in herds. If one elephant is injured, the rest will help it. Elephants eat huge amounts of grass and leaves every day.

There are two kinds of elephant. The Indian elephant can be trained to work. But the larger African elephant is not easily tamed.

ELIZABETH I (1533–1603)

When Elizabeth was born, her father, Henry VIII, was furious.

He wanted a son to succeed him as King of England. But when Elizabeth became queen in 1558, she proved a strong ruler. She never married, and for 45 years successfully protected England against its chief enemies, France and Spain. Daring seamen, such as Francis Drake, and brilliant writers, such as William Shakespeare, made her reign one of the most exciting in English history.

ENERGY

When a piece of wood is set on fire, it burns and gives out light you can see and heat you can feel. Heat and light are two common forms of energy.

Wood is one kind of fuel, which releases energy when it is burned. Coal, gasoline, and natural gas are other fuels. When gasoline is burned in a car engine, the energy produced makes pistons turn the car wheels.

The *chemical energy* in the fuel has been changed into *mechanical energy* to turn the car wheels. When the car is moving it has *kinetic energy,* the energy of motion. A rock balancing on top of a cliff has *potential energy*—the energy of position.

ENGINE

We use many kinds of engines in the modern world. Some work the machines in our homes and factories, and others transport us in the air and on the roads. Most engines burn a fuel that produces energy to move the machine parts. Most car engines burn gasoline; trucks and buses have diesel engines, which burn oil. Airplanes have jet engines, which burn kerosene. There are all kinds of internal combustion engines, in which fuel is burned in an enclosed space. Steam engines and turbines burn fuel outside the engine.

See also ENERGY; FUEL; JET ENGINE.

ESKIMO

The Eskimos live in the cold Arctic regions. All Eskimos once hunted for their food. They traveled in skin canoes, called kayaks, and on sleds. In summer they lived in skin tents and in winter they built igloos. Most Eskimos now live in modern settlements.

▼ **An automobile engine,** with the side cut away to show the piston and crankshaft.

Piston

End of crankshaft

EUROPE

The continent of Europe is smaller than any of the other continents except Australia. Yet a fifth of the world's people live in Europe.

Most of Europe has fertile soil and good rainfall. Europe's farmers produce meat, grain, fruit, and vegetables. Europe is also rich in coal, iron ore, and other raw materials.

Europe lives by trade. It has good roads, railways, airports, and canals. Ships carry goods across the Baltic Sea, the North Sea, and the Mediterranean Sea, and to all parts of the world.

The people of Europe are made up of many different nationalities. Each has its own language and customs. In the past, European countries have fought wars with one another. European wars affected the rest of the world, because European countries were so powerful. Two world wars in this century have begun in Europe.

Today, the European countries are among the richest in the world. They try to live peacefully together. But there are divisions still. Most of the countries of Eastern Europe have communist governments; the western countries are democracies.

EUROPEAN ECONOMIC COMMUNITY

The European Economic Community, or EEC, is also known as

▶ **Europe** is a continent of contrasts – from cold frozen tundra and pine forests in the north, to the sun-parched plains of the south. There are lush green valleys and snowcapped mountains, open farmlands and crowded cities. Europe is a center of art and learning. Its many famous buildings show some of the continent's fascinating history.

BRITISH ISLES

FRAN

Atlantic Ocean

The Pyrenees

PORTUGAL SPAIN

AFRICA

the Common Market. It is a group of countries in western Europe. There are ten members: Belgium, the Netherlands, Luxembourg, France, Greece, West Germany, Italy, Denmark, Ireland, the United Kingdom,

Spain, and Portugal. They work and trade together. The EEC has a parliament and a court.

EVOLUTION

Evolution is the gradual process by which all living things have changed since life began millions of years ago. Fossils show us how creatures have changed.

The first creatures were very simple forms of life. They evolved into more complicated plants and animals. Fishes evolved

103

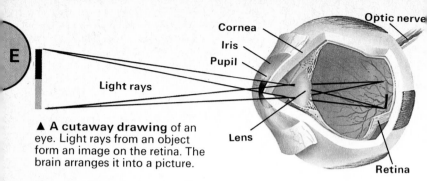

E

Light rays

▲ **A cutaway drawing** of an eye. Light rays from an object form an image on the retina. The brain arranges it into a picture.

Optic nerve
Cornea
Iris
Pupil
Lens
Retina

from smaller sea creatures. Some fish began breathing air and crawled onto dry land. These were the first amphibians. The amphibians evolved into reptiles. All birds and mammals, including humans, evolved from reptiles.

EXPLORERS

People have always had the urge to explore the unknown. Some explorers have gone in search of lands to settle. Others were greedy for riches, and some journeyed only in search of knowledge.

To the ancient peoples of Europe, "the world" meant the lands around the Mediterranean Sea. Only the Phoenicians dared sail out into the gray Atlantic Ocean beyond.

In the 900s the Vikings sailed in their small, fragile ships as far as North America. But until the invention of the magnetic compass in the 1300s, long sea voyages were very dangerous.

To reach the East, with its gold, spices, and silks, European merchants had to travel overland. Marco Polo reached China in 1275. Then the Portuguese

▼ **Roald Amundsen** was the first to reach the South Pole, in 1911.

discovered they could arrive at India by sailing around the coast of Africa. In 1492 Columbus reached America, the New World. By 1522 Magellan's sailors had proved that the world was round by sailing around it.

After this, explorers went out from Europe eager to find lands to settle as colonies. The last continent to be explored by Europeans was Africa. During the 1800s several explorers crossed this unknown continent. Then in 1909 Peary reached the North Pole, and in 1911 Amundsen beat Scott to the South Pole. Today few parts of the earth are unexplored.

See also COLUMBUS; COOK; DA GAMA; MAGELLAN; MARCO POLO; VIKINGS.

EYE

Our eyes are very delicate. Each eye is a ball full of liquid. In the center of the front is a black hole called the *pupil*. This lets in light. Behind the pupil is a *lens*. The lens focuses an image of whatever we are looking at onto a screen called the *retina*. Then messages are sent along a nerve to the brain. The brain arranges the messages into a picture again, and we "see."

The colored part of the eye is called the *iris*. It is a ring of muscle which makes the pupil larger or smaller. In bright light, the pupil gets smaller. But in dim light, it gets larger to let in as much light as possible.

FARMING

Farming is the world's most important industry. By raising animals and growing crops, farmers provide us with food. Civilization became possible only when people stopped being nomadic and settled down to farm.

Gradually, people learned how to plant seeds and grow crops, and how to keep and breed animals such as chickens, cattle, and sheep. Slowly, tools were devised to help.

In the 1800s and 1900s machines were invented to do the work of people and animals. There were better plows, seed drills, threshers, and reapers, and tractors replaced the horse and ox. Discoveries about crop rotation, fertilizers, and chemicals allowed farmers to grow larger crops.

FEMINISM

Feminism is a name given to the beliefs of the women's rights movement—that is, that women have the right to be equal to men as citizens under the law. Until the 1900s, women did not have these rights. Women could not

105

▶ **Campaigners for women's right** to the vote, or *suffrage*, became known as suffragettes. In 1918 American women won the right to vote.

own property or vote. Their earnings legally belonged to their husbands. Feminist leaders such as Elizabeth Cady Stanton, Susan B. Anthony, and Julia Ward Howe began the fight for equal rights in the United States. The modern feminist movement has fought for abortion reform, equal employment opportunity, and equal pay for women.

FERN

Ferns are primitive plants. There have been ferns on earth for over 300 million years. Some prehistoric ferns were as tall as trees.

Ferns have no flowers or seeds. Instead they have tiny cells called spores under their leaves. The wind scatters the spores onto the ground and they grow into tiny plants. Later these plants grow into new ferns.

FERTILIZER

A fertilizer is a substance that contains food which plants need. Plants use about twelve different foods from the soil. They need some, such as nitrogen, phosphorus, and potassium, in greater amounts than are usually found in the soil. So fertilizers are added to the soil.

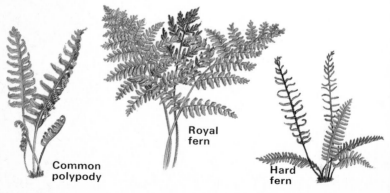

Common polypody

Royal fern

Hard fern

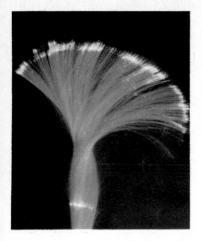

▲ **A bundle** of optical fibers.

Some fertilizers are made from natural substances; others are mainly chemicals.

FIBER OPTICS
An optical fiber is a glass or plastic strand along which light, including laser light, can be sent on a curved path. Each fiber can be as little as 0.0005 to 0.006 inch thick. The fibers are most often used together in bundles. Fiber optics may soon be used instead of metal wires for telephone systems, since a single fiber can carry thousands of telephone conversations at the same time.

See also LASER.

FINGERPRINT
The tiny ridges and furrows arranged in patterns on the tips of the fingers and thumbs are called fingerprints. No two people have the same fingerprints.

Even if the outer skin is damaged, the pattern does not change. This is why fingerprints are so helpful to the police in identifying criminals.

F

FINLAND
Finland is a northern European country that lies between Scandinavia and the Soviet Union. Part of it stretches north of the Arctic Circle. A land of lakes and forests, Finland produces wood and wood products, such as paper. Most Finns speak Finnish and Swedish. Finland was ruled by Sweden and then by Russia, but became an independent republic in 1917.

See also page 78.

FISH
Fishes are animals that spend their lives in water. Some fishes live in salt water and some live in fresh water. Some spend part of their lives in the sea, and part in rivers.

▲ **Some standard** fingerprint patterns.

Most fishes have bony skeletons. But a small group, including sharks, have skeletons made of gristle, or cartilage. Like all animals, fishes have to breathe oxygen. Their gills take oxygen out of the water. Some fishes breathe through their skin as well, and a few have lungs.

Fishes eat water animals, including other fishes, and plants. They swim by bending their bodies from side to side and by moving their tails. They use their fins to keep them upright and for steering and braking.

Most fishes are covered with scales. Some fishes have a line of special scales along each side of the body. This is called the lateral line. It helps the fish detect underwater vibrations. Most fishes have an air bladder inside their bodies to keep them at any level they choose. But the more primitive cartilage fishes do not

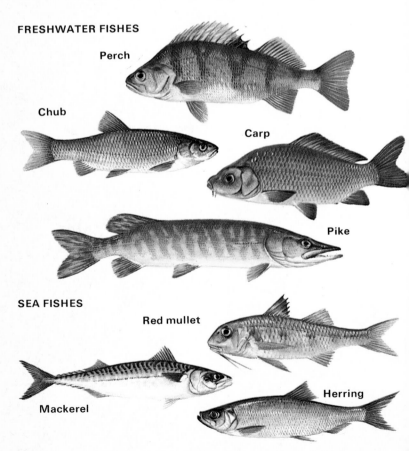

FRESHWATER FISHES

Perch

Chub

Carp

Pike

SEA FISHES

Red mullet

Mackerel

Herring

have this "swim bladder." If they stop swimming, they sink.

During the breeding season some fishes migrate over long distances to reach their spawning grounds. Most fishes lay their eggs and leave them floating in the water. Out of millions of eggs, only a few survive. Other fishes lay fewer eggs but take more care of them.

See also SEA HORSE; SHARK.

FISHING

Most fishes are caught in the sea; but in some countries river and lake fisheries are important. The best fishing grounds are in the Atlantic and Pacific oceans.

The most important food fishes are cod, mackerel, haddock, herring, flatfishes (such as flounder and sole), sardine, tuna, and salmon. Shellfishes, such as shrimps, lobsters, and oysters, also make valuable catches.

Most sea fishes are caught in nets. *Trawls* are long, bag-shaped nets towed along under water. A *purse seine* net is drawn around a shoal of fishes, then pulled up. *Gill nets* look rather like curtains: the fishes swim into them and are caught in the mesh. Fishes can also be caught on baited lines. This method is known as *lining* or *trolling*.

FLAG

Every country has its own flag. Organizations such as the United Nations and the Red Cross have flags, and kings and queens have their own personal flags.

The first flags were ornamental streamers. In battle, flags or standards, raised high on poles,

▼ **Some of the nets** and a trap used in sea fishing.

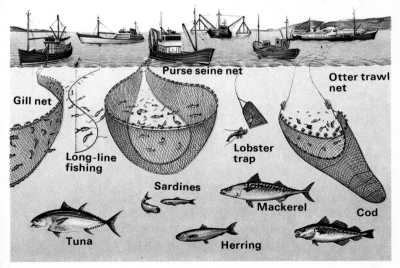

Gill net

Purse seine net

Otter trawl net

Long-line fishing

Lobster trap

Sardines

Mackerel

Cod

Tuna

Herring

FLAGS

1. Albania	37. N. Korea
2. Algeria	38. S. Korea
3. Argentina	39. Lebanon
4. Australia	40. Liberia
5. Austria	41. Malaysia
6. Belgium	42. Malta
7. Bolivia	43. Mexico
8. Brazil	44. Morocco
9. Bulgaria	45. Netherlands
10. Burma	46. New Zealand
11. Canada	47. Nigeria
12. Sri Lanka	48. Norway
13. Chile	49. Pakistan
14. China	50. Peru
15. Colombia	51. Philippines
16. Cuba	52. Poland
17. Czechoslovakia	53. Portugal
18. Denmark	54. Romania
19. Ecuador	55. Saudi Arabia
20. Ethiopia	56. Sierra Leone
21. Finland	57. Singapore
22. France	58. South Africa
23. E. Germany	59. Spain
24. W. Germany	60. Sweden
25. Ghana	61. Switzerland
26. Greece	62. Thailand
27. Hungary	63. Trinidad & Tobago
28. Iceland	64. Tunisia
29. India	65. Turkey
30. Indonesia	66. United Kingdom
31. Iraq	67. United States
32. Ireland	68. Uruguay
33. Israel	69. U.S.S.R.
34. Italy	70. Venezuela
35. Jamaica	71. Yugoslavia
36. Japan	72. Zaire

were easily seen rallying points for soldiers.

In the Middle Ages there were several flags of different shapes (gonfalons, banners, and pennons), but today most are rectangular. Flags are also used at sea to identify ships and to send messages.

FLEA

The flea is a small, wingless insect. It has three pairs of strong legs that are especially good for jumping. It is a parasite that lives on and sucks the blood of birds and animals, including humans. Fleas can be dangerous because they carry diseases.

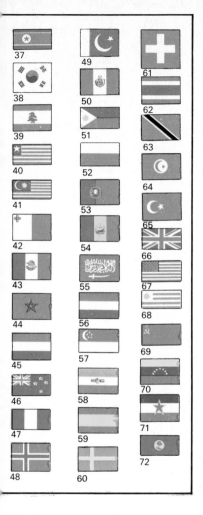

world. The Kennedy Space Center at Cape Canaveral is the launch site for U.S. space missions.

See also page 263.

FLOWER

Most plants have flowers. The flower is the part of the plant where the seeds develop. Without it, the plant could not reproduce itself. Inside each seed is all the "information" needed to make a new plant grow. Most flowers appear in the summer when the plant is fully grown. Flowers come in all shapes and sizes, but they all have the same basic parts.

The most important parts are called *stamens* and *carpels*. The

▼ **Florida's Seaquarium** in Miami, built in 1938, led the way as the first aquarium of its kind in the world.

FLORIDA

The state of Florida lies on a peninsula bounded on the east by the Atlantic and on the west by the Gulf of Mexico. Called the Sunshine State, Florida has a tropical to subtropical climate. Lining its coast are some of the most famous beaches in the

111

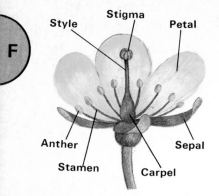

▲ **This diagram** shows the parts of a typical flower. Some flowers have only one ovule. Others have hundreds. After they are fertilized, ovules develop into seeds.

stamens are male parts, which produce a powder called *pollen*. The carpels are female parts. Each carpel has a sticky top, called a *stigma*. It is sticky so that pollen will cling to it. When this happens, the *ovule* in the lower part of the carpel can develop into a seed.

See also FRUIT; PLANT.

FLY

There are more than 750,000 different kinds of flies—one of the largest groups of insects in the world. Flies have only one pair of wings.

Some flies are harmless, but many carry germs and spread dangerous diseases. For example, a housefly will land on a piece of human food and vomit up a drop of its own last meal. It sucks up most of it, but millions of bacteria remain behind.

FOG

A cloud that forms close to the ground is called fog. Fog is formed when warm, moist air passes over cool land or water, or when cool air moves over warm water or moist land. The water vapor in the air turns into tiny drops of water. That is why fog feels damp. After a clear, warm day, heat from the land may cause a thin fog to form.

FOOD

Our bodies need energy to live and grow. This energy comes from the food we eat. The three most important substances in food are *carbohydrates, fats,* and *proteins.* Carbohydrates are food "fuels." They give us energy to work, move, and keep warm. Sugar and starch are carbohydrates. We eat carbohydrates in bread, potatoes, rice, desserts, and cakes. Cream, butter, and the fat in meat provide us with fats. These are also good fuels.

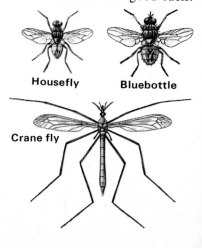

Housefly   **Bluebottle**

Crane fly

But if we eat too many carbo-hydrates or fats, our bodies store what we cannot use. Then we get fat. Proteins build the body's cells and are vital to good health. Protein-rich foods are eggs, lean meat, cheese, fish, and beans.

FOOTBALL
Football is one of the most popular team sports in America. Two teams of 11 players each try to get the ball past their opponents' goal to score points. The game involves kicking, passing, carrying the ball, and tackling, and each team member has a job to do. Football is played at every level in the United States, from professional to little league. Its popularity has recently begun to spread to other countries.

FORD, Henry (1863–1947)
Henry Ford was an American automobile manufacturer. He was the first man to develop assembly-line methods of production. In mass production the parts of the car are added to the car body on a conveyor belt. Ford could produce many cars very cheaply. Between 1908 and 1927 he mass-produced 15 million Model T cars alone.

FOREST
Land that is covered with trees is forest. Today about a third of the earth's land surface is covered by forests. There are about 20,000 different kinds of trees, of which 1,000 produce good timber.

In cold lands the forests are mainly of conifers, such as pines and firs. The largest coniferous forests are in northern Europe, Canada, and Siberia.

Milder countries have forests of broad-leaved trees, such as oaks, elms, beeches, birches, and maples. These trees are deciduous: that is, they shed their leaves every year.

In the hot, wet lands close to the equator there are tropical forests of trees such as ebony and mahogany, whose wood is very hard. There are vast rain forests in South America, central Africa, and southeast Asia. Swamp forests of mangroves are often found near the coasts.

FOSSIL
Fossils are the hardened remains of dead animals and plants that lived thousands of years ago.

▼ **This fossil** of the *Eoplatax* fish is about 50 million years old.

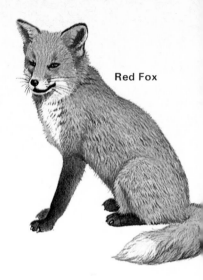

Red Fox

They tell us what life was like before written records were kept.

Some fossils are the impressions made by remains which have since disappeared. They are often found in rock because the plants and animals were covered by mud or sand which later turned into rock.

Sometimes a whole body is preserved, including the hair and skin. Sometimes the body has dissolved away and the space it left filled with mud or sand that slowly turned into rock. Most commonly, though, fossils show us the hard parts of animals, such as bones or shells.

▲ **Thousands of people** visit Paris, the French capital, each year. In the background is the Arc de Triomphe.

FOX

Foxes belong to the dog family. They hunt by night for rabbits, mice, and voles. The female fox is called a vixen. She rears her cubs in an underground den.

Farmers dislike foxes because they raid hen houses. Foxes are often hunted or shot. Silver and blue Arctic foxes are bred on special farms for their fur. The little fennec fox lives in the desert.

FRANCE

France is the largest country in western Europe. Its beautiful scenery includes forests, plains, valleys, mountains, and rivers.

France has fertile soil and a mild climate. Many of its people are farmers. Throughout France grapes are grown to make wine. French cheeses are also famous. France has many industries and

114

Benjamin Franklin

is a member of the European Economic Community. Its capital city is Paris.

In 1789 the French people overthrew their king and set up a republic. This important event is called the French Revolution.

See also page 78.

FRANKLIN, Benjamin
(1706–1790)
Benjamin Franklin was an American politician, scientist,

and patriot. He began as a printer, publishing an almanac that made him a fortune. He was a signer of the Declaration of Independence, and at the end of the Revolutionary War he helped draw up the peace treaty with Britain. His inventions include bifocal eyeglasses and the lightning rod.

FREUD, Sigmund (1856–1939)
Sigmund Freud was a Viennese doctor who made a great contribution to the study of the human mind. He taught that the *subconscious*, the activity of the mind that we are not aware of, provides clues to a person's mental state. He also developed the system of *psychoanalysis*, a kind of examination of the mind.

FROG AND TOAD
These animals are amphibians. They can live on land, but must

▼ **The life cycle** of the frog. The eggs or spawn grow into tadpoles. Tadpoles breathe like fish, through gills. As they grow they develop legs, and their gills become lungs. After three months they become baby frogs.

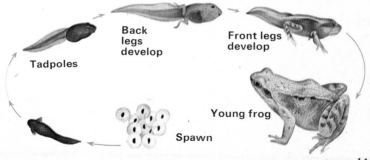

Back legs develop

Front legs develop

Tadpoles

Young frog

Spawn

115

return to the water to lay eggs.

Frogs and toads look rather alike. But frogs use their long back legs to hop. Toads crawl or run. Both eat insects and worms, catching their prey with their long, sticky tongues.

In spring frogs and toads travel to ponds and streams to breed. They lay eggs called spawn. The eggs hatch into tadpoles. Tadpoles swim like fish and breathe through gills. But soon they grow legs, lose their tails, and develop lungs. Finally, they become tiny frogs or toads.

FRUIT

We all recognize apples, bananas, and oranges as fruits. But pea pods, walnuts, cucumbers, acorns, and dandelion "clocks" are also fruits. Growing fruit is an important industry.

The fruit is the part of a plant that protects the seed. It helps to

▲ **A frog,** hind legs poised to leap, rests on a waterside rock.

spread the seed, so that new plants can grow. Some fruits have wings (such as the sycamore) or light, fluffy heads (such as the dandelion) so that the seeds will blow away. Other fruits are sweet and juicy, so that animals will carry them away as food. Burrs are fruits that cling to the fur of passing animals.

See also FLOWER; PLANT.

FUEL

Fuels are substances that release energy when burned. This process is called combustion.

Fuel may be solid, liquid, or gas. Coal, wood, charcoal, and peat are solid fuels. The most important liquid fuels come from petroleum. Natural gas, a compound of hydrogen and carbon, is often found near petroleum.

GAGARIN, Yuri (1934–1968)

Yuri Gagarin was a Russian pilot who became the first man in space. After training in the air force and as a cosmonaut, Gagarin manned the spacecraft *Vostok I* on its launch on April 12, 1961. He went 200 miles above the earth at more than 17,500 miles per hour—higher and faster than anyone before him.

▼ **The Andromeda Galaxy** is very much like our own galaxy.

GALAXY

Our sun is part of a great family of stars. We call this family the Milky Way galaxy, or just the galaxy. A galaxy is a big group of stars that move together through space. Each galaxy contains about 100,000 million stars and probably many planets. Some stars are grouped together in giant *clusters*. The galaxies also contain great clouds of gas and dust called *nebulae*.

GALILEO (1564–1642)

Galileo was an Italian astronomer. In 1609 he became the first person to look at the sky through a telescope. He saw the mountains on our moon and the moons of the planet Jupiter.

Galileo was skilled at mathematics and carried out scientific experiments. He discovered how

a pendulum swings and showed that different weights fall to the ground at the same rate.

GAMA, Vasco da (*c*.1460–1524)
This Portuguese explorer was the first to find a sea route to India. He sailed from Lisbon in July 1497, rounded the Cape of Good Hope in November, and went on to land in southwestern India in May 1498. He returned to Portugal with two ships laden with spices.

GANDHI, Mohandas Karamchand (1869–1948)
Gandhi helped to free India from British rule. Known as the Mahatma, or Great Soul, he believed that all violence was wrong. So he used "peaceful non-cooperation" as a weapon against his opponents. He was born in India. From 1893 to 1915 he worked against racial hatred in South Africa.

When India became indepen-

dent in 1947, Muslims and Hindus began fighting. Gandhi failed to make peace between them, and was shot by a Hindu fanatic on January 30, 1948.

GARIBALDI, Giuseppe (1807–1882)
Garibaldi was an Italian patriot. In his time Italy was made up of several separate states, and large

◀ **Galileo** and the telescope with which he discovered the moons of Jupiter.

▼ **Gandhi** lying in state after his assassination in 1948. Vast crowds came to mourn at his funeral.

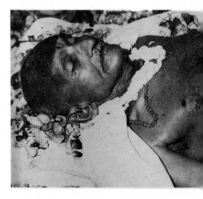

parts of northern Italy belonged to Austria. Garibaldi fought to make Italy one country from 1834 until 1860. Then Victor Emmanuel became king of the whole of Italy.

GAS
All the substances that make up our world can exist in three forms—as a solid, liquid, or gas.

Gases are different from the other two forms because they have no shape and completely fill anything they are put in.

The air we breathe is a gas, or rather a mixture of gases. It contains mainly oxygen and nitrogen. All living things need oxygen to live. We breathe in oxygen and breathe out another gas—carbon dioxide.

Some gases, such as natural gas and hydrogen, are valuable as fuels. Others, such as chlorine, carbon monoxide, and hydrogen sulfide, are very poisonous.

See also FUEL; OXYGEN.

GASOLINE

Gasoline is a fuel used to power most cars, outboard boat engines, motorcycles, and small airplanes. It is a mixture of chemical compounds called *hydrocarbons*. Most gasoline comes from petroleum and is separated out by a process called *distillation*. The gasoline that runs your car also contains chemicals to help keep the engine clean, increase mileage, and burn the gas more smoothly.

GEM

Some rocks contain beautiful crystals that can be cut to show great brilliance and sparkle. They are called gems, or gemstones. They can be set in gold, platinum, and silver to form beautiful pieces of jewelry.

The finest gems are diamonds. Red rubies, green emeralds, and blue sapphires are also valuable. Some gems are not crystals, but lovely stones. They include opal and lapis lazuli. Pearls are gems that oysters produce in their shells.

See also CRYSTAL.

GENETICS

The science of genetics explains why living things look and behave as they do. Advanced animals have two sexes, male and female. Each individual produces sex cells. If a male and female sex cell join, the female cell grows into a new individual. Each parent passes on certain characteristics to its offspring. This process is called *heredity*.

Heredity works in an amazing way. Inside every cell are tiny *chromosomes*, largely made of a chemical called DNA. Different

▼ **Polished opals** photographed in front of the rock, or ore, in which they are found.

119

PARENTS

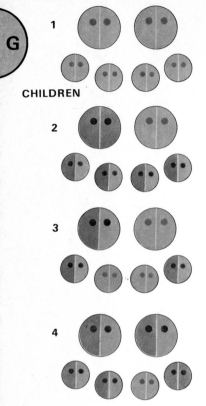

CHILDREN

◀ **Genetic patterns.** If both parents have two blue eye genes (1), all their children will have blue eyes. If one parent has two brown eye genes and the other has two blue eye genes (2), the children will all have brown eyes because the brown gene is dominant. But those children will have what is called a recessive blue eye gene. If they have children with a blue-eyed person (3), or another person with a recessive blue gene (4), some of their children may have blue eyes.

GENGHIS KHAN (1167–1227) Genghis Khan was one of the most feared men in history. He was born Temujin, son of a Mongol prince, but became known as Genghis Khan, meaning "conqueror of the world." The Mongols came from central Asia. Wherever Genghis Khan led his Mongol army, terrible tales were told of his cruelty. He conquered many tribes in China, Russia, Afghanistan, and Persia and so won an enormous empire for the Mongols.

GEOLOGY

Geology is the study of the substances that make up the earth and of the forces that act upon it to change it. Geologists work to find what kinds of rocks the earth is made of and how they got there. They study volcanoes and earthquakes for clues about the underground movements of the earth. To understand the earth as it is today, geologists study the history of the planet

parts of each chromosome carry different *coded messages*. Each part is called a *gene*. The genes carry all the information needed to make a new plant or animal. They decide its sex, what it looks like, and also what characteristics it inherits.

Some inherited characteristics are stronger than others. They are *dominant*. Weaker ones are *recessive*. Genes for brown eyes, for example, will always dominate over the weaker genes for blue eyes.

120

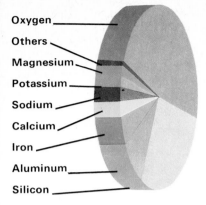

Oxygen
Others
Magnesium
Potassium
Sodium
Calcium
Iron
Aluminum
Silicon

▲ **This pie chart** shows the chief elements in the earth's crust. By weight, oxygen makes up about 46 percent and silicon about 28 percent. Aluminum, iron, calcium, sodium, potassium, and magnesium make up 24 percent.

from its beginnings four billion years ago.

Geologists can help us to locate valuable mineral resources such as coal and oil. They can also help engineers in choosing sites for bridges or tunnels.

GEORGIA

Georgia is a southeastern state bordering the Atlantic Ocean north of Florida. Sometimes called the Empire State of the South, Georgia is a busy industrial and agricultural state, the nation's top producer of poultry and peanuts. Atlanta, the capital, is the commercial and industrial center of the southeast. Other Georgia cities are Macon, Savannah, and Columbus.

See also page 263.

GERMANY

Two countries in Europe are called Germany. Until 1945 each was part of a single country, called Germany. Germany began two devastating wars in this century—World War I (1914–18) and World War II (1939–45). After World War II the Russians controlled the eastern part (now East Germany or the D.D.R.), while the Western Allies held the rest (West Germany). Berlin, the old capital, was also divided.

Northern Germany has a seacoast on the North and Baltic seas. Here the land is mostly flat. Central Germany is hilly and wooded, and in the south are high mountains and thick forests.

Germany has fertile soil and a mild climate. Farmers grow

▼ **The Mosel Valley** in West Germany is a famous wine-producing region.

G

121

cereals, potatoes, and sugar beets, and make grapes into wine. They raise cattle and pigs.

Germany has plenty of coal, iron ore, timber, and hydroelectric power. So industry is important. There are many factories, especially in the Ruhr valley in West Germany.

Both Germanies have built up new, modern industries. West Germany is a member of the EEC (p. 102). East Germany is not so rich and the people have less freedom.

See also page 78.

GEYSER
A geyser is a spring that spouts hot water and steam into the air from time to time. It is a small sign of the searing heat deep inside the earth.

A geyser consists of a hole which goes down to a layer of hot rock (usually uncooled lava) and water. When the water is super-

Giraffe

heated by the rocks, it erupts or shoots into the air.

Geysers are found in many volcanic regions. The most famous are in Japan, the United States, and New Zealand.

See also VOLCANO.

GIRAFFE
The giraffe is the tallest animal in the world. It can reach nearly 20 feet in height. Giraffes live in Africa. They eat leaves, not

◄ **The Diamond Geyser,** Rotorua, New Zealand, erupts to over 30 feet.

122

► **A glacier** in the Swiss Alps.

grass, and when they drink, they have to spread their legs wide in order to reach the water. They run swiftly to escape their enemies.

GLACIER

A glacier is a slow-moving river of ice. It flows down the slopes of mountains from an ice cap or high snow field. Glaciers push stones and boulders along with them. They scrape the soil from the land, smooth the hills, and scoop out valleys. The rocky mounds piled up by glaciers are called *moraines*.

During the Ice Ages glaciers spread across the Northern Hemisphere. Boulders carried with the ice can still be seen, even though the glaciers melted long ago.

See also ICE AGE; ICEBERG.

GLASS

Glass is a useful material. It is transparent, easy to shape, and cheap to make. It can be made as flat sheets for windows, or into curved lenses for cameras, microscopes, and other instruments. It can be blown to make bottles, tumblers, and other objects.

Glass is made from some of the cheapest materials you can think of—sand, limestone, and soda ash. These three ingredients are mixed together and heated in a very hot furnace. They melt and become glass.

GOAT

The goat was one of the earliest animals to be tamed. Its milk, meat, wool, and skin have been useful to people for thousands of years.

The goat is tougher than its

Goat

relative the sheep. It can live in dry, rocky country. It climbs well and can eat almost anything. Herds of hungry goats have turned good pastures into deserts. Wild goats live on high mountain crags.

123

▲ **Gold bars** stacked in a vault.

GOLD

Gold is a heavy, yellow metal. It has been used for thousands of years to make jewelry and ornaments because it is beautiful and does not lose its shine. It is also easy to shape. It can be drawn into fine wire or beaten into thin sheets without snapping. Gold is precious because it is scarce. It is found in the ground as a metal. Sometimes large lumps of gold, or nuggets, are mined in the rocks. But usually gold is found in lodes, or veins, in rocks. Half the world's gold is mined in just one part of South Africa.

See also METAL.

GOLD RUSH

Gold is one of our most valuable metals. It is also rare. Whenever a new source of gold has been discovered, it has set off a gold rush. People have flocked to the area to "strike it rich." The most famous gold rush in the United States began with the discovery of gold in California in 1848. Another took place in 1896 along the Klondike Creek in the Yukon valley of Alaska and Canada.

GOLF

In golf, a sport that originated in Scotland, players hit a ball from hole to hole around a course of 9 or 18 holes, using a long, slender club. A player starts off from a *tee,* hitting the ball along the *fairway* to the *green,* a closely mown grassy area that contains the hole. The golfer using the lowest number of strokes to get around is the winner. A variety of clubs is used, carried in a bag

▼ **A golfer** drives the ball toward the hole, which can be 100 to 600 yards from the tee.

124

or a cart around the course. Professional golfers are experts and earn their living from the sport, but amateur players of all ages play for sport and enjoyment.

GOVERNMENT
Government was needed as soon as people began living in groups. People living together in a group have to agree on what jobs must be done and who should do them. In a primitive tribe the best hunter or strongest warrior might become the ruler or chief.

The ancient Greeks were the first to try a form of government called *democracy*, or "rule by the people." The people met to discuss new laws and to decide what taxes should be paid. This was the beginning of the modern legislature.

Today every country has a head of state. In the United States the president is head of state and head of the government. He also commands the armed forces. Presidents are elected every four years. The legislative body is Congress, which is divided into the House of Representatives and the Senate.

Britain is a monarchy, so the head of state is the queen. But the country is ruled by a government of ministers. The head of the government is the prime minister. Parliament is divided into two parts, the House of Commons and the House of Lords.

In a democracy more than one

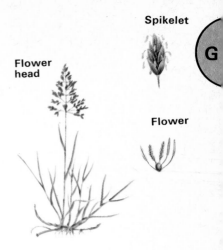

▲ **Grasses** have thin, wiry roots. The flowers are arranged in groups called spikelets.

political party is allowed. But in Communist countries, only the Communist party takes part in the government.

See also COMMUNISM; DEMOCRACY.

GRASS
Most grasses are slender, with hollow stems and pointed leaves. The plants keep growing even when the leaves are cut.

Cereals are grasses that are also valuable foods. Many farm animals eat grass, fresh in summer and dried as hay in winter. Sugarcane is a kind of grass.

GRASSHOPPER
Grasshoppers are insects. They live in fields and meadows and feed on green plants. They can

▲ **This mountain grasshopper** is well camouflaged against the stony ground.

hop as far as 30 inches. The male grasshopper chirps to attract a mate. He does this by rubbing the inside of his back legs against his wings.

GRAVITY

Throw a ball into the air and it will fall back to the ground. This is because the earth pulls it back. The earth's pull is called gravity. Gravity is one of the basic forces in the universe. Magnetism is another. Sir Isaac Newton first stated the laws of gravity. He said that every object in the universe has an attraction for every other object.

Gravity is what keeps all the heavenly bodies in their paths through the heavens. It keeps the moon moving in a circle around the earth. It keeps the earth moving around the sun. If there were no gravity, the moon and earth would fly off into space.

GREAT DEPRESSION

This is the name given to the period in American history that followed the stock market crash of 1929. Many small stores and businesses had to close because people could not afford to buy their goods and services. Large companies were forced to cut production and lay off thousands of workers. The government under President Roosevelt started many new projects to provide jobs for Americans.

GREECE, ANCIENT

The ancient Greeks built one of the greatest of all civilizations. It

▼ **The stock market crash** on Wall Street in 1929 brought crowds to the New York Stock Exchange at the start of the Great Depression.

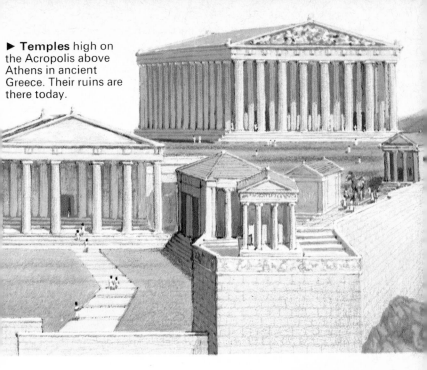

► **Temples** high on the Acropolis above Athens in ancient Greece. Their ruins are there today.

began some 4,000 years ago when wandering tribes from central Europe came to the land that we now call Greece.

Over the centuries, the Greek civilization developed. Cities were built. Craftsmen made beautiful gold ornaments and bronze weapons. Art, music, and poetry developed.

About 2,500 years ago the Greeks of Athens set up a new form of government, called *democracy,* which means "rule by the people." All the citizens had a right to say how they were to be ruled. This was an important new idea.

Life in Athens was relaxed. The Athenians built fine temples

and public buildings. For entertainment, the Athenians played music on flutes and lyres or they went to the theater. The Athenians loved to hear stories of great Greek heroes and their deeds. The greatest of these stories were told by the poet Homer in two long poems, called the *Iliad* and the *Odyssey.* The beauty of life in Athens can be seen from the ruins which still remain.

Athens was only one of a number of city-states in Greece. The states often quarreled. The greatest rival of Athens was Sparta, and the two states were very different. Sparta was a military state, ruled by all-powerful kings. Its people were soldiers and the Spartans had no use for art, philosophy, or comfortable homes.

The Greeks were very fond of athletics, such as running, javelin and discus throwing, and wrestling. The first Olympic Games, named after Mount Olympus, home of the Greek gods, took place in 776 B.C. The Greeks had many gods, but the greatest was Zeus, king of the gods.

The age of the city-states ended in Greece in 338 B.C. Then, King Philip of Macedonia brought all of Greece under his rule.

Greek ideas have survived many centuries and have had great influence. The way we live and think today owes a great deal to the civilization of ancient Greece.

GUATEMALA
Guatemala is a small country in Central America, south of Mexico. It is a land of jungles, volcanoes, and hot, dry desert. About half the people are Indians; most of the rest are of mixed Spanish and Indian blood. Agriculture is the main industry: farms produce coffee, cotton, and bananas. Guatemala was once the heart of the Maya empire. The ruins of their magnificent palaces and temples can still be seen.

See also page 79.

GUINEA PIG
The guinea pig is a member of the rodent family. Guinea pigs have

Guinea pig

Hamster

four toes on their front feet and three on their hind feet.

All varieties of guinea pig are descended from the wild cavy of the Andes. Long before Europeans went to America, the Indians there had tamed it and kept it for its meat.

GULF STREAM
The Gulf Stream is a very important warm ocean current. It is surface water that flows in a clockwise direction around the north Atlantic Ocean. It begins near the equator and drifts past Florida up the coast of the United States toward Newfoundland and then moves toward Europe.

Part of the Gulf Stream washes the shores of France, the British Isles, Norway, and Iceland. Because it is warm, winter in these countries is much milder than that of other places just as far north.

GUN
Guns are weapons that fire bullets or shells. Small arms, also called firearms, include pistols,

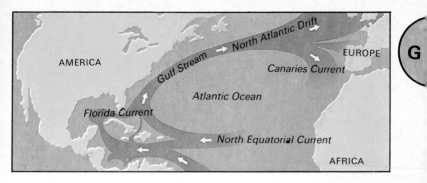

▲ **The path** of the Gulf Stream across the Atlantic Ocean.

revolvers, shotguns, and rifles. Big military guns—artillery pieces—include field guns, howitzers, and mortars.

All guns work in roughly the same way. A gun has a long, hollow, metal *barrel*. The *bore* of a gun is the width of the hole in the barrel. One end of the barrel, the *breech,* is closed; the other end, the *muzzle,* is open. When the gun is fired, an explosive charge inside a *cartridge* sends a bullet down the barrel and out of the muzzle with great force.

GUTENBERG, Johannes
(*c*.1398–1468)
Gutenberg invented movable type for printing in about 1439. His invention meant that books could be produced cheaply. Knowledge, once available only to a few people, spread more rapidly through Europe.

GYMNASTICS
Gymnastics consists of exercises that develop and strengthen the body. There are two main types of gymnastics—Swedish and German. They were developed in the early 1800s. Gymnasts use apparatus such as beams, rings, and horizontal and parallel bars.

Gymnastics forms part of the Olympic Games. Mastery of this sport calls for strength, artistic feeling, and technical skill.

▼ **A gymnast** requires both strength and grace.

H

HALLEY'S COMET
Halley's Comet is named after Edmund Halley, the English astronomer who discovered it. Visible from earth every 76 years, it was most recently seen in 1986. Space probes from earth showed details of the "dirty snowball" nucleus of the comet. The nucleus alone was about nine miles long.

HANDEL, George Frideric
(1685–1759)
Handel was a German-born English composer who was famous for his operas, concertos, and oratorios. His best known works are the *Messiah, Fireworks Music,* and *Water Music.*

HANNIBAL (247–183 B.C.)
Hannibal, a general and statesman, was one of ancient Rome's greatest enemies. He came from Carthage in North Africa. In 218 B.C. he invaded Italy by crossing the Alps with his entire army including war elephants. He fought the Romans for fifteen years but was never able to crush them.

HARVEY, William (1578–1657)
Harvey was an English physician who showed how the heart functioned and proved that the blood circulates around the body.

HAWAII
Hawaii became the fiftieth state of the Union in 1959. It is a group of islands in the north Pacific.

▲ **This photograph** of Halley's Comet and Venus was taken in South Africa in 1910.

The seven largest are Hawaii, Molokai, Maui, Oahu, Kauai, Lanai, and Niihau. The most important is Oahu, which has the state capital, Honolulu. The international airport at Honolulu is the busiest in the Pacific.

See also page 263.

HEART
Your heart beats about 70 times every minute. It is a pump—a

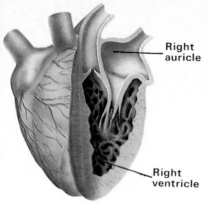

Right auricle

Right ventricle

▲ **A diagram** of the heart.

bag of extra-strong muscle that pumps blood around the body.

The pump is divided into four parts: a left and right *auricle* above a left and right *ventricle*. The two sides of the pump work independently. Blood fresh from the lungs enters the left auricle and is forced through a valve down to the left ventricle. From there it is forced into the body's main artery, the aorta, and out of the heart, ready to flow around the body.

On the other side, "stale" blood from the body enters the right auricle, passes into the right ventricle, and is forced out toward the lungs, where it will dump its carbon dioxide and pick up vital oxygen.

HELICOPTER

A helicopter is a machine that can fly forward, upward, downward, and sideways. This is because it has a rotor, or rotating (turning), wing. Ordinary airplanes have fixed wings and their engines can drive them forward only. The helicopter's rotor consists of metal blades mounted on top of the body. Turned by the engine, the rotor screws itself into the air to lift the helicopter off the ground. When flying forward, the rotor blades are angled so that they push the air backward.

HERALDRY

Heraldry is the study of coats of arms, and the people who control and design them are known as heralds. Heraldry began during the Middle Ages. It was difficult to tell if a knight in armor was a friend or an enemy, so knights put *crests* on their helmets and painted designs called *devices* on their shields.

Each knight had his own coat

▲ **A helicopter** landing on an aircraft carrier.

131

of arms, which became his family badge or emblem.

HERCULES

Hercules is a hero of ancient Greek and Roman mythology. In a fit of madness, he killed his wife and children. The god Apollo ordered Hercules to perform Twelve Labors in punishment. Today the word "Herculean" is used to describe a mammoth or difficult task.

HIBERNATION

In winter when food is scarce, many animals go into a long, deep sleep. This is called hibernation.

During late summer and fall, while food is still plentiful, the animal eats until its body is fat. Then it digs itself into the ground or finds a sheltered place to sleep. While the animal is asleep, its heartbeat and its breathing slows. It uses so little energy that it can live solely on the fat in its body.

◄ **These hibernating** animals all live in North America.

Dormouse

Woodchuck

American badger

Frog

HIEROGLYPHIC

This was a system of writing used in ancient Egypt. Hieroglyphics began before 300 B.C. with a very simple kind of picture writing in which each picture stood for an object. Later, pictures came to represent ideas. Finally, pictures were used to represent sounds in the spoken language.

Hieroglyphics fell into disuse and remained unread until a Frenchman called Champollion deciphered inscriptions on a stone slab, the Rosetta Stone, in 1822.

HIPPOPOTAMUS

The huge hippopotamus lives in the rivers of Africa. Its name means "river horse" but it is actually related to the pig.

Despite their gaping jaws and tusks, hippos eat only plants. They spend the day in the water, floating or walking along the river bottom, and come ashore at night. They love to wallow in mud. Hippos can be dangerous if annoyed.

▼ **A mother hippo** splashing about with her young.

HINDU

Hinduism is a religion. Hindus believe that God is present in all things. Their most important holy books are the *Vedas*. Hindu priests, or Brahmins, worship the supreme God. Ordinary people worship lesser gods, such as Vishnu, God of Life.

HISTORY

History is the story of the past. Historians are mostly interested in famous people and great events, because these things affect nations. But history is also concerned with people's lives.

Science, medicine, art, religion, and architecture all have histories of their own. History is revealed in many ways: by digging for it, by reading about it in old books and manuscripts, and by listening to people talk.

See the history chart on pages 134–137.

B.C.	AFRICA
c.8000	Farming begins
c.4000–3500	Wheel, plow, and sail in Egypt
c.3500	Early writing in Egypt
c.2700–c.2200	Age of Pyramids in Egypt
2050–1800	Middle Kingdom under Theban rulers
670	Assyrians conquer Egypt
525	Persians conquer Egypt
500	Nok civilization founded in Nigeria
332	Alexander the Great conquers Egypt
306	Ptolemy I founds new dynasty in Egypt
30	Death of Antony and Cleopatra; Rome conquers Egypt

A.D.	
100	Kingdom of Ethiopia founded
429–44	Vandals occupy North Africa
533–4	Belisarius reconquers North Africa for Justinian
800s	Civilization of Ghana
969	Fatimids conquer Egypt

	ASIA
c.6000	Rice cultivation in Far East
c.4000	Farming, plow, wheel in Mesopotamia
c.3000	Civilization of Sumeria
c.2700–1750	Harappan civilization in Indus Valley
c.2000–c.1200	Hittite civilization in Turkey
c.1750–1000	Shang dynasty in China
c.1200–650	Domination of Assyrian Empire
1000–c.500	Chou dynasty in China
551	Birth of Confucius
c.550–330	Achaemenid Empire in Persia
530s	Buddha preaching
334–323	Campaigns of Alexander the Great
c.320	Mauryan Empire in India
200 B.C.–A.D. 220	Han dynasty in China
c.6	Birth of Jesus
c.30	Crucifixion of Jesus, founder of Christianity
226–636	Sassanid Empire in Persia
304–8	Huns invade China
c.320	Gupta Empire in Ganges Valley: "Golden Age" of Hindu culture
c.300–500	Main spread of Buddhism in China
c.520	Decimal system invented in India
540	Persian-Byzantine War begins
618–906	T'ang dynasty in China
622	Muhammad founds religion of Islam
636–750	Arabs conquer an empire from Spain to the Indus Valley
794	Japanese capital moves to Kyoto
?960–1280	Sung dynasty in China

134

EUROPE	
c.6500	Farming begins in Greece and the Aegean
c.2000	Bronze Age in north Europe
c.2000–1200	Minoan and Mycenean civilization in Crete and Greece
753	Rome founded
c.750–c.550	Greeks and Phoenicians colonize Mediterranean and Black Sea
490–479	Battles of the Persian Wars
431–404	Peloponnesian War
c.380–300	Work of Plato, Euclid, and Aristotle
c.327–300	Main Roman expansion
27	Octavian takes title of Augustus: end of Roman republic

AMERICA AND AUSTRALASIA   **B.C.**

EUROPE	
c.43	Romans occupy Britain
284–305	Roman Empire reorganized and divided into East and West.
313	Freedom of Christian worship in Roman Empire
378	Valens defeated by Visigoths at Adrianople
410	Sack of Rome
496	Baptism of Clovis, king of the Franks
c.600	Slavs move into Balkans
711	Muslims invade Spain
768–814	Charlemagne builds Frankish empire
800s	Vikings invade and settle northwest Europe
1054	Break between Greek and Roman Churches
1066	Norman conquest
1096–1300	The Crusades

A.D.

AMERICA AND AUSTRALASIA	
c.300–c.900	Mayan civilization in Central America
c.750	First Maoris arrive in New Zealand
c.1000	Greenland Vikings reach America

AFRICA	
1250	Mamluks seize power in Egypt
1300s	Mali Empire in west Africa
1400s and 1500s	European settlements on west coast
1500s	Songhai Empire replaces Mali Empire
1652	Dutch found Cape Colony
1869	Suez Canal opened
1880s	Scramble for Africa
1899–1902	Boer War
1914	All Africa except Liberia and Ethiopia colonized by European nations
1952–80	African states win independence
1981	President Anwar Sadat of Egypt assassinated
1984–86	Severe famine in East Africa, millions face starvation
1985–86	Renewed unrest in South Africa results in international pressure for reform of apartheid

ASIA

1096	First Crusade
1192	Yoritomo first shogun in Japan
1206–80	Mongols conquer empire in central Asia
1368–1644	Ming dynasty in China
1486–98	Voyages of Bartolomeu Dias and Vasco da Gama
c.1500–1870	African slave trade
1522–1680	Mughal expansion in India
c.1550–c.1650	Russians colonize Siberia
1630s	Japan isolates itself from rest of world
1644–1911	Manchu dynasty in China
1757	Battle of Plassey; British defeat French in India
1805	Beginning of East India Company's dominance in India
1839–42	Opium War; Britain takes Hong Kong
1857–59	Indian Mutiny
1867	Shoguns lose power in Japan
1900	Boxer Rebellion in China
1911	Republic established in China under Sun Yat-sen
1920–38	Career of Mustapha Kemal, Atatürk, in Turkey
1937	Japan invades China
1941	Japanese attack Pearl Harbor
1945	U.S.A. drops atomic bombs on Japan
1947	Indian independence
1948	State of Israel founded
1949	Communist victory in China.
1957–1973	Vietnam War
1979	Peace treaty signed between Israel and Egypt
1980	Iran-Iraq War
1982	Israel invades Lebanon
1984	Prime Minister Indira Gandhi of India is assassinated
1986	President Marcos regime in the Philippines is overthrown

EUROPE

1337	Beginning of Hundred Years' War in France
1347–50	Black Death
c.1450	Gutenberg starts printing
1450–53	English driven out of France
1453	Constantinople falls to Ottoman Turks
1455–85	Wars of the Roses
1521	Martin Luther leads Protestant split from Roman Church
1618–48	Thirty Years' War
1642–48	English Civil War
1643– 1715	Reign of Louis XIV
1750	Start of Industrial Revolution
1756–63	Seven Years' War
1789	French Revolution begins
1799	Napoleon seizes power in France
1815	Battle of Waterloo; Congress of Vienna
1821–29	Greek War of Liberation
1848	Year of revolutions throughout Europe
1854–56	Crimean War
1870–71	Franco-Prussian War
1885–95	Daimler and Benz work on automobile; Marconi's wireless
1914–18	World War I
1917	Bolshevik revolution in Russia begins
1933	Hitler becomes German Chancellor
1936–39	Spanish Civil War
1939–45	World War II
1941	Germany invades U.S.S.R.
1945	Defeat of Germany. Cold War begins
1957	U.S.S.R. launches first space satellite. Treaty of Rome: formation of European Economic Community
1980	Polish solidarity trade union confronts Communist government
1982	Argentina attempts takeover of Falkland Islands
1986	Prime Minister Olof Palme of Sweden is assassinated

AMERICAS AND AUSTRALASIA

c.1325– 1520	Aztec civilization in Mexico
c.1400– 1525	Inca civilization in Andes
1492	Columbus reaches America
1519	Cortés begins conquest of Aztec Empire
1532	Pizarro begins conquest of Inca Empire
1608	French colonists found Quebec
1620	*Mayflower* Puritans (Pilgrim Fathers) settle in New England
1645	Tasman discovers New Zealand
1770	James Cook claims Australia for Britain
1776	American Declaration of Independence
1788	British colony founded at Botany Bay, Australia
1817–24	Careers of Simon Bolívar and José de San Martín
1840	Britain annexes New Zealand
1846–48	Mexican War
1861–65	American Civil War
1898	Spanish-American War
1911	Mexican Revolution
1914	Panama Canal opened
1917	U.S.A. enters World War I
1929	Wall Street Crash begins Great Depression
1941	U.S.A. enters World War II
1945	United Nations set up
1959	Cuban Revolution
1963	President Kennedy assassinated
1969	Neil Armstrong lands on the moon
1981	First Space Shuttle flight
1983	U.S. troops invade Grenada after Marxist takeover
1986	Jean Claude Duvalier's regime in Haiti is overthrown

HITLER, Adolf (1889–1945)

Hitler became *Fuhrer* (leader) of Germany in 1933. He was an evil dictator whose Nazi party led Germany into World War II. German armies conquered most of Europe and millions of people were murdered on Hitler's orders. Britain, the United States, the U.S.S.R., and their allies defeated the Nazis. To avoid capture, Hitler killed himself.

HOCKEY

This is one of the most popular field games in the world. It can be played on any smooth, level surface in all seasons. It calls for speed and endurance.

Hockey is played by two teams of 11 players per side. The object of the game is to hit a small, hard ball with a curved stick into the other team's goal.

HOLOCAUST

Holocaust means a great destruction of life by fire. In recent times the word has been used to refer to the murder of six million Jews and thousands of others by the Nazis in Germany and German-occupied countries before and during World War II. Many of these victims were sent to concentration camps to be tortured, starved, and made to work under horrific conditions before being executed.

HOMER

Two very famous poems called the *Iliad* and the *Odyssey* are said

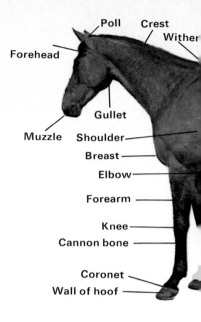

Poll Crest Wither Forehead Gullet Muzzle Shoulder Breast Elbow Forearm Knee Cannon bone Coronet Wall of hoof

to have been the work of Homer. The poems were written in Greece about 800 B.C. Both poems are about the Trojan War. The *Iliad* tells the story of how the Greeks captured the city of Troy. The *Odyssey* describes the homeward journey of the Greek hero Odysseus.

HORSE

The first horse was an animal no larger than a small dog. It is known as *Eohippus* or the "dawn horse." It had four toes on its front feet and three toes on its back feet. Gradually, over millions of years, the horse lost all its toes except one.

No one knows when horses were first tamed. Their first use was to pull war chariots, and

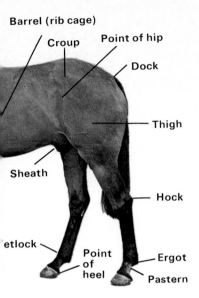

Barrel (rib cage)
Croup
Point of hip
Dock
Thigh
Sheath
Hock
etlock
Point of heel
Ergot
Pastern

cavalry played an important part in wars until early in this century. Horses were the fastest form of transportation until the invention of the steam locomotive. Also, horses' strength made them invaluable on farms where they could pull wagons and plows.

Many different types of horses have been bred. Among the largest are the Shire and Clydesdale breeds. The Shetland pony is one of the smallest.

HUMAN BEING

People exactly like us have lived for only a few thousand years. We belong to a group of mammals called the primates. Our scientific name is *Homo sapiens,* which means "thinking man."

Fossil remains of our primitive ancestors have been found in Africa and Asia. These early humanlike creatures walked on two legs, and their skulls and teeth were a lot like our own. But their brains were much smaller, about the same size as an ape's. After these "ape-men," however, came creatures much more like modern human beings. They had bigger brains and they could use tools. Having a bigger brain made it possible for primitive people to develop until *Homo sapiens* appeared perhaps about 100,000 years ago.

The human brain gave human beings the power to hunt, kill, capture, and tame other animals. Human beings developed skills far greater than those of any other creature. This made it possible for them to control the

▼ **Four reconstructions** from fossils of the heads of early people.

Homo habilis   Homo erectus   Neanderthal man   Homo sapiens

139

environment in which they lived. They learned to make and use fire, to grow food, and to make metal tools. They settled in villages and towns, and used language and writing to store and pass on the knowledge they had gained. In this way, civilization developed.

HUMAN BODY

Our bodies are made of millions of tiny cells which are grouped together into separate tissues and organs. Skin protects us from heat, cold, injury, and germs. Our bones give us our shape and allow us, with the help of our muscles, to move about.

Our bodies need oxygen and food. We get the oxygen from the air when we breathe. The blood carries the oxygen to every cell of the body. It also carries digested food, which is burned by the oxygen to give us energy.

The body produces lots of

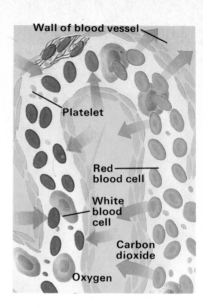

Wall of blood vessel
Platelet
Red blood cell
White blood cell
Carbon dioxide
Oxygen

▲ **The blood** carries nutrients and oxygen to all parts of the body. Red cells carry oxygen; white cells fight disease. Platelets help blood to clot in a wound.

▼ **This hummingbird** rolls its tongue into a tube to suck nectar from a flower.

waste. Some of this is excreted through the skin when we sweat, some (carbon dioxide) when we breathe out. Other waste is removed via the bowels and the bladder.

The only organs which are different in a man and a woman are the reproductive organs. A woman has a vagina and ovaries which contain ova (eggs). A man has a penis and testes which contain sperm. The fertilization of a female egg cell by a male sperm cell produces one new cell which has all the makings of a complete new human body.

See also BLOOD; BRAIN; BREATHING; CELL; EAR; EYE; HEART; REPRODUCTION; SKIN.

HUMMINGBIRD
Hummingbirds are the smallest birds in the world. Most kinds live in the great forests of South America. Hummingbirds are marvelous fliers. They can hover in midair and even fly backward. Their wings beat so fast they make a humming noise.

HYDROFOIL
The hydrofoil is a type of watercraft that has large, winglike structures attached to the hull. As the craft gains speed, the hull rises out of the water on these ski-like projections. Because the hull no longer has to push against the water, the craft can travel at much greater speeds than an ordinary boat. Hydrofoils are in use for ferry services

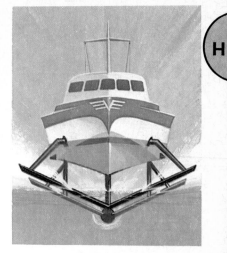

▲ **Most modern hydrofoils** have V-shaped foils for stability.

in the United States and Europe and in the U.S. Navy.

HYDROGEN
Hydrogen is an element. It is a colorless gas and has no smell and no taste. It is very light—more than 14 times as light as air. Hydrogen is easily set on fire.

Atoms of deuterium (heavy hydrogen) can be made to join together, or *fuse,* at a very high temperature to release huge quantities of energy. This is the principle of the hydrogen bomb.

HYENA
Hyenas are ungainly doglike creatures. They live in Africa and Asia, where they are useful scavengers. The strange howl of the laughing hyena sounds like weird human laughter.

ICE AGE
The Ice Ages were times of intense cold. Sheets of ice spread southward from the North Pole, covering much of Europe, North America, and Asia. The most recent Ice Age ended about 11,000 years ago. Glaciers (rivers of ice) carried soil and rocks along with them like huge bulldozers. They scraped the land clear of soil, smoothed hills, and scooped out valleys.

During the recent Ice Age many plants and animals were killed by the cold. Human beings had to find ways of keeping warm. They took to the shelter of caves and made clothes from the skins of animals. In time the ice sheets melted and the climate grew warmer. Today, the possibility of another ice age in the future cannot be ruled out.

ICEBERG
Icebergs are islands of ice that drift in the cold polar seas. They are formed from masses of ice that break off the end of a glacier or ice sheet and float off into the sea. An iceberg can weigh millions of tons, but only the tip of the iceberg shows above water. Nine times as much is hidden beneath the surface.

See also GLACIER.

IDAHO
Idaho is a Rocky Mountain state in the northwest. It has over 50 mountains higher than 10,000 feet, and 40 percent of the state is covered with forest. Idaho has a small population of less than a million. Idaho farms produce potatoes (25 percent of the nation's crop), peas, and sugar beets; lumbering and mining are also important.

See also page 263.

▼ **A gold knife** used in Inca ceremonies.

142

ILLINOIS

Illinois is the home of the nation's second largest city—Chicago. It is also a great farming state, producing more soybeans than any other state, and, after Iowa, the most corn. Located at the southern tip of Lake Michigan, Chicago is well connected by water, road, and rail to the rest of the nation, and is a major industrial and communications center.

See also page 263.

INCA

Hundreds of years ago the Incas ruled an empire in the Andes Mountains. Its heart lay in the South American country we now call Peru. All the people living in the mountain valleys had to work for the Incas. In return, the Incas made sure that everyone had a home and enough to eat.

The Incas became very rich. In 1532 Spanish explorers came seeking gold. They had horses and guns and they captured the Inca king, Atahualpa. They made themselves rulers of Peru.

INDIA

India is a large country, (about 1,266,000 square miles). 784 million people live in India. The north is cut off from the rest of Asia by the Himalaya Mountains. Great rivers, such as the Brahmaputra and Ganges, flow across the plains south of these mountains.

Parts of India are dry and hot.

▲ **A market** in the holy city of Varanasi (Benares), India.

It is cooler in the mountains, but most people live in the fertile river valleys. India gets most of its rain during the monsoon season. Many Indians are poor farmers who live in small villages. Others live in crowded cities like Calcutta. Industry is developing in India. There are steelworks, mines, and textile and engineering factories.

Most Indians follow the Hindu religion. But there are also Buddhists, Sikhs, Muslims, and Christians. Civilization began 4,500 years ago in the area that includes India. From the late 1700s until 1947 most of India was ruled by Britain. Then it became independent.

See also GANDHI and page 79.

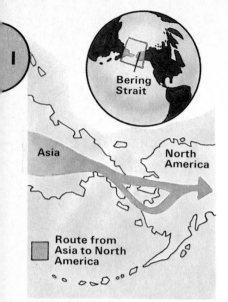

▲ **The American Indians'** route from Asia to the Americas.

▼ **Sitting Bull** led the Sioux in the final stages of Indian resistance against the settlers.

INDIANA
Indiana is a midwestern state lying between Ohio and Illinois. Oil refineries, steel mills, and other industries rise up from the shores of Lake Michigan to the north. Corn, soybeans, and wheat are grown on the southern plains. Two-thirds of Indiana's population live in cities such as Indianapolis (the capital), Fort Wayne, Gary, and Evansville.

See also page 263.

INDIANS, AMERICAN
American Indians are the native peoples of the Americas. They are thought to have come from Asia about 20,000 years ago, crossing the land "bridge" where the Bering Strait is now. Over the centuries they gradually spread into Central and South America, developing different ways of life depending upon where they lived.

In the woodlands of eastern North America, tribes such as the Iroquois and Algonquin made domed wigwams of bark and hunted deer. On the plains, the Indians were nomadic, following the herds of buffalo that provided them with food, clothing, and shelter. In the deserts of the Southwest, tribes such as the Hopi built villages of sun-dried brick *adobe*.

As America was settled by Europeans, the Indians were pushed farther and farther west. Many were killed fighting for their hunting grounds. By the late 1800s almost all the tribes had been given land on reservations by the U.S. government. In 1968 the American Indian Movement was formed to fight for Indians' civil rights.

INDUSTRIAL REVOLUTION

This is the name given to the great change that took place in Europe and America when goods began to be produced in factories. Before that time, many things were made by hand by craftworkers in their own homes. When James Watt harnessed the power of steam in the mid-1700s, all this changed. England's textile industry was revolutionized by the invention of machines that would spin thread and weave cloth. Cities grew as more and more people left farming areas to seek jobs in the factories.

The Industrial Revolution soon spread to the United States. The new factories created wealth. Railroads and canals were built; coal was mined to fuel steam engines and to make steel. The new wealth was not for everybody, however. Workers often lived in crowded conditions in the towns that grew up around the factories. They worked long hours, often for little pay. These bad conditions eventually led to the formation of labor unions, which fought for better pay and conditions.

▲ **The Navajo** are skilled weavers, turning the wool from their flocks of sheep into brightly colored rugs and blankets.

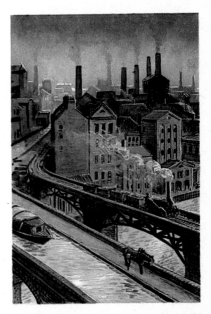

▶ **The Industrial Revolution** led to increased wealth but also to overcrowded, smoky factory towns.

145

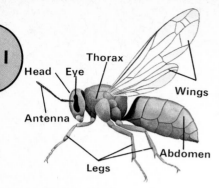

▲ **The parts** of an insect.

INSECT

Insects are found in every part of the world. There are hundreds of thousands of different kinds of insects, but they are all built on a similar plan. The body is divided into three sections. An insect's *head* has eyes, jaws, and antennae, or feelers. The middle part, or *thorax*, carries three pairs of jointed legs and sometimes two pairs of wings as well. The end part is called the *abdomen*.

Most insects reproduce by laying eggs. Instead of bones, they have a hard case covering the outside of their bodies. As the insect grows, it has to shed this case and grow another.

Some young insects develop

▼ **The growth cycle** of an insect.

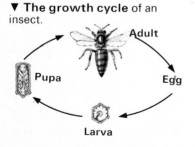

Pupa

Adult

Egg

Larva

INVENTIONS AND INVENTORS

Wheel

Abacus

B.C.	
*c.*3000	Wheel in Asia
*c.*500	Abacus – the Chinese
*c.*300	Geometry – Euclid (Gr.)
*c.*200	Screw – Archimedes (Gr.

A.D.	
105	Paper – the Chinese
*c.*1000	Gunpowder – the Chinese
*c.*1440	Printing press (movable type) J. Gutenberg (G.)
1593	Thermometer – Galileo (It
1608	Telescope – Hans Lippershey (Neth.)
1642	Calculating machine – B. Pascal (Fr.)
1712	Steam engine – T. Newcomen (Eng.)
1800	Electric battery – A. Volta (It.)
1836	Revolver – S. Colt (U.S.)
1837	Telegraph – S. Morse (U.S.)

Telephone

Steam engine

into adults without changing shape. They are called *nymphs*. But many kinds of insects go through two big changes in shape. At each stage, the insect looks different and has a different way of life. Butterflies lay eggs. They hatch into larvae called caterpillars. A caterpillar

146

Gunpowder Printing press

1866	Dynamite – A. Nobel (S.)
1876	Telephone – A. Bell (Sc.)
1879	Electric light – T. Edison (U.S.)
1887	Automobile engine – K. Benz, G. Daimler (G.)
1895	Wireless – G. Marconi (It.)
1899	Tape recorder – V. Poulsen (Den.)
1925	Television – J. L. Baird (Sc.)
1944	Digital computer – H. Aitken (U.S.)
1960	Laser – T. Maiman (U.S.)

Eng. = England;
G. = Germany; It. = Italy;
Gr. = Greece;
Neth. = Netherlands;
Fr. = .France; U.S. = United
States; Sc. = Scotland;
Den. = Denmark; S. = Sweden

Television
Radio
Microcomputer

other insects pollinate flowers. The silkworm makes silk.

See also ANT; BEE; BEETLE; BUTTERFLY AND MOTH; FLY; GRASSHOPPER; MOSQUITO; WASP.

INTERNATIONAL DATE LINE

Geographers have divided the globe into sections with lines that run from pole to pole. These lines are called meridians. Each section is in a different time zone, because as the earth rotates the sun faces different parts of the earth at different times. The world's nations have agreed that the date changes at the 180th meridian. This imaginary line is called the International Date Line. Each date begins on the west side of the line and ends on the east side.

INVENTION

Throughout history people have created new things. Most of these new products, or inventions, have given us an easier and better life. We can all benefit from machines and equipment such as cars and airplanes, radio and TV, newspapers and books. But some inventions, such as guns and bombs, are very destructive.

Many inventors invent to fulfill a need. English engineer James Hargreaves saw the need for a machine to spin cotton faster, and he invented the spinning jenny.

Other inventors just seem to

grows and turns into a pupa, or chrysalis. Finally, the adult butterfly emerges from the pupa. This process of change is known as *metamorphosis*.

Some insects are harmful. Insects such as the mosquito and the tsetse fly carry diseases. But many insects are useful. Bees and invent for the love of it. Thomas Edison was one of these. In his lifetime he registered, or patented, more than a thousand inventions.

Inventions are often the product of many people. The airplane was first flown by the Wright brothers, but they did not invent most of its parts. They drew upon the work of others who had gone before. The German engineers Daimler and Benz built the first successful cars by extending other people's ideas and adding some of their own.

See also EDISON; GALILEO; GUTENBERG; MARCONI; WATT.

▲ **The Masjid-i-Shah** (Royal Mosque) in Isfahan, Iran.

ION
An ion is an electrically charged atom. Most atoms have equal numbers of protons ($+$) and electrons ($-$). This means they are electrically neutral. But if an atom gains or loses an electron, it becomes electrically charged, either negatively (if it gains an electron) or positively (if it loses one).

IOWA
Iowa is a midwestern state lying between the Mississippi and Missouri rivers. Its rolling plains are very fertile, which makes it one of the nation's most important farming regions. About 95 percent of its land is farmed, producing corn, soybeans, and oats. It is also the leading hog-raising state. More than half of all Iowans live in cities such as Des Moines, the capital, Cedar Rapids, and Davenport.

See also page 263.

IRAN
Iran is a Muslim country that lies between the Caspian Sea and the Persian Gulf. It has mountains, deserts, and green valleys, and the remains of the ancient Persian civilizations. Today Iran is one of the world's top oil producers. In 1979 the emperor, or shah, was forced out and the country became an Islamic Republic. A long and costly war with Iraq followed.

See also page 79.

IRAQ
Iraq is a country in southwest Asia, in the region between the

Tigris and Euphrates rivers, where Western civilization began. The country is one of the biggest oil producers in the world. Farmers in the river valleys grow rice, cotton, wheat, and dates. In the 1980s, Iraq went to war with Iran.

See also page 79.

IRELAND
Northern Ireland is part of the United Kingdom. Southern Ireland is a republic. In the republic most people are Roman Catholic. Most of the people in Northern Ireland are Protestant.

Ireland is mainly a farming country. It has fertile soil and a mild, moist climate. The center of Ireland is flat, but there are mountains near the coast.

Ireland has had a troubled history. From the 1500s it was ruled by England. Many Irish people were poor and thousands emigrated to England and the United States. In 1921, 26 of the 32 Irish counties set up an independent country, which became the Republic of Ireland in 1949. Many people in the south want the six northern counties to become part of the republic. In Northern Ireland quarrels between Protestants and Catholics have led to fighting, bombings, murders, and riots.

See also page 78.

IRON AGE
This is the name given to a period when people began to use iron to make knives, axes, and swords. Iron was first used about 2300 B.C. in Asia Minor. It reached Britain in about 500 B.C. The Iron Age followed the Bronze Age.

Iron ore is found in many places in the world and can be smelted (made into iron) fairly simply on charcoal fires.

See also BRONZE AGE.

IRON AND STEEL
Steel is our most important metal. No other metal that is so strong is so cheap.

Steel is not a pure metal. It is an alloy made up mainly of iron, together with small amounts of carbon and one or two metals. Iron by itself is quite soft and weak, but adding the other ingredients makes it hard and strong.

▼ **Giant steel-making** machinery.

149

Steel is like iron in other ways. It is magnetic, and it rusts easily. But by adding metals, such as chromium and nickel, we can make a steel that does not rust. It is called stainless steel.

Iron is found in the form of a mineral, or ore, in the ground. Crude iron is made in a blast furnace by heating iron ore with coke and limestone. Steel is made by purifying the crude iron in other furnaces.

See also ALLOY.

IRRIGATION
Irrigation waters the land to help crops to grow. In many places not enough rain falls each year, or it rains only at certain times of the year. Farmers have to get their water from rivers, wells, or lakes.

The ancient civilizations of Egypt, India, China, Assyria, and Babylon depended on irrigation. Today, engineers build dams to make artificial lakes. The water can then be released into pipes, earth channels, or river systems as it is needed.

ISLAM
Islam is one of the world's great religions. It was begun in A.D. 622 in Arabia by Muhammad, and today has more followers than any other religion except Christianity. Its followers are called Muslims, and its holy book is the Koran. Muslims believe in one god (Allah) and in Muhammad as his prophet. Islam today is most widespread in North Africa and southwest Asia.

See also MUHAMMAD.

ISRAEL
Israel is a country bordering the Mediterranean Sea in southwest Asia. Most Israelis are Jews, and the main language is Hebrew. Many Arabs also live in Israel. Much of the country is hot desert, but farmers grow oranges, cotton, and grain on fertile plains and in fields watered by irrigation. Israel maintains an uneasy peace with its Arab neighbors after conflicts in the 1960s and 1970s.

See also page 79.

▼ **The Romans** used their engineering skills to irrigate dry fields. They built great aqueducts to carry water over long distances.

▲ **The Wailing Wall** in Jerusalem, the capital of Israel, is one of the oldest and holiest places in Jewish history.

ITALY

On the map Italy looks like a boot sticking out into the Mediterranean Sea. The islands of Sardinia and Sicily are also part of Italy. In the north the Alps form a wall between Italy and the rest of Europe.

Southern Italy is warm and fairly dry. In the north it is cooler, with more rain. Both agriculture and industry are important. Most of the factories are in northern Italy. Italy is famous for its wine and for pasta—foods such as spaghetti, macaroni, and ravioli.

Most Italians are Roman Catholic. The center of the Catholic Church is the Vatican, a tiny independent state in the middle of Rome. Italy has many old and beautiful buildings. A lot of them are in Rome, because 2,000 years ago the Romans ruled Italy. Later separate city-states grew up. The greatest were Genoa, Florence, and Venice.

See also page 78.

▶ **Milan Cathedral** in Italy.

JAPAN

The islands that make up the country of Japan lie off the northeast coast of Asia. The largest islands are Honshu, Hokkaido, Kyushu, and Shikoku. Earthquakes are common and there are volcanoes and hot springs. Japan has heavy rainfall and a cool climate.

Most Japanese live in cities. Rice, fish, and vegetables are the main foods. There are many factories making all kinds of goods,

▼ **The highest mountain** in Japan, Mount Fuji, is an old volcano.

from cars and ships to radios and zippers.

The Japanese came from mainland Asia perhaps 3,000 years ago. Ancient Japan was ruled by warrior lords. Until the 1850s Japan had little contact with the world outside. But then its rulers decided to allow trade with European countries.

Japan became powerful, and its rulers became warlike. During World War II Japan joined Germany and Italy, and Japanese forces conquered much of Asia. But in 1945 Japan surrendered. Today Japan's emperor no longer has any power. There is an elected parliament and a government led by a prime minister.

See also page 79.

JENNER, Edward (1749–1823)

Jenner was an English physician. He discovered that people who had had cowpox, a mild disease, never caught smallpox, a painful and dangerous disease. He developed a vaccine from cowpox germs that protected people from smallpox.

JESUS CHRIST

Jesus Christ was the founder of Christianity. Christians believe that he was the son of God. He taught people to trust in God and lead good, peaceful lives and he promised eternal life in heaven. The Bible tells of miracles he performed, healing the sick, lame, and blind. Jesus' followers said he was the Messiah, but

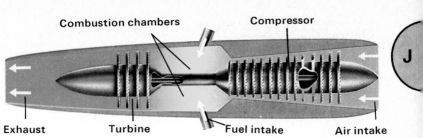

Combustion chambers   **Compressor**

Exhaust   Turbine   Fuel intake   Air intake

▲ **A gas turbine** jet engine. Air is drawn into the engine and compressed. Fuel is sprayed into the combustion chambers and burns in the air. The gases expand and drive the turbine. The exhaust gases thrust it forward.

others feared he was just a troublemaker. The Romans, who were harsh rulers of the Jews, thought so too. Jesus was arrested and executed on the Cross. But his followers went on teaching others what he had taught them, even though the Romans at first tried to stop them. Many of these early Christians died for their belief in Jesus.

JET ENGINE

The jet engine was developed by both Britain and Germany. In 1930, Frank Whittle, a British engineer, patented the first gas turbine for jet propulsion. Germany flew the first successful jet plane, the Heinkel 168, in 1939.

The aircraft gas turbine consists of a rotating shaft with a compressor at the front and a turbine wheel at the back. When the shaft turns, air is drawn into the engine and compressed. It enters combustion chambers where it mixes with liquid fuel

such as kerosene. This mixture burns. The hot gases produced are allowed to escape from the back of the combustion chambers. As the fast jet of gas moves backward out of the exhaust, it thrusts the engine forward.

The jet engine is smaller and lighter than the piston engine which it has largely replaced. It works efficiently at high speeds and produces great power.

JOAN OF ARC (1412–1431)

In 1429, France was at war with England. Joan was a French girl who believed that God had told her to save France. She persuaded France's Charles VII to let her lead his army and won five battles. Captured by the English, she was burned as a witch.

JUDAISM

Judaism is one of the world's oldest religions. Its followers are called Jews. They believe in one god, and the Bible is their holy book. Christians include the Hebrew Bible in their Bible, calling it the Old Testament. Today, though Israel is their spiritual home, Jews live in all parts of the world.

153

K

KANGAROO
Kangaroos live in Australia. They are the largest of the marsupials, the animals that carry their young in pouches.

Kangaroos eat grass and leaves. They travel around in groups called mobs, led by an old male known as a boomer. With their powerful hind legs and long tails for balance, kangaroos can leap long distances.

▼ **A kangaroo** with its young, called a joey, in its pouch.

KANSAS
Kansas grows more wheat than any other state. This land of high plains and prairies lies in the center of the United States. Farms that stretch as far as the eye can see produce wheat, sorghum, and corn. Cattle ranching is also important. Industries include food processing and the production of farm machinery and aircraft.

See also page 263.

KENNEDY, John F. (1917–63)
John F. Kennedy was the 35th president of the United States. In 1961, he became the first Roman Catholic to be elected to this office. He tried to help the poor and underprivileged. He was assassinated in Dallas, Texas.

KENTUCKY
Kentucky is sometimes called the Bluegrass State. It stretches west from the Allegheny Mountains to the Mississippi. The Bluegrass region, so-called because the lush grass has a bluish tint, is famous for breeding thoroughbred horses. Whiskey and tobacco are two more Kentucky products. The state's largest cities are Louisville and Lexington.

See also page 263.

KING, Martin Luther (1929–68)
Martin Luther King was a black American clergyman and leader in the struggle for racial equality in the United States. Because he admired the teachings of Gan-

▲ **Horses graze** in Kentucky's lush Bluegrass region near Lexington.

dhi, he preached nonviolence in the fight for civil rights. Dr. King won the Nobel Peace Prize in 1964. He was assassinated in 1968.

See also CIVIL RIGHTS MOVEMENT.

KING AND QUEEN

In the past most countries were ruled by monarchs—kings or queens. Usually the king's eldest

▲ **A portrait** of Elizabeth I, nicknamed Good Queen Bess.

KINGS AND QUEENS OF ENGLAND SINCE THE NORMAN CONQUEST (1066)

William I	1066–1087 *
William II	1087–1100
Henry I	1100–1135
Stephen	1135–1154
Henry II	1154–1189
Richard I	1189–1199
John	1199–1216
Henry III	1216–1272
Edward I	1272–1307
Edward II	1307–1327
Edward III	1327–1377
Richard II	1377–1399
Henry IV	1399–1413
Henry V	1413–1422
Henry VI	1422–1461
Edward IV	1461–1483
Edward V	1483
Richard III	1483–1485
Henry VII	1485–1509
Henry VIII	1509–1547
Edward VI	1547–1553
Mary I	1553–1558
Elizabeth I	1558–1603

KINGS AND QUEENS OF GREAT BRITAIN FROM 1603

James I (VI of Scotland)	1603–1625
Charles I	1625–1649
Commonwealth	1649–1660
Charles II	1660–1685
James II	1685–1688
William III and (to 1694) Mary II	1689–1702
Anne	1702–1714
George I	1714–1727
George II	1727–1760
George III	1760–1820
George IV	1820–1830
William IV	1830–1837
Victoria	1837–1901
Edward VII	1901–1910
George V	1910–1936
Edward VIII	1936
George VI	1936–1952
Elizabeth II	1952

*Dates refer to length of reign.

155

son succeeded him, which mean that the same royal family might reign for hundreds of years.

English kings ruled with the help of their barons. In 1215 the barons forced King John to sign the Magna Carta, which said that the king should not misuse his powers. Later, English monarchs had to take the advice of Parliament. Britain is now a "constitutional monarchy." The Queen is the head of state, but her powers are limited by law. She *reigns* (holds office), but she does not *rule* (govern).

KIWI

The kiwi is the national bird of New Zealand. It cannot fly, but it waddles about the forest, searching for worms and insects to eat. The kiwi has hairlike feathers, no tail, strong claws, and a long bill. It is the only bird that has nostrils at the tip of its bill.

KNIGHT

A knight in medieval times was a warrior who had vowed to be courageous yet gentle. This code of behavior was called *chivalry*. A knight gave military service to a lord or an organization such as the church. In return he was granted land.

The training to become a knight was long and hard. A boy of noble birth began as a page at the age of 7. At 14, he became a squire and began to learn the skills of a knight. He took vows of knighthood at about 21.

156

KNOT

A knot is a way of tying rope, string, or thread. We all use knots to tie packages, but many special knots were first developed by sailors to perform different jobs on a sailing ship. A *bend* is used to tie ends of rope together; a *hitch* is used to tie a rope to a post. Common knots are the *square knot, bowline, clove hitch, half hitch, slipknot,* and *sheet bend*.

KOALA

Although it looks like a small bear, the koala is a marsupial

▲ **The kiwi** looks for food after dark.

(p.169). It lives in Australia. Koalas are good climbers. They live in eucalyptus trees, feeding on the leaves.

KORAN

The Koran is the holy book of Muslims. It is believed to have been dictated to Muhammad, the great prophet of Islam, by the archangel Gabriel. The Koran contains rules for both everyday and spiritual life. It was written down between A.D. 610 and 632.

Square knot

Two half hitches

Slipknot

Sheet bends

▲ **A square knot** joins two ropes of equal thickness; a sheet bend is useful for tying ropes of different thicknesses. A slipknot will pull tight around a post, and two half hitches make a quick fastening.

KOREAN WAR

The Korean War broke out in 1950 when communist North Korea invaded pro-West South Korea. The United Nations stepped in, and a U.N. force made up mostly of U.S. troops went to South Korea's defense. Although truce talks began just over a year later, the fighting continued for two more years until July 1953, when agreement was reached to end the war.

KREMLIN

The Kremlin is the oldest part of the city of Moscow. It was once the fortress home of the kings, or czars, of Russia. A high wall surrounds the old palaces and gold-domed cathedrals of the Kremlin, still the seat of the Soviet government today.

KU KLUX KLAN

The Ku Klux Klan was an organization set up in 1866 by white southerners to prevent newly freed blacks from voting and exercising other rights. Members, dressed in white sheets and hoods, beat up blacks and public officials. The KKK used violence against both black and white civil rights workers in the South in the 1960s and is still recruiting new members.

▲ **A young koala** rides on its mother's back after leaving the pouch.

157

LAKE

Many lakes were formed during the Ice Ages by glaciers scooping out hollows in the land. When the ice melted, the hollows filled with water. Some lakes are artificial—created when dams are built across rivers.

Some lakes are so big that they are called seas. The Caspian Sea in Asia is the largest lake in the world. Its water is salty because the lake has no outlets. The water evaporates. The largest freshwater lake is Lake Superior, one of the Great Lakes.

See also ICE AGE.

LANGUAGE

When we speak, we are using language. Language is a collection of "sound signs" or words. We use it to communicate with one another. There are more than 2,800 different languages in the world and many more *dialects* or local variations. Chinese is the language spoken by the largest number of people. English is spoken in more countries than any other language.

All languages change. People make up new words and often "borrow" foreign words.

LASER

A laser is an instrument that produces a thin beam of very pure light. The beam from some lasers is so powerful that it can blast a hole through metal. Other lasers can be used in surgery to remove diseased body tissues, and to repair tissues in the eye.

An exciting new use of lasers is in communications. Laser beams can relay television signals and telephone messages. Sending telephone calls by laser may soon replace our present telephone system in which we send electric signals along copper wires.

▼ **Laser beams** are very intense and narrow.

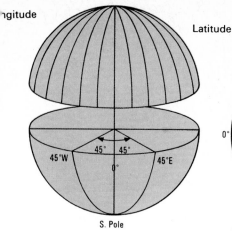

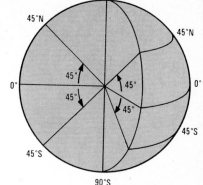

S. Pole

LATITUDE & LONGITUDE

Because we know that the world is round, we can show it on a globe and divide it into sections with accurately drawn lines.

The lines that run east and west and are parallel to the equator are called *parallels* of latitude. Those that run north and south through the poles are called *meridians* of longitude.

These lines are measured in degrees. By using them we can give the position of any place in the world. Washington, D.C., is latitude 38° 52′N, longitude 77° 0′W.

LATTER DAY SAINTS

Members of the Church of Jesus Christ of Latter Day Saints are usually called Mormons. The sect was founded by Joseph Smith in 1830. Their center is Salt Lake City, Utah. Mormons were once criticized for their practice (now illegal) of *polygamy*—men often had more than one wife.

▲ **Lines of latitude** and longitude are measured in degrees. Each line lies at a certain angle to the center of the earth.

LAW

All countries have rules that tell people how to behave and that must be obeyed. They make up the law of a country.

Law is made and works differently in different societies. In many countries groups of men and women are chosen by other people to make the laws. These people are called legislators and the law they make is *statute law*. Some law is made by judges. It is called *case law*. The law that comes from the customs of the people is called *common law*.

Lawyers are trained especially to understand the law. The police and the courts arrest and punish people who break the law.

LEAD

Lead is one of the heaviest metals. It is soft and easy to

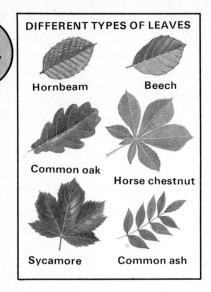

DIFFERENT TYPES OF LEAVES

Hornbeam

Beech

Common oak

Horse chestnut

Sycamore

Common ash

xylem, and the carbon dioxide enters the leaf through little holes called *stomata*. The energy for photosynthesis comes from sunlight.

Leaves of plants growing in mild climates wither and fall off in the fall. Lack of sunlight in winter makes them unnecessary. First the water supply to the leaves is cut off. This destroys the green color and gives the leaves beautiful red and orange tints.

LEAGUE OF NATIONS

The League of Nations was formed after World War I and was the forerunner of the United Nations. The United States never joined the League, however, and this weakened it. Gradually other nations dropped out. Despite its failure, it served as a model when the United Nations was founded after World War II.

LENIN, Vladimir (1870–1924)

Lenin is remembered as the man who made Russia a Communist country. When he was 17, Lenin decided to work against the Czar (emperor) of Russia, because he thought the Czar's rule was harsh and unjust. He became a Bolshevik (Communist), and in 1917 was the leader of the Communist revolution.

LENS

A lens is a specially shaped piece of transparent glass or plastic that refracts, or bends, rays of

shape and does not rust. Lead is mixed with other metals to make useful alloys such as pewter, which contains lead and tin. The metal used for printer's type contains lead. Solder used to join electrical wires and pipes also contains lead. Lead is also used in some car batteries.

LEAF

All of a plant's food is manufactured in its green leaves. Light, water, and carbon dioxide are used to make a form of sugar. From the sugar the plant makes starch and other kinds of food.

The process that makes the food is called *photosynthesis.* It relies on the green coloring inside a leaf called *chlorophyll.* The carbon dioxide comes from the air. The water comes from the soil through tiny veinlike tubes called light. It makes an object look bigger or smaller. A lens that is thicker in the middle is called *convex*. It makes objects seen through it look bigger. A lens that is thicker at the edge is called *concave*. Objects seen through it look smaller.

LEONARDO DA VINCI
(1452–1519)
Da Vinci was a great Italian artist, scientist, and inventor. He was fascinated by the way in which the human body, machines, and the universe worked. He designed war engines, a sort of helicopter, a parachute, and diving gear. His *Last Supper* and *Mona Lisa* are among the best-known paintings in the world.

LEOPARD AND CHEETAH
The leopard lives in Africa and Asia. It is an expert tree climber and sometimes lies in wait for its prey in a tree. It can drag a half-eaten antelope into the branches, out of reach of hyenas.

The cheetah of Africa is the fastest land animal. It hunts by

L

Leopard

Cheetah

161

stalking its prey and then chasing it at great speed. Not even the swift antelope can escape, for the cheetah can run at over 65 miles an hour, though only in short bursts.

Leopards and cheetahs belong to the cat family.

LIBYA
Libya is a country in North Africa. Most of it lies in the Sahara Desert and is rich in oil. One of the Arab nations, Libya was an Italian colony until the

of tiny plants called lichens. A lichen is really two plants in one. One part is a fungus. The other part is a green plant called an alga. The fungus cannot make its own food. Instead it takes in water and minerals for the alga. The alga uses the water and sunlight to make food for itself and the fungus.

LIGHT
The sun is a huge furnace that gives out vast amounts of energy as heat and light. Its light is one

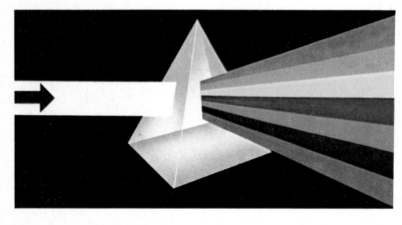

end of World War II. It became an independent monarchy in 1952, but in 1969 army officers overthrew the king and Colonel Mu'ammar el Qaddafi became the head of a revolutionary government.

See also page 78.

LICHEN
You often see a gray crust on rocks and tree trunks. It is made

▲ **White light** splits into the seven colors of the rainbow – the spectrum – when it passes through a prism.

of the most important things to us on earth. It enables us to see by day. We see things because objects reflect light into our eyes. Sunlight also gives green plants the energy to make their food. And all animals, including ourselves, rely on plant food to live.

▲ **Light rays** bend when they pass from air to water, a denser medium, making straight objects appear to bend too.

Light travels in straight lines—you cannot shine a flashlight around a corner. But you can reflect the beam around a corner with a mirror. Light also bends when it passes from air into glass or water. This is called *refraction*. The bending of light by curved pieces of glass, or lenses, makes it possible to magnify objects, as in the microscope and telescope. When light is bent by a wedge of glass (a prism), it splits up into bands of color. A laser is a powerful beam of very pure light.

See also COLOR; LASER; SUN.

LIGHTNING

Lightning is a gigantic electric spark that zigzags between the clouds in a thunderstorm. It also travels down to the ground,

where it can cause great damage. It can split trees and set fire to buildings. Tall buildings have to be protected from lightning by a lightning conductor.

L

LINCOLN, Abraham
(1809–1865)
Lincoln is remembered as one of the greatest of all U.S. presidents. As president during the Civil War, he was determined to end slavery and to hold the Union together. Lincoln was assassinated by John Wilkes Booth, a supporter of the South, in 1865.

See also CIVIL WAR.

LINDBERGH, Charles
(1902–1974)
Lindbergh was an American pilot who performed a remarkable feat of daring and endurance. He flew nonstop in his single-engine plane, *The Spirit of St. Louis*, from New York to Paris in May 1927. The flight took $33\frac{1}{2}$ hours

Charles Lindbergh

163

and caught the imagination of the world.

LION

The lion is called "the king of beasts." With the tiger, it is the largest member of the cat family.

Lions live in groups called *prides*. Only the males have manes. The females, called lionesses, do most of the hunting.

Lions feed mainly on antelopes and zebras. They creep up on their prey and kill it after a short chase.

Lions once lived in Europe. Now wild lions are found only in parts of Africa and in a special reserve in India.

LISTER, Joseph (1827–1912)

Lister was an English surgeon who did much to make operations safe. He used carbolic acid to clean instruments and to kill germs. He was also the first person to use catgut in surgery for stitching wounds.

▼ **A lion and lioness** dozing in the African sun.

LIZARD

Lizards are reptiles. Most lizards have four legs, but some are legless. The blindworm is a legless lizard. Unlike snakes, lizards have movable eyelids and visible ears. Their skins are dry and scaly, and are shed from time to time.

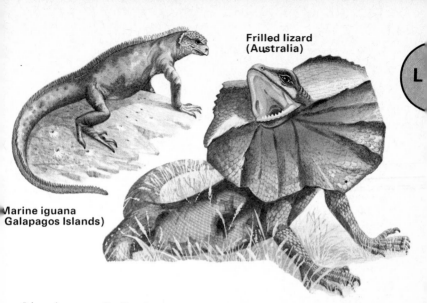

Frilled lizard (Australia)

Marine iguana (Galapagos Islands)

Lizards generally live in warm climates. Most kinds lay eggs, but some produce live young. Lizards feed on insects, small mammals, or plants. They prefer dry land, but the marine iguana is a good swimmer.

See also DINOSAUR; REPTILE.

LLAMA
The llama looks like a small, woolly camel without a hump. It lives in the Andes Mountains of South America.

Llamas are useful because they can carry loads along narrow mountain tracks. They also provide people with meat, wool, skins for making leather, and fat for candles.

LOUISIANA
Louisiana, one of the Gulf states, lies at the mouth of the Mississippi River. The port city of New Orleans has been an important center for river and ocean trade for several hundred years. Once part of the Louisiana Purchase, the state is today a leading producer of oil and natural gas and has a large fishing industry.

See also page 263.

LUTHER, Martin (1483–1546)
Luther was a monk who thought the Roman Catholic Church had moved too far away from the teachings of the Bible. He also objected to the custom of selling people pardons for their sins. Many Christians agreed with Luther. They started a great religious movement—the Reformation. Martin Luther and others who broke away from the Roman Catholic Church became known as Protestants.

See also REFORMATION.

165

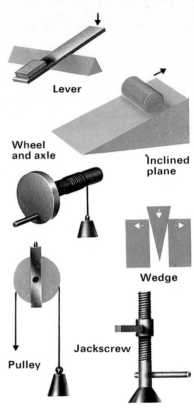

Lever

Wheel and axle

Inclined plane

Wedge

Pulley

Jackscrew

MACHINE, SIMPLE

Machines are devices that put energy to work. Most machines are complicated devices, but they are all based on six types of simple machines: the lever, the inclined plane, the wheel and axle, the pulley, the wedge, and the screw (see illustrations, right).

Starting from these simple machines, engineers have developed machines that can do a vast range of things. All machines, whether the simple lever or a giant crane, make it possible for people to do things more quickly and easily than they could by hand.

MAGELLAN, Ferdinand
(1480–1521)

Magellan was a Portuguese navigator in the service of Spain. He sought a sea route westward to the Moluccas where spices were grown. He set out with four ships, found the route to the Pacific through what he named the Strait of Magellan, and went on to the Philippines. There he was killed by natives. One of his ships completed the first voyage around the world in 1522.

MAGIC

Before people understood what caused such things as storms or disease, many thought that nature was controlled by good and evil spirits. They believed that magic gave them power over these spirits. Some magic was good, or "white"; but other magic was bad, or "black." The clever tricks of stage magicians today really have nothing to do with magic.

MAGNET

Magnets can pick up or attract pieces of metal, particularly iron and steel. This power is called magnetism. The magnetism is most powerful at the ends of the magnet. If you hang a bar magnet from thread, it always points its ends toward the earth's north and south magnetic poles. So we call the two ends its north and south poles. The magnet always points north-south because the earth itself acts like a giant magnet. And one magnet affects another. The needle in a compass is a magnet.

▲ **This mammoth** was preserved in the frozen soil of Siberia.

MAINE

Maine is a hilly, forested state, the largest in New England. Its coastline is rocky and irregular and has many fine harbors. Potatoes, apples, and blueberries are the state's chief crops. Many tourists come to Maine's beautiful coast in summer to escape the heat farther south. Maine was once part of the colony of Massachusetts but became a separate state in 1820.

See also page 263.

MAMMAL

Mammals are the most advanced animals. They are vertebrates (animals with backbones) and they are warm blooded. They can control the temperature of their bodies by sweating or panting when it is hot and shivering when it is cold. Because of this, mammals can live in hot and cold climates. They have hairy or furry skin.

Almost all mammals, including human beings, give birth to live young, rather than laying eggs. The female feeds the young with milk from her body and cares for them until they can look after themselves.

Mammals range in size from tiny shrews to huge whales. Most mammals are land animals, but dolphins and whales spend all their lives in the sea. Bats are flying mammals.

MAMMOTH

The mammoth was a hairy elephant. It lived during the Ice Age but is now extinct. Mammoths had long, woolly hair and a thick layer of fat to keep out the cold. Prehistoric people hunted mammoths for food and drew pictures of them inside caves.

167

MAO ZEDONG (MAO TSE-TUNG) (1893–1976)

M

Modern China was founded by a farmer's son, Mao Zedong. He led the peasants in a revolution that changed China's government and way of life. He became a Communist, and for many years the Communists fought against the government. Mao was their leader, and in 1949 he led his armies to victory. China became a Communist state.

See also CHINA; COMMUNISM.

MAP

A map is a drawing that shows all or part of the earth's surface. It can show how cities, roads, railroads, rivers, mountains, and other features are arranged.

A flat map cannot be really accurate because the earth is round. Maps are drawn by methods called *projections*.

Maps are drawn to scale. For example, a distance of half an inch on the map may represent a mile on the ground.

Political maps show countries, and often cities, roads, and railroads. Physical maps show mountains, rivers, and other land features.

MARCO POLO (*c.*1254–1324)

The book *The Travels of Marco Polo* recorded the adventures of this Venetian merchant. With his father and his uncle he journeyed to China in 1275. The emperor, Kublai Khan, favored Marco and made him first a court attendant and later an official. He served the emperor for 17 years. The Polos returned home with great wealth in 1295.

MARCONI, Guglielmo (1874–1937)

Marconi worked with and made important discoveries about

▼ **These drawings** show how difficult it is to make an accurate map. When the surface of the round earth is stretched out, some parts must be squashed out of shape or distorted.

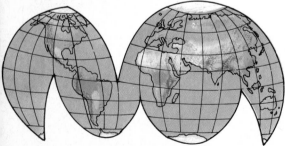

168

▲ **The swamp wallaby** is a marsupial.

radio waves. He patented wireless telegraphy and, in 1901, he sent the first wireless message across the Atlantic.

MARSUPIAL
Marsupials are primitive mammals. Most marsupials live in Australia and New Guinea. The opossum lives in the Americas.

A marsupial is born tiny. It crawls into its mother's pouch, where it sucks milk until it is big enough to leave.

MARX, Karl (1818–1883)
Marx was the founder of the modern Communist movement. His writings greatly changed the way many people thought about society. He helped write *The Communist Manifesto* in 1848, arguing that all old forms of government had to be overthrown. In *Das Kapital* he wrote that working people should rule and run the factories.

MARYLAND
Maryland is a Middle Atlantic state. The eastern part of the state is divided by Chesapeake Bay into the Eastern Shore and the Western Shore. Maryland produces iron and steel, electric and electronic goods, and fish and shellfish. The capital is Annapolis, also home of the U.S. Naval Academy. Baltimore is the state's largest city.

See also page 263.

MASSACHUSETTS
Massachusetts is a New England state and has been an important manufacturing center since the Industrial Revolution. The textiles produced by its early industry have given way to electronic equipment, scientific instruments, chemicals, and printed materials. The state was the center of anti-British feeling in the years before the Revolutionary War, which began at Concord, near Boston.

See also page 263.

▼ **Boston,** the capital of Massachusetts, lies along the Charles River.

◀ **The Pilgrims** stepped ashore in the New World in 1620.

MATHEMATICS

Mathematics is a science that deals with numbers and shapes. Arithmetic is one branch of mathematics. The other main branches are algebra, geometry, trigonometry, and calculus. Arithmetic deals with figures. Algebra deals with figures and symbols. Geometry deals with shapes. Trigonometry deals with measurement of triangles and problems based on this. Calculus deals with changing quantities.

MAYA

The Maya Indians developed a civilization in Central America from the A.D. 400s. They built great cities of stone, with palaces, temples, pyramids, and observatories. The Maya were astronomers and mathematicians, and they developed an advanced kind of writing. Like the other early civilizations in the Americas, they never developed the wheel. They did not have metal tools until late in their history, and most of their great engineering feats were accomplished using stone tools. Descendants of the Maya still live on and near the Yucatán Peninsula.

MAYFLOWER

The *Mayflower* was the ship that brought the Pilgrims from Plymouth, England, to Massachusetts in 1620. Persecuted for their Puritan beliefs in England, this intrepid band planned to start a settlement in Virginia, but storms blew the *Mayflower* off course. After more than two months at sea the settlers reached what is now Cape Cod. They crossed Cape Cod Bay and founded the colony of Plymouth in December 1620. The *Mayflower* returned to England the following April.

MEASUREMENT

How long is your desk? How heavy are you? How much water is in the bottle? We find the answers to these questions by measurement. To measure length we use a ruler. For weight, we use scales. For volume, we use a measuring cup.

Although the numbers on the

various scales may be the same, they mean different things. On the ruler, 8 may mean 8 inches; on the scales, 8 pounds; and on the cup, 8 ounces, or half a pint. The inch, pound, and pint are different units of measurement. They are units of length, weight, and volume. In the metric system of measurement, these units would be expressed as centimeters, kilograms, and milliliters.

MEDICI FAMILY

The Medicis were a family that ruled the city-state of Florence in Italy for 300 years during and after the Renaissance. They made Florence into a prosperous and beautiful city and had magnificent palaces, museums, and churches built. Two of the most famous of the Medici rulers were Cosimo (1389–1464) and Lorenzo the Magnificent (1449–1492). The Medicis became virtual dictators, allowing the people very little freedom. The last of the Medicis to rule died in 1737.

MEDICINE

Since very early times people have searched for medicines to heal wounds and cure diseases. The first drugs came from berries and herbs that had healing powers.

The ancient Greeks and Romans knew what the inside of the human body looked like. But they did not know how the different parts worked or what made them go wrong.

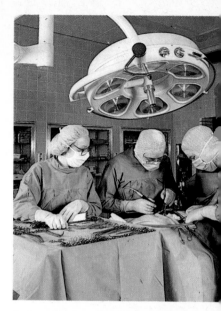

▲ **A patient** undergoing surgery in a sterilized operating room.

ADVANCES IN MEDICINE	
1590	Microscope – Zacharias Janssen
1593	Thermometer – Galileo
1628	Blood circulation – William Harvey
1796	Vaccination – Edward Jenner
1846	Anesthetic – William Morton
1865	Antiseptic surgery – Joseph Lister
1877	Germs cause disease – Louis Pasteur
1895	Psychoanalysis – Sigmund Freud
1895	X rays – William Roentgen
1898	Radium – Pierre and Marie Curie
1928	Penicillin – Alexander Fleming

171

Medicine made little progress until the 1600s, when doctors began studying anatomy (the parts of the body). By cutting up dead bodies, they began to find out how the ·body works. But since no one knew about germs, doctors did not bother very much about cleanliness. Many patients died because hospitals were dirty places.

Over the next 200 years progress in medicine was slow. But in the 1700s *vaccination* was discovered as a way of preventing disease, and later *antiseptics* were developed to kill harmful germs. *Anesthetics* came to be used to deaden pain during operations. In the 1900s the discovery of X rays meant that doctors could examine the insides of their patients to find out what was wrong without cutting them open. Powerful new drugs called *antibiotics* were also discovered.

See also DISEASE; DRUG; X RAY.

MENDEL, Gregor (1822–1884)
Mendel was an Austrian monk who studied the way in which physical characteristics are passed on from parent to child. He observed that the color and shape of peas are passed on from generation to generation according to certain laws.

His discoveries went unnoticed until improved microscopes finally made it possible to see chromosomes, the minute

▲ **Electricity** is used to extract aluminum from bauxite.

threadlike bodies that carry these hereditary characteristics.

See also GENETICS.

METALS
There are over 60 different metals. They make up the most important group of elements. They are very different from the other elements. Metals pass on, or conduct, electricity and heat well. Most nonmetals do not. Many metals have a silvery, shiny surface. They are tough and strong, but can be bent and hammered without breaking.

Most metals are found in the form of mineral ores. They must be separated out before they can be used. There are several different ways of taking, or extracting, a metal from its ore. Iron is extracted by smelting, aluminum by means of electricity.

Metal may be shaped by casting, hammering, rolling, forcing through holes, and cutting.

See also ALUMINUM; COPPER; GOLD; IRON AND STEEL; MINING.

METEOR
On some nights you may see bright streaks in the sky. Though they look like falling stars, these glowing trails are actually made by meteors, lumps of rock or metal. As they shoot through the upper part of the earth's atmosphere they burn up in a flash of light.

METRIC SYSTEM
The metric system of measurement is used for measuring length, weight, and volume. It is a decimal system: that is, it is based on units of ten. The metric system was devised in France in the late 1700s and has been in use in Europe most of this century. In the United States, conversion to the metric system has been on a voluntary basis.

MEXICO
Mexico is a republic and lies just south of the United States. Most of it consists of a broad, central plateau that is flanked on both sides by mountain ranges. On the west is the Pacific Ocean and on the east, the Gulf of Mexico and the Caribbean Sea. There are three main kinds of climate— cool, temperate, and hot—and a huge variety of plant life.

Over a third of Mexico's 81,700,000 people work on the land, growing corn, beans, coffee, wheat, cotton, sugar, and vegetables.

Mexico is rich in minerals. Its silver and gold originally attracted the Spanish. There is also oil. Mexico's factories produce a wide variety of goods.

See also page 79.

MICHELANGELO
(1475–1564)
Michelangelo was a sculptor, architect, painter, and poet who lived in Italy at the time of the Renaissance. Among his most famous statues are the *Pietà* and *David*. He painted a scene on the ceiling of the Sistine Chapel in

▼ **A sculpture** by Michelangelo.

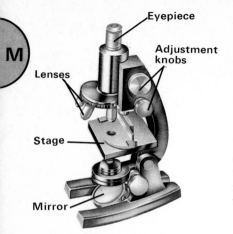

Eyepiece

Adjustment knobs

Lenses

Stage

Mirror

▲ **An optical microscope.** It has a base, a tube containing the lenses, and a body, or upright, to hold the tube. Objects to be studied are put on glass slides.

the Vatican depicting the creation of the world.

See also RENAISSANCE.

MICHIGAN
The state of Michigan lies on two peninsulas, almost surrounded by the waters of the Great Lakes. The Upper Peninsula is a land of lakes and woodland and is popular with people who like to camp and fish. The Lower Peninsula is the heart of the automobile industry, with its center in Detroit. Other major products include machinery, steel, and chemicals.

See also page 263.

MICROSCOPE
A microscope makes small objects look bigger, so that we can see things that are invisible to the naked eye.

Ordinary microscopes magnify by bending light rays with glass lenses. The bent rays make an image that is bigger than the original object. Electron microscopes are much more powerful than ordinary microscopes, and can magnify things hundreds of thousands of times. They magnify by bending beams of electrons, rather than light rays.

See also LENS; LIGHT.

MIDDLE AGES
The Roman Empire fell in A.D. 476 and it took 1,000 years for strong nations to grow out of the confusion that followed. In between lay the Middle Ages. In the early Middle Ages, Europe was overrun by barbarians. They sacked and burned towns, and soon the art and learning of Rome was forgotten, except by monks.

To defend themselves, people banded together under the protection of strong leaders, or kings. The peasants became the vassals of rich nobles and knights. They traded crops and services for protection. The nobles became vassals of the king. In return for the king's protection they promised to supply soldiers in war. This is known as the *feudal system.*

Life in the Middle Ages was often harsh and cruel. Anyone who broke the law was severely punished. And anyone who questioned the Church's teachings was punished harshly too. But slowly knowledge grew. Beautiful cathedrals were built. Universities and schools were founded. Gradually government became more settled, and trade flourished. With the voyages of discovery in the 1400s and the Renaissance, the Middle Ages came to an end.

MIDDLE EAST
The desert lands of southwest Asia and northeast Africa are often called the Middle East. This area stretches from Egypt to Iran. Most of the people are Muslim Arabs. Many are poor, but oilfields have made some Middle East countries rich.

In 1948 the Jews founded the state of Israel in what had been British-ruled Palestine. The Arabs would not accept this. There have been five wars between Israel and the Arab countries since 1948.

See also page 79.

MIGRATION
Many swallows spend the summer in Europe. But in the fall they fly south to the warmth of Africa. This journey is called migration.

Many animals migrate to find food or to breed. Caribou move south to escape the Arctic winter. African antelope migrate during the dry season to find water and fresh grass.

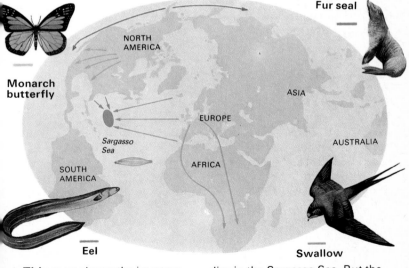

Fur seal

Monarch butterfly

NORTH AMERICA

ASIA

EUROPE

Sargasso Sea

AUSTRALIA

SOUTH AMERICA

AFRICA

Eel

Swallow

▲ **This map** shows the journeys made by some animals in the fall. The eel is the only one that does not return in spring. It breeds and dies in the Sargasso Sea. But the elvers (young eels) will eventually return to the rivers their parents once lived in.

175

Some birds fly very long distances. The Arctic tern flies from the Arctic winter to the Antarctic summer, and back again.

Frogs, toads, and newts spend most of their time on land. But they return to ponds and streams to lay their eggs.

MINERAL

A mineral is any substance that can be mined. There are nearly 3,000 kinds of minerals. Some, such as gold and silver, are pure elements. But most, such as salt and coal, are combinations of the 92 naturally occurring elements. Pure minerals are made up of atoms arranged in regular patterns known as crystals. This is what makes jewels such as diamonds and emeralds sparkle.

See also DIAMOND; GEM; MINING.

MINING

Mining means taking minerals from the ground. It is one of our most important industries and supplies many other industries with their raw materials.

Sometimes mineral deposits can be dug out from the surface. Other deposits lie just below the surface. The soil is first stripped off, then explosives break up the deposits. Power shovels load the mineral into trucks.

Often the mineral deposits are buried deep in the ground. Miners have to travel by elevator down shafts and in trains along tunnels to reach them.

▲ **Lake Calhoun**, Minnesota.

MINNESOTA

Minnesota is a north-central state bordering on Canada. It has more than 25,000 lakes of 25 acres or more, as well as many rivers and streams. The industrial center around Minneapolis–St. Paul produces computers, farm equipment, and mining machinery. Minnesota is also known for its dairy products.

See also page 263.

MISSILE

A missile can be anything that is thrown or fired at a target. Today the word usually means a military weapon that has an automatic control system. Many are powered by a rocket engine and carry an explosive *warhead*. A *guided missile* is controlled by radio or radar and stays within the earth's atmosphere. A *ballistic missile* goes beyond the atmosphere under rocket power, but returns to earth in an unguided path called a ballistic trajectory. Missiles can be launched from planes in the air, or from the ground at targets in the air or on land.

MISSISSIPPI
Mississippi is one of the Gulf states; the Mississippi River forms its western border. The fertile delta region was once one of the most important cotton-farming areas in the nation. Even today, cotton is the state's leading crop. Other industries produce lumber, clothing, transportation equipment, oil, and natural gas.

See also page 263.

MISSOURI
A midwestern state, Missouri lies at the point where the Missouri and Mississippi rivers meet. Missouri cities such as St. Louis, St. Joseph, and Jefferson City all began as river ports and the starting point for pioneers going west. Today Missouri's income comes from manufacturing, agriculture, and tourism.

See also page 263.

MOLLUSK
Mollusks are animals with soft bodies. To protect themselves, many mollusks have shells.

Some mollusks, such as the mussel, stay inside their shells and hardly ever move. Others, such as the clam, use their single foot to move around. Snails and slugs crawl very slowly.

The largest and most active mollusks are the octopus, which has no shell, and the squid, which has its shell inside its body.

MONASTERY
A monastery is the home of a religious community. The monks who live in the monastery take

M

▼ **A battery** of surface-to-air (SAM) missiles.

▼ **The Mississippi River** at Memphis, Tennessee.

religious vows promising not to marry, not to have possessions or money, and to do whatever work they are asked to do. They spend the day working, studying, or in prayer. The long tunic many monks wear is known as a *habit*.

The first Christian monasteries were started about 200 years after the death of Christ. By the Middle Ages there were several important "orders" of monks and friars (friar means brother).

Some monks work outside the monastery as missionaries and teachers. Others remain in the monastery and lead strict lives.

▼ **A selection** of coins from different countries.

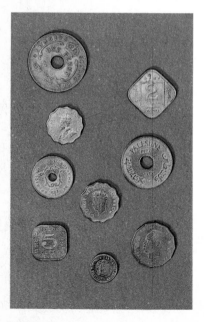

MONEY

Originally, people did not use money. They bartered or traded. When people settled in towns, trade became more complicated. The barter system was too clumsy. So *token goods,* such as cattle or shells, were used. This was the beginning of the money system. Later small pieces of metal, or coins, came into use.

Merchants in the Middle Ages began to exchange pieces of paper, promising payment for goods bought. They set up banks in which to keep their gold safe. The banks began to issue paper money, and people gradually accepted that this had the same value as gold.

Today the government controls how much money is made by minting coins and printing paper money. The money we use is token money: that is, modern coins are made of cheap metals and have little value in themselves. The real value of money is the amount of goods it will buy.

See also COIN.

MONKEY

Monkeys belong to the group of animals called primates. Old World monkeys live in Africa and Asia. New World monkeys live in Central and South America. New World monkeys have *prehensile* tails, which can grasp a branch like an extra hand. Old World monkeys cannot do this.

Monkeys are lively, intelligent

MONKEYS

Black howler monkey

Long-nosed proboscis monkey

Squirrel monkey

Golden spider monkey

animals. They use their hands and feet to hold things. Most monkeys live in groups. They eat fruit and other parts of plants, insects, small mammals, and birds' eggs.

MONTANA
Montana is one of the Rocky Mountain states, bordering on Canada. Spectacular scenery in the Rockies in the western part of the state attracts tourists to such places as Glacier National Park. In the east lie the Great Plains, where cattle and crops are raised. Lumber, mining, and food processing are other Montana industries.

See also page 263.

MOON
The moon is a ball of rock, about a quarter the diameter (width) of the earth. It has no atmosphere. Because there is no air, there is no weather on the moon, and no

▼ The moon shows "phases" as it moves around the earth. It takes $29\frac{1}{2}$ days to complete these phases, as more or less of its surface is lit by the sun. First it waxes (from crescent, or new, moon to full moon) and then wanes (from full back to crescent).

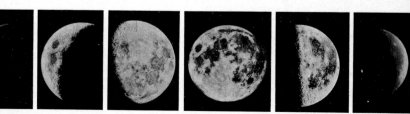

sound. There is no water and no life at all. It is very hot in the sunlight, but cold in the shade.

The moon's surface is not smooth. There are great, flat plains and jagged peaks and mountain ranges. Everywhere on the moon there are pits, or craters. The whole surface is covered with loose rocks and a thick layer of fine dust.

The moon travels around the earth once a month. The shape of the moon appears to change during the month. What changes is the area we can see which is lit by the sun. This area changes because of the moon's movement around the earth.

See also ECLIPSE.

MOSQUE
Mosques are the buildings in which the services of the religion Islam take place. Most mosques

▼ **Muslims** worship God in a mosque. This one is in Iraq.

have a dome; a minaret, from which the faithful are called to prayer five times a day; and a prayer niche.

MOSQUITO
The mosquito is a fly with a small body and long legs. Some mosquitoes spread diseases such as malaria. The male is harmless, but the female mosquito feeds on the blood of animals, including human beings. The insect pours a juice into the wound to stop the blood clotting, or hardening, and this can pass on a disease.

Mosquitoes lay their eggs in water. In warm countries, where mosquitoes are most dangerous, eggs and larvae are destroyed.

MOSS
Mosses are simple plants. They do not have flowers, but reproduce by sending out tiny off-shoots. Spores, or cells, grow on these shoots. When the spores are ripe, they are blown away by the wind. New moss plants develop from them.

MOTION PICTURE
One of the earliest inventions in the development of moving pictures was Thomas Edison's kinetoscope, built in 1891. This was soon followed by the *cinématographe,* built by two French brothers, Auguste and Louis Lumière. It projected pictures from a piece of film onto a screen. The pictures were shown one after another, so quickly that

M

▲ **Charlie Chaplin,** master of film comedy.

▶ **Box office hits:** *The Sound of Music* (top) and *The Godfather*.

the images seemed to move. Soon people all over Europe and North America were making films. The first "talkie," with sound, was *The Jazz Singer* (1927). The United States was the leader in the movie world, producing films using hundreds of actors, singers, and dancers and special "sets," or back-grounds. After World War II, more realistic movies, many made in Europe, became popular. After the 1960s movies lost some of their popularity to television and home videos.

MOTORCYCLE

A motorcycle is a vehicle that has two and sometimes three wheels.

1894 Hildebrand and Wolfmuller   **1980s Honda 500**

▶ **On a mountain,** different plants grow in zones at various heights. On the lower slopes are deciduous trees. Higher up there are conifers. Above the tree line are shrubs, alpine flowers, and then lichens and mosses. Snow covers the highest peaks.

HIGHEST MOUNTAINS		
Asia	**Feet**	
Everest	29,028	
Godwin Austen	28,250	
Kanchenjunga	28,208	
Makalu	27,824	
Dhaulagiri	26,810	
Nanga Parbat	26,660	
Annapurna	26,504	
Gasherbrum	26,470	
Gosainthan	26,291	
Nanda Devi	25,645	
South America		
Aconcagua		22,834
North America		
McKinley		20,320
Africa		
Kilimanjaro		19,340
Europe		
Elbrus		18,481
Mont Blanc		15,771
Antarctica		
Vinson Massif		16,864
Oceania		
Wilhelm		14,763

The first motorcycles were built at the end of the 1800s when men such as Edward Butler, an Englishman, and Gottlieb Daimler, a German, began making powered bicycles and tricycles. The first motorcycle races in 1907 encouraged improvements in design. They soon brought the motorcycle to something like its present form, with electric ignition, variable gears, and the engine mounted low down between the two wheels.

MOUNTAIN

Mountains are masses of rock that rise at least 2,000 feet above the surrounding land.

Mountains are usually grouped together in ranges, chains, or massifs. Some mountains are the cones of volcanoes. But most are formed by folding and sideways movements of the crust, or outer skin, of the earth. These movements push up the rocks to build mountains. Mountain building occurs over millions of years. It is still going on today in parts of the earth. The rocks are worn away by rain, wind, ice, and snow.

The height of a mountain is always measured in height above sea level. The world's highest mountains are in the Himalayas in Asia.

MOZART, Wolfgang Amadeus (1756–1791)

The Austrian composer Mozart was a musical genius. He began writing music at the age of five. Two years later his father took him to play at concerts in the great cities of Europe. Mozart wrote church music, operas, and nearly 50 symphonies. He worked hard but earned little money, and died very poor at the age of 35.

MUHAMMAD (A.D. 570–632)

The Arab prophet Muhammad founded the religion of Islam. He taught people to stop worshiping idols and follow the "true God," called Allah. In 622 Muhammad's enemies drove him out of his birthplace, Mecca. He fled to the city of Medina and converted many people to the new religion. By the time he died, Islam had spread throughout Arabia.

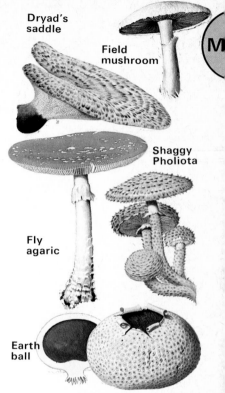

Dryad's saddle

Field mushroom

Shaggy Pholiota

Fly agaric

Earth ball

MUSHROOM AND TOADSTOOL

These plants belong to the fungus group. Fungi are not green. They contain no chlorophyll, so they cannot use sunlight to make their food like other plants. Instead they feed on dead and decaying plant and animal matter. Some are parasites. Fungi reproduce by means of cells.

See also PHOTOSYNTHESIS.

MUSIC

Music is a set of sounds arranged in a way that is pleasant to hear. It has rhythm (the beat), harmony (the total sound when several notes are played together), and usually melody (the tune). Music is made up of *notes* which may be long or short, loud or soft, high or low.

At first music had a simple melody and rhythm. But it gradually grew more complicated. Two or three tunes were played together. This rich sound was called *counterpoint*.

People who make up music and write it down are called *composers*. Two great composers

183

FAMOUS COMPOSERS

Antonio Vivaldi, Italian (1678?–1741)

Johann Sebastian Bach, German (1685–1750)

Wolfgang Amadeus Mozart, Austrian (1756–1791)

Ludwig van Beethoven, German (1770–1827)

Franz Schubert, Austrian (1797–1828)

Hector Berlioz, French (1803–1869)

Frédéric Chopin, Polish (1810–1849)

Robert Schumann, German (1810–1856)

Franz Liszt, Hungarian (1811–1886)

Giuseppe Verdi, Italian (1813–1901)

Richard Wagner, German (1813–1883)

Johannes Brahms, German (1833–1897)

Peter Ilyich Tchaikovsky, Russian (1840–1893)

Antonín Dvořák, Czech (1841–1904)

Edvard Grieg, Norwegian (1843–1907)

Edward Elgar, British (1857–1934)

Giacomo Puccini, Italian (1858–1924)

Gustav Mahler, Austrian (1860–1911)

Claude Debussy, French (1862–1918)

Jean Sibelius, Finnish (1865–1957)

Sergei Rachmaninov, Russian (1873–1943)

Igor Stravinsky, Russian (1882–1971)

Dmitri Shostakovich, Russian (1906–1975)

Benjamin Britten, British (1913–1976)

of counterpoint were Bach and Handel. Much great music has been written for orchestras by composers such as Haydn, Mozart, Beethoven, and Brahms. They wrote *symphonies* (long pieces of music for orchestras) and *chamber music* (for smaller groups of instruments). They also wrote music for choirs. Some composers have written operas— musical plays in which all the words are sung.

People often call this kind of music "classical" music. There are many other kinds of music, including folk songs, jazz, and pop music. Modern music is very different from the music of the 1800s. It has difficult rhythms and sounds, and sometimes requires electronic instruments as well as wind, stringed, and percussion instruments.

See also BACH; BEETHOVEN; MOZART; OPERA.

MUSICAL INSTRUMENT

Musical instruments have been made for thousands of years. There are three main groups of instruments. *Wind instruments* are played by blowing down a hollow wooden or metal tube with holes cut in it. By covering some holes with the fingers, different notes are produced. Wind instruments include flutes, clarinets, trumpets, and horns.

The *stringed instruments* have strings stretched across a hollow box. The strings are bowed, as in a violin, or plucked, as in a guitar, to make different notes. Short strings make high notes and long strings make low notes. Stringed instruments include violins, violas, cellos, guitars, banjos, and lutes.

Instruments such as drums, cymbals, and bells, which are hit with hammers or sticks, are called *percussion instruments*.

See also ORCHESTRA.

MYTHOLOGY

Mythology is the study of the myths, or stories, that ancient peoples told about their creation and origins, their gods and goddesses. The most familiar to us are the myths the ancient Greeks and Romans created. Myths were a part of their religion, for they believed that many gods and goddesses inhabited the earth—gods of the sun and moon, gods of war, of the sea and forests, of rain and thunder. The Greek gods lived on Mt. Olympus, and the stories told about them were full of heroic adventures and amazing feats. The Greek poets Hesiod and Homer recorded many of these myths in writing. The Romans adopted many of the Greek myths and told dramatic stories about their own gods and heroes that were similar to the Greek myths.

The Norse people of Scandinavia also developed a rich mythology. Norse and Roman myths are kept alive today in our names for the months and the days of the week.

MUSICAL INSTRUMENTS

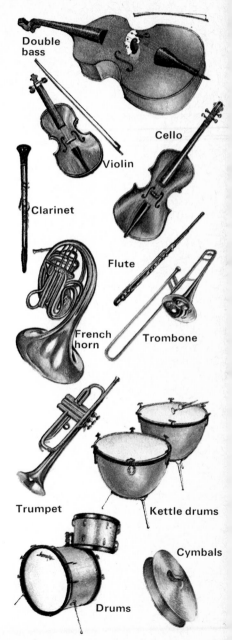

Double bass

Cello

Violin

Clarinet

Flute

French horn

Trombone

Trumpet

Kettle drums

Cymbals

Drums

N

NAPOLEON BONAPARTE
(1769–1821)
After the French Revolution in 1789, Napoleon conquered much of Europe. In 1804 he made himself Emperor of France. But in 1812 his army had to retreat from Russia, and in 1815 the British and Prussians beat the French at the Battle of Waterloo. He was exiled, and died on the island of St. Helena.

NASSER, Gamal Abdal
(1918–1970)
Nasser was an Egyptian revolutionary and army officer. He helped to depose King Farouk in 1952 and became president in 1956. He tried to modernize Egypt. In 1956 he nationalized, or took over, the Suez Canal.

NEBRASKA
Nebraska lies in the heart of the Great Plains and is one of the nation's great farming states. Leading crops include corn, wheat, sorghum, and soybeans. Omaha, the state's largest city, is an important meat-packing center. Cattle raised in north-central Nebraska are brought to market

▲ **The nest** of the harvest mouse.

here. Industries include the production of chemicals and farm machinery.

See also page 263.

NELSON, Horatio (1758–1805)
Nelson was a great British admiral whose statue stands above Trafalgar Square in London.

He fought and defeated the French fleet led by Napoleon

near Alexandria in 1798 (the Battle of the Nile). His most famous battle was at Trafalgar in 1805, though he was shot and killed during this battle.

NEST
Many animals build nests for their young. Usually they are well hidden and out of reach of enemies. Some are simple: just scrapes in the ground or untidy piles of twigs. But many are elaborately built of mud, grass, moss, feathers, or wax. Birds, fish, insects, reptiles, and mammals build nests.

NETHERLANDS
The Netherlands is a small country in Europe. It is largely flat, but in the south and east there are low hills and moorlands.

The Netherlands is well known for its dikes and canals. Two-fifths of the land has been reclaimed from lakes, marshes, or the sea. The canals drain the land to make new land for farming. Much of the Netherlands is below sea level. Dikes keep the water out.

Dairy farming, horticulture, and food processing are very important, but industry has grown rapidly in recent years. The port of Rotterdam is the busiest port in the world.

The Netherlands is a kingdom. See also page 78.

▼ **The low-lying** Netherlands countryside is drained by dikes and canals.

NEVADA
Nevada is a desert state lying between California and Utah. Rain falls chiefly in the mountains surrounding the desert highlands. Most of Nevada's people live in or around the cities of Las Vegas and Reno, gambling and entertainment centers. Tourists also go to Lake Tahoe, a winter resort in the Sierra Nevada range.

See also page 263.

NEW HAMPSHIRE
New Hampshire is a hilly, forested state in New England, lying between Maine and Vermont. Its beaches, mountains, and lakes attract many visitors each year who are eager to get away from the large cities of the East Coast. Most of New Hampshire's industry is in the south, where factories produce machinery, paper and wood products, and leather goods.

See also page 263.

▲ Shiprock Butte rises sharply out of New Mexico's tableland.

NEW JERSEY

New Jersey is a Middle Atlantic state and one of the most densely populated of all the states. It lies between the urban centers of New York City and Philadelphia and has a number of large cities of its own, including Newark, Jersey City, and Paterson. An important transportation center, it is the leading producer of chemicals and pharmaceuticals.

See also page 263.

NEW MEXICO

New Mexico is a southwestern state, bordering on Mexico. The eastern part of the state is in the Great Plains; west of the Pecos River are the Rocky Mountains. Mining produces oil, natural gas, uranium, and copper. The U.S. government employs many New Mexicans at the atomic research center at Los Alamos and other test sites.

See also page 263.

NEW YORK

New York State has more people than any other state apart from California. Over 7 million live in New York City, the largest city in the United States. The state is the business and industrial capital of the nation. Factories produce clothing, electrical machinery, and food products. Much of the state is hilly or mountainous, though there are farms along the Hudson and Mohawk river valleys.

See also page 263.

NEW ZEALAND

Two long and narrow islands, the North Island and South Island, and a few smaller islands make up the country of New Zealand. It lies in the south Pacific Ocean.

New Zealand has high mountains, volcanoes, hot springs, fast-flowing rivers, and glaciers. Most of the towns and cities are on the coast. The climate is mild.

The grasslands are ideal for sheep and cattle farming. New Zealand is famous for its butter, cheese, and meat, and for fruit.

The native Maoris settled in New Zealand about 700 years ago. Although the Dutch explorer Abel Tasman discovered and named New Zealand in 1642, the country was mainly settled by people from Britain.

See also page 79.

NEWTON, Isaac (1642–1727)

Newton was one of the greatest scientists and mathematicians the world has known. He was the first person to explain the force of gravity, which holds the universe together. Newton carried out many experiments with light and split up light into a spectrum, or band of color. He built the first reflecting telescope and he invented calculus.

Newton was born in England and studied mathematics and science at Cambridge University.

See also COLOR; GRAVITY; LIGHT; TELESCOPE.

▼ **Skyscrapers** on Manhattan Island, the heart of New York City.

NIAGARA FALLS

Niagara Falls are waterfalls along the Niagara River, on the border between Canada and New York. They formed where the river drops from Lake Erie to Lake Ontario. Each minute about 500,000 tons of water plunge 165 feet over a cliff into the gorge below. The falls are divided into two wide sections: the Horseshoe Falls and the American Falls.

NIGERIA

Nigeria is a large country in West Africa. It has a tropical climate and the largest population in Africa.

Nigeria produces oil, hardwoods, palm oil, groundnuts, cocoa, and various fruits and vegetables. A great variety of animals live in the country including gorillas, chimpanzees, lions, and elephants.

Most Nigerians are black Africans who belong to different tribes. Many speak different languages. Nigeria is a member of the Commonwealth.

See also page 78.

▼ **Students** at Ibadan University in Nigeria.

NOMAD

Nomads are groups of people who wander from place to place with their animals and possessions. They do not build permanent houses. Some nomads keep flocks and herds and move to find fresh grazing land for their animals.

NORTH AMERICA

This is the third largest of the earth's continents. It stretches from the cold wastes of Alaska in the north to the hot deserts cf

NOBEL PRIZE

Every year six Nobel Prizes may be awarded, for outstanding work in chemistry, physics, medicine, literature, economics, and the cause of peace. Two or three people may share a prize, and the prizewinners may come from any part of the world. To win a Nobel Prize is a very great honor. The money for the prizes was given by Alfred Nobel, a Swedish chemist, who invented the explosive dynamite.

Mexico and the tropical forests of Central America in the south. Canada and the United States of America cover most of North America. North America covers about a sixth of the earth's land surface.

Down the western side of North America run the rugged Rocky Mountains. In the center of the continent are wide prairies, or grasslands. The Canadian Shield, a wild region of lakes and forests in northern Canada, has

valuable minerals, such as coal and oil. In the south of the continent are coastal plains, swampy in places. The longest river in North America is the Mississippi, which joins another long river, the Missouri. The Great Lakes are the largest freshwater lakes in the world.

Crops grown in North America include wheat, fruit, vegetables, and cotton. Forestry and furs are important in the north, and fishing is a major activity. Canada and the United States are great industrial countries, endowed with plentiful raw materials.

191

North America is a continent of great contrasts. It has some of the world's largest cities, such as Mexico City and New York. But there are huge areas with hardly any people at all. The United States is one of the richest countries in the world. But in Central America the countries are small and poor.

The first people in North America came from Asia. They were the ancestors of the American Indians and Eskimos. Much later Europeans came, bringing with them black slaves from Africa.

See also page 79.

NORTH CAROLINA

North Carolina is a southeastern state bordering on the Atlantic. In the west are the Blue Ridge Mountains. North Carolina grows more tobacco than any other state. Factories turn out textiles, tobacco products, and

▼ **The Great Smoky Mountains** form a backdrop to Fontana Lake in North Carolina.

furniture. Along the coast are the Outer Banks, a string of long, sandy islands. Cape Hatteras is a famous landmark on the Outer Banks.

See also page 263.

NORTH DAKOTA

The state of North Dakota lies along the Canadian border, in the very center of North America. Fertile farmland in the east produces wheat—only Kansas grows more. In the west are the Badlands, a dry, barren region of spectacular rock formations. Cattle are raised on the Great Plains. North Dakota industries produce food products and farm machinery.

See also page 263.

NORWAY

Norway is a country in Scandinavia. Its long, rocky coast is pierced by narrow inlets called *fiords*. The sixth largest country in Europe, Norway has the largest fishing catch of any European country. Much of the country is covered by mountains and forests. The Arctic Circle runs through the north. The North Sea oil wells belonging to Norway are among Europe's richest.

See also page 78.

NUCLEAR ENERGY

Under certain conditions atoms of uranium can be made to split. When they do so, large amounts of energy are released as heat and

▲ **A Norwegian fiord,** a long, narrow, and steep-sided inlet of the sea.

light. The splitting of the atom, or rather of its nucleus, is called nuclear fission.

Scientists can now control the fission of uranium and use the energy is releases to produce nuclear power. In furnaces called reactors, great heat is produced when the nucleus of the atom splits., This heat is used to drive turbines and generate electricity. Nuclear power is also used to drive some ships.

In atomic bombs, the nuclear reaction is uncontrolled and all the energy is released, causing devastation over a huge area.

NUT
Some trees bear fruit called nuts. Inside the tough shell of the nut is a seed. Many animals crack or gnaw at nuts to get at the seed inside. Ripe nuts fall to the ground in the autumn. The seed sends a new shoot pushing through the shell, and a new tree begins its life.

NUTS

Hazelnut

Peanut

Acorn

Coconut

OASIS

An oasis is a fertile area in a desert. Sometimes water comes to the surface naturally. Sometimes wells are sunk to tap it. Some oases cover many square miles and may support a city. Others have only a few huts.

▼ **An oasis** on the desert coast of Peru, South America.

OCEAN

About 70 percent of the earth's surface is covered by water. The large areas of salty water that separate the continents are called oceans.

194

▲ **At its outer edge** the continental shelf plunges down to the ocean floor, or abyss, a plain crossed by rivers and trenches.

There are five oceans. The biggest and deepest is the Pacific Ocean, which separates America and Asia. Next come the Atlantic Ocean and the Indian Ocean. The Antarctic and Arctic Oceans surround the poles.

Around most coasts a shelf of land runs out under the sea. This is the *continental shelf*. It lies up to 600 feet deep and may stretch for hundreds of miles. Beyond the continental shelf, the ocean floor drops away steeply. It flattens out again at a depth of about 12,000 feet. The bottom of the ocean is called the abyss. It is a flat plain, crossed by ridges, high mountains, and deep trenches.

Life abounds in the oceans. Today, sea creatures range in size from enormous whales to tiny drifting animals, too small to be seen without a microscope. There are many plants, including huge seaweeds.

The oceans are never still. The rise and fall of the tides, which takes place roughly every twelve hours, is caused by the gravitational pull of the earth and the moon. The surface of the water is moved by waves, caused by the wind.

See also TIDE; WIND.

OCTOPUS AND SQUID

The octopus and squid are soft-bodied mollusks that live in the sea. Octopus means "eight feet," though we usually call its tentacles "arms." A squid has ten tentacles. Suckers on the tentacles seize and hold prey, which the animals eat with a sharp, horny "beak" in the center of their bodies. If danger threatens, an octopus can squirt an inky liquid that forms a cloud in the water, behind which the octopus can escape. A giant squid can measure up to 30 feet in length, including the tentacles.

OHIO

Ohio is a midwestern state and one of the leading industrial states. Its central location bordering the Great Lakes gives it an excellent transportation network. Ohio's natural resources include limestone, gravel, rock salt, and clay. Industries centered around Cleveland, Dayton, Toledo, Akron, and Cincinnati produce iron and steel, machinery, books, chemicals, and clothing.

See also page 263.

OIL

Oil is a greasy substance that does not mix with water. There are three kinds of oil: mineral, fatty, and "essential."

Mineral oil is distilled from petroleum. It comes from the earth's crust and is used for fuels and lubricants.

Fatty oils come from both animals and vegetables. Linseed oil, lard, butter, and margarine are fatty oils.

▲ **An oil rig** being towed out to oil fields in the North Sea.

Essential oils give scents and flavors to flowers and fruits. Lemon oil from lemon rind and cinnamon from bark are kinds of essential oils.

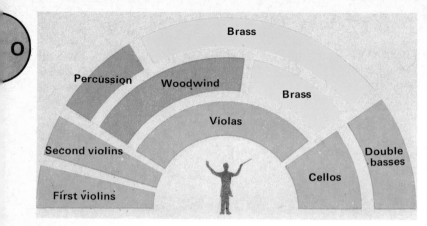

Brass

Percussion   Woodwind
                                Brass
              Violas
Second violins   Double
                                    basses
First violins   Cellos

▲ **A plan** of a symphony orchestra. About two-thirds of the musicians play stringed instruments.

OKLAHOMA

Oklahoma is a south-central state to the north of Texas. Most of the state is dry plains, especially in the west. In the east are rolling hills and prairie. Over five million head of cattle graze in Oklahoma; wheat and cotton are also produced. The state's most important industry is oil refining.

See also page 263.

OLYMPIC GAMES

Between 776 B.C. and A.D. 393, the ancient Greeks held athletic contests at Olympia every four years. The idea was taken up again in 1896, when the first modern Olympics were held in Athens. The Games are now held every four years, each time in a different country, and many nations take part in the different sports. The winners receive gold, silver, and bronze medals.

OPERA

An opera is a play in which the actors sing the words of the story. The first operas were written in Italy in the 1600s. The actors recited the story to music. Later, complete songs called arias were added. Famous composers of operas include Monteverdi, Mozart, Verdi, Puccini, and Wagner.

ORCHESTRA

The word orchestra is used to describe any group of musicians, large or small, that plays together under a conductor. There are various types: large symphony orchestras of about a hundred musicians, small chamber orchestras, orchestras with stringed instruments only, and theater orchestras.

The conductor directs and interprets the music, giving it its life and character. He also indicates the speed and rhythm.

OREGON

Oregon is a northwestern state lying between Washington and California. East of the coastal plain is the rugged Cascade Range, which has some of the tallest mountains in North America. Oregon's forests produce quantities of timber and wood products. Factories also make machinery and metal products. Most of the state's people live in the lush valley of the Willamette River.

See also page 263.

OWL

Owls are birds of prey. Their large eyes see well in the dark and they fly noiselessly on their broad wings. Hunting by night, they swoop down on small animals such as mice and voles, and carry them off in their strong claws. The owl rips flesh with its hooked beak but it cannot digest fur, skin, and bones. It spits them out in the form of a pellet.

OXYGEN

Oxygen, a colorless, odorless gas, is the most common element on earth. It combines easily with minerals and other substances. Oxygen is found in air, water, and many different rocks.

All living things need oxygen. Animals need extra oxygen to move around, and fire needs oxygen in order to burn. Plants give out oxygen in photosynthesis.

See also BREATHING; PHOTOSYNTHESIS.

Eagle owl

Short-eared owl

Brown form   Gray form

Tawny owl

197

P

FAMOUS PAINTERS

Giotto, Italian (*c*.1266–1337)
Jan van Eyck, Flemish (*c*.1387–1440)
Sandro Botticelli, Italian (*c*.1444–1510)
Leonardo da Vinci, Italian (1452–1519)
Albrecht Dürer, German (1471–1528)
Michelangelo, Italian (1475–1564)
Titian, Italian (1477–1576)
Raphael, Italian (1483–1520)
El Greco, Spanish (*c*.1541–1614)
Rubens, Flemish (1577–1640)
Velázquez, Spanish (*c*.1599–1660)
Rembrandt van Rijn, Dutch (1606–1669)
Goya, Spanish (1746–1828)
J.M.W. Turner, English (1775–1851)
Edouard Manet, French (1832–1883)
Paul Cézanne, French (1839–1906)
Henri Rousseau, French (1844–1910)
Vincent van Gogh, Dutch (1853–1890)
Vassily Kandinsky, Russian (1866–1944)
Henri Matisse, French (1869–1954)
Pablo Picasso, Spanish (1881–1973)
Jackson Pollock, American (1912–1956)

PACIFIC OCEAN

The Pacific Ocean is the largest and the deepest of all the world's oceans. Its deepest part is deep enough to cover the world's highest mountain. The Pacific washes the shores of western North and South America, eastern Asia, and Australia, stretching from the Arctic to the Antarctic. Thousands of islands in the Pacific were formed from volcanoes. Movements in the earth's crust around the fringes of the Pacific often cause earthquakes and sometimes tidal waves.

PAINTING

The oldest known paintings were made by Stone Age people in caves thousands of years ago. Much later, people started to decorate their homes and temples with paintings. Egyptians, Greeks, Romans, and Chinese painted vases, pottery, and walls.

During the Middle Ages in Europe most paintings were done for churches. So painters often painted stories from the Bible. Later Italian painters began to paint Bible characters that looked like real people.

During the Renaissance, painters often took scenes from history and Greek and Roman legends as their subjects. They also painted portraits of people from life, and realistic scenes from nature. During the 1700s many painters worked for fashionable society. They painted

▲ **Raphael** is one of the most famous painters of the Renaissance. He painted many beautiful pictures of the Madonna and Child.

▼ **A scene** of country life painted by the Flemish painter Pieter Brueghel in the 1500s.

▲ *Light Red over Black,* an abstract painting by the American Mark Rothko (1950s).

P

people in family groups, often against a background of a garden or a fine house.

Artists have always experimented with new ideas. "Impressionist" painters, for instance, loved to paint light and shadow, and ignore the details, which could be captured perfectly in a photograph. By the early 1900s some were making pictures as designs and shapes, rather than as copies of objects. This is called *abstract* painting.

See also ART; LEONARDO DA VINCI; MICHELANGELO; PICASSO.

PANAMA

Panama is a small country that occupies the narrow strip of land that links North and South America. The country is cut in two by the Panama Canal Zone, which connects the Atlantic and Pacific. Panama produces rice, sugarcane, and bananas; coffee is grown in the highlands.

See also page 79.

PANDA

One of the world's rarest animals is the giant panda. It looks like a furry black and white bear.

Pandas live in bamboo forests in the mountains of China. They eat mostly bamboo shoots and leaves. Pandas do not breed easily in captivity, so few have been seen in zoos outside China.

PAPER

The word *paper* comes from *papyrus,* the reed the Egyptians used to make paper. The type of paper we use today was invented by the Chinese about A.D. 105. It was made of mulberry bark. Small pieces of bark were soaked to separate the fibers, then dried into flat sheets. The use of paper spread after it was discovered by Arabs in the 700s.

With the invention of the printing press in the 1400s the demand for paper grew. In 1799 Louis Robert invented a machine to produce a continuous reel of paper. Today, most paper is made on machines from wood pulp obtained from tree fibers.

PARACHUTE

A parachute is a safety device for pilots and passengers of military airplanes. It is a canopy about 25 feet across, made of silk or nylon and worn on a harness. It inflates when the wearer pulls a *ripcord.*

▲ **Pandas** are related to raccoons.

200

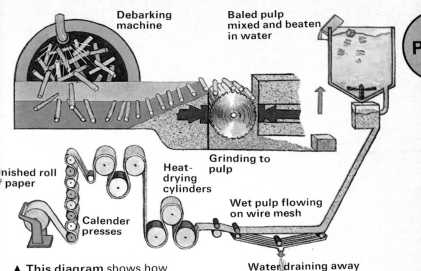

Debarking machine

Baled pulp mixed and beaten in water

Grinding to pulp

Heat-drying cylinders

nished roll paper

Calender presses

Wet pulp flowing on wire mesh

Water draining away

P

▲ **This diagram** shows how paper is made from timber. Logs are chopped into small pieces, then ground into pulp. The pulp is mixed with water and poured onto a wire mesh belt. The water drains away, leaving a web of fibers which is dried and rolled.

Parachutes today have other uses besides saving lives. They can be used to drop food and supplies in places where planes cannot land, or at the sites of accidents or forest fires. Racing cars and fast fighter planes use parachutes to act as extra brakes.

PASTEUR, Louis (1822–1895)
Pasteur was a French scientist. He proved that bacteria and other germs cause diseases. Pasteur injected weakened germs into animals and people to stop them catching the diseases those germs usually caused. He invented *pasteurization:* a way of heating milk and cooling it quickly to make it safe to drink. Pasteur also found out how tiny yeast cells turn sugar into alcohol.

PEARL HARBOR
Pearl Harbor, on the island of Oahu in Hawaii, was the site of the surprise Japanese air attack on the U.S. Pacific Fleet on December 7, 1941. In less than two hours, five battleships and 188 planes were destroyed. More than 2,000 Americans lay dead and 1,200 were wounded. The United States declared war on Japan as a result and entered World War II on the side of the Allies.

See also WORLD WAR II.

PENGUIN
Penguins are sea birds that live on coasts around the Antarctic. Unable to fly, penguins use their

201

▲ **The emperor penguin's** chick sits on its parent's feet under a warm flap of feathers.

wings as paddles and are excellent swimmers. They have a layer of thick fat to keep out the cold. Some kinds of penguins lay their eggs in rough nests on the rocks.

PENICILLIN
Penicillin is a kind of mold which, when processed, is used to stop the growth of many kinds of germs. It was the first antibiotic—a drug which kills bacteria.

PENNSYLVANIA
Pennsylvania is a Middle Atlantic state and a leading industrial center. Its rich deposits of coal and oil have enabled it to smelt iron ore brought from Minnesota via the Great Lakes, and it has become a major producer of iron and steel. The state is

named for William Penn, who founded Philadelphia, an early U.S. capital.

See also page 263.

PERFUME
Perfume is a fragrant essence in which more than a hundred natural aromatic (sweet-smelling or spicy) materials may be blended. The materials come from about 60,000 different flowers, leaves, fruits, seeds, woods, barks, resins, and roots.

PERISCOPE
A periscope is an instrument used for looking over walls and around corners. A simple periscope can be made from two mirrors, at a 45° angle, at either end of a tube. More complicated periscopes are used in submarines.

PHILIPPINES
The Philippines is a nation made up of over 7,000 islands in the western Pacific. It is a producer of chromite, nickel, and copper, as well as sugarcane, fruits, and Manila hemp. Governed first by Spain and then by the United States, it became independent in 1946. In 1986 its virtual dictator, Ferdinand Marcos, was ousted, and in democratic elections Corazón Aquino came to power.

See also page 79.

PHOTOGRAPHY
Photography was invented in 1839 by Louis Daguerre in

France and William Fox Talbot in England.

Today there are cheap cameras that work automatically as well as the complex equipment, processes, and techniques used by television and motion pictures and in medical and scientific research.

See also CAMERA.

▲ **An early camera** called a *daguerreotype* after its inventor Louis Daguerre.

PHOTOSYNTHESIS

This is the process by which plants make food. Water from the soil and carbon dioxide gas from the air are combined to form sugars. This process can take place only in living plant cells that contain the green coloring matter chlorophyll. The energy comes from sunlight.

See also LEAF.

PICASSO, Pablo (1881–1973)

Picasso was a Spanish artist who greatly influenced art in this century. His painting changed from a realistic style to abstract styles such as cubism, which uses shapes that include cubes and triangles.

PIG

The pig is a very useful, intelligent animal. We eat its meat as pork, sausages, bacon, and ham. Its skin can be made into leather and its bristles go into brushes. Male pigs are called *boars,* and females *sows.* Pigs are unjustly accused of being dirty. They wallow in mud to keep themselves clean as well as cool.

PIRATE

Until about 150 years ago sea voyagers had more to fear than sudden storms. They faced the added danger of pirates. These fierce bands of sea robbers sailed the seas in fast, well-armed ships. When they saw a merchant ship, they chased and captured it. They stole its cargo and robbed the passengers.

Some pirates became rich. Most were caught and hanged. By the 1800s ships could sail most seas without fear of pirates.

P

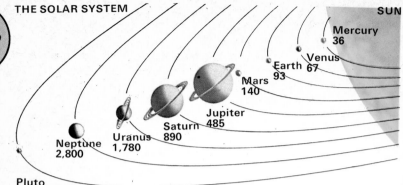

THE SOLAR SYSTEM

P

SUN

Mercury
36

Venus
67

Earth
93

Mars
140

Jupiter
485

Saturn
890

Uranus
1,780

Neptune
2,800

Pluto
3,650 million
miles from sun

PLANET

Planets are small bodies that circle around the sun. Unlike stars, planets do not produce their own light. They shine because they reflect the sun's light. There are nine known planets circling the sun: Mercury (the planet nearest the sun), Venus, Earth, Mars, Jupiter, Saturn, Uranus, Neptune, and Pluto. There may be other planets beyond Pluto which have yet to be discovered. Jupiter is the largest planet—it is over 1,000 times larger than Earth. Mercury and Pluto are the smallest planets.

The planets can be divided into two groups, *gaseous* and *rocky*. Earth is the biggest of the rocky planets, which also include Mercury, Venus, Mars, and Pluto. Pictures taken by spacecraft have shown what the first three planets are like. They have a rough surface covered with great pits, or craters, and strewn with rocks. We know little about the planet Pluto because it

is so far away from Earth.

The other planets are made up mainly of gases. The giant planet Jupiter, for example, contains mostly hydrogen. Much of it is in very cold liquid form. The other gaseous planets are probably similar. Saturn and Neptune are surrounded by rings of gas and dust.

Earth is the only planet known on which life can exist. Mercury and Venus are too hot for life to exist. And the outer planets are too cold. It is just possible that some kind of life could exist on Mars. But there are other planets in the universe, circling around other suns.

PLANKTON

This is the drifting life on the sea. It is made up of tiny and microscopic plants and animals which float at or near the surface. Every sea animal depends in some way on plankton, because small fish feed on it and are eaten in turn by larger fish.

PLANT

There are more than 335,000 kinds of plants. Most plants are green. The green color is caused by a substance called *chlorophyll*. This is used by the plant to make its food. The way it does this is called *photosynthesis*.

The plant kingdom includes several groups. The simplest plants of all are algae. Some algae are simply a single cell, which reproduces itself by splitting in two. Others, including seaweeds, are much bigger.

Fungi are plants that have no chlorophyll, so they are not green and cannot make their own food. Instead they feed on rotting or dead matter.

Mosses and liverworts are another group. They live on land. But, like fungi, they have no proper roots and no flowers. Ferns are more advanced. They have stems, leaves, and roots, but they cannot make flowers and seeds.

There are two sorts of flowering plants. *Monocotyledons,* such as lilies, bluebells, daffodils, and grasses, have long, straight leaves. *Dicotyledons,* such as peas, roses, and many trees, have broad leaves.

Seed-bearing plants produce male and female cells. The cells join to form a fertile seed which grows into a new plant.

See also ALGAE; FERN; FLOWER; GRASS; LEAF; LICHEN; MOSS; MUSHROOM AND TOADSTOOL; PHOTOSYNTHESIS; SEAWEED; SEED; TREE.

P

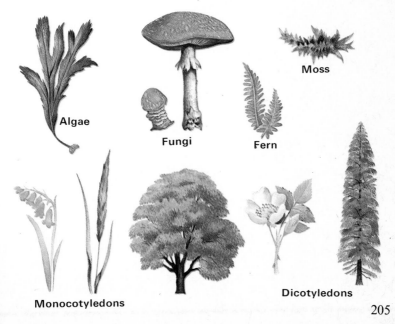

Algae

Fungi

Moss

Fern

Monocotyledons

Dicotyledons

Platypus

PLASTIC

Plastics are man-made materials that have a wide variety of uses. They can be made into furniture, car bodies, clothing, and crockery. There are many different kinds of plastics, all of which can be shaped easily. Many are shaped by blowing, squirting, or pressing into molds.

Important plastics include nylon, polyethylene, PVC, and polystyrene. All are made with chemicals obtained from oil. Some plastics are made from wood.

PLATYPUS

The curious platypus is a mammal that lays eggs. It lives in Australia. It has webbed feet, a tail like a beaver, thick fur, and a ducklike bill. The platypus lives in a burrow in a river bank and feeds under water on insects, worms, and shellfish.

PLAY

Plays were first performed in ancient Greece. Some were *tragedies*, plays that tell a serious story and often have sad endings. Others were *comedies*, plays with happy endings.

In the Middle Ages people performed *miracle* and *mystery* plays—stories from the Bible— or *morality* plays, in which the hero (main character) met a number of good and bad characters.

Some of the first indoor theaters were built in England in the

---

FAMOUS PLAYWRIGHTS

Aeschylus, Greek (c.525–456 B.C.)
Sophocles, Greek (496–406 B.C.)
Euripides, Greek (480–406 B.C.)
Aristophanes, Greek (450–c.388 B.C.)
William Shakespeare, English (1564–1616)
Ben Jonson, English (1572–1637)
Jean Baptiste Racine, French (1639–1699)
Richard Brinsley Sheridan, Irish (1751–1816)
Henrik Ibsen, Norwegian (1828–1906)
Oscar Wilde, Irish (1854–1900)
George Bernard Shaw, Irish (1856–1950)
Anton Chekhov, Russian (1860–1904)
Jean Cocteau, French (1889–1963)
Bertolt Brecht, German (1898–1956)
Samuel Beckett, Irish (born 1906)
Tennessee Williams, American (1911–1983)
Eugène Ionesco, French (born 1912)
Harold Pinter, English (born 1930)

▲ **Kabuki** is a special kind of drama created by the Japanese in the 1600s.

1500s. Companies of actors performed the plays of Shakespeare, Marlowe, and Jonson. There was little scenery, and actors wore the clothes of their own day. Boys took women's parts, as women were not allowed to act.

Since the 1700s and 1800s plays have become closer to real life. They are written in simple, everyday language, and the plots (the stories) are usually about the lives of ordinary people.

POE, Edgar Allan (1809–1849)
Edgar Allan Poe was a great American writer of poems, short stories, essays, and criticism. He is perhaps best known for his mystery and horror stories, such as *The Fall of the House of Usher*, and for melancholy poems such as "The Raven."

POETRY

The oldest stories we know were first told as poetry. In a poem the words are often arranged to a musical beat or rhythm. Poetry that is written in a meter, or rhythm, is known as verse. But the rhythm does not have to be regular all the time. This would be dull. Blank verse has a rhythm, but it does not rhyme. Shakespeare used blank verse in his plays. Modern poets often prefer free verse, which does not rhyme or have a strict rhythm.

There are different styles and forms of poetry. Story-poems with short verses and, often, with exciting stories are called *ballads*. Long story-poems are called *epics*. The greatest of the ancient epic poems, full of the deeds of brave heroes, are the *Iliad* and *Odyssey* of Homer, a Greek, and the *Aeneid* of the Roman poet Virgil.

Expressions of poets' feelings

207

are called *lyrics*. They include such forms as the song, sonnet, ode, elegy, and pastoral. Plays are sometimes written in poetry and these are called *dramatic* poems.

POISON

A poison is a substance that attacks the body and can cause sickness or death. Some poisons are dangerous when swallowed. Others damage the lungs, the skin, and the nervous system. Chemicals, drugs, gases, acids, and bad food can all be poisonous. Some medicines are also poisonous if used wrongly. So it is important always to follow the directions carefully.

POLAND

Poland is the seventh largest country in Europe. Most of its

▼ **Smoke** from factory chimneys pollutes the air.

▲ **The long, spiny quills** on a porcupine's back are a good protection against enemies.

area is low-lying farmland where crops such as potatoes, wheat, and flax are grown. In the south there are also forests and mountains.

Coal mining is important in Poland and there are also many factories and industries in the big cities such as Warsaw, Gdansk, Poznan, Krakow, and Wroclaw.

See also page 78.

POLLUTION

Pollution is the contamination of soil, water, or the atmosphere by harmful substances. Chemicals used to kill insects and weeds can build up and damage the soil. Sewage, waste from factories, and oil from tankers pollute rivers and oceans. Smoke from chimneys and fumes from cars pollute the air.

Pollution can threaten our health and even make it impossible for plants and animals to live. People are trying to find ways of preventing pollution.

POPE

The Pope is the head of the Roman Catholic Church and

bishop of Rome. St. Peter was the first bishop of Rome. The Pope lives in the Vatican, a tiny independent state in Rome. His chief advisers are the cardinals. They elect each new pope.

POPULATION
The population is the total number of people who live in a particular area. The word comes from *populus,* the Latin word for "people." Every city, state, and nation needs to know its population in order to govern itself and plan for the future. Most countries count their population every ten years by taking a *census.* The United States took its last census in 1980. A census can also tell the government where most people live and how they live. Scientists are worried about the world's rapidly expanding population. In many countries governments urge people to have no more than two children.

PORCUPINE
Porcupines are rodents. They live in forests and eat twigs, leaves, and fruit. The porcupines of Africa and Asia live on the ground, but American porcupines are good climbers.

PORTUGAL
Portugal is the most westerly country of mainland Europe. The land varies from high plateaus in the north to lowlands with gentle hills and marshy plains in the south.

Many people work in agriculture or fishing. The chief crops are wheat, corn, fruit, grapes, and olives. There are huge forests of cork oak.

See also page 78.

POST OFFICE
In early times messages were carried by runners or by riders on horseback. Fresh messengers and horses waited at "posts," usually inns, along the road. Later, post coaches were used. The cost of delivering a letter was usually very expensive.

In 1840 a cheap postal system was started in Britain by Rowland Hill. For a standard charge of one penny (which bought a postage stamp) a letter was delivered anywhere in the country.

See also STAMP.

POTATO
Potatoes are important food plants. The part you eat is a

Potato

tuber, a swollen underground stem, in which the plant stores food. New plants grow from the "eyes" in the tubers.

The potato plant grows wild in the Andes of South America. Explorers brought potatoes to Europe in the 1500s.

POTTERY

Objects made of molded clay and baked hard in an oven are called pottery. Since earliest times people have made pottery bowls, jugs, plates, and cups as useful containers and decorative items. Today most pottery is stoneware or porcelain. Porcelain is fine pottery made of white China clay. Stoneware is thicker and grittier. The shaped clay is *glazed* and *fired* in a *kiln* to make it hard and smooth.

PREHISTORIC ANIMALS

The first animals appeared in the sea more than 700 million years ago. They may have looked like tiny blobs of jelly. Later some kinds developed protective shells. One common group, trilobites, looked like woodlice. All were invertebrates.

The first vertebrate animals (animals with backbones) were the fishes, which appeared about 450 million years ago. The first fishes had armored bodies and heads.

At this time the land was still almost empty. There were plants and insectlike creatures but no vertebrates. Then, about 400

▲ **A Stone Age woman** makes coiled and molded pottery.

million years ago, some fishes crawled out of the water onto the land. They slowly developed legs instead of fins, and lungs with which they could breathe. They were the first amphibians.

Then came the reptiles. They adapted to different ways of life. Many were plant eaters, but some were hunters, preying on other reptiles. About 200 million years ago some reptiles gave rise to dinosaurs. For millions of years dinosaurs ruled the earth.

The first true birds may have evolved from dinosaurs that lived in trees and could just manage to glide from branch to branch.

The first mammals were small, insect-eating animals. For a long period of time they remained unimportant, and the dinosaurs

▶ **This chart** shows how life developed in prehistoric times. A primitive form of life probably began in Precambrian times, over 4,600 million years ago.

210

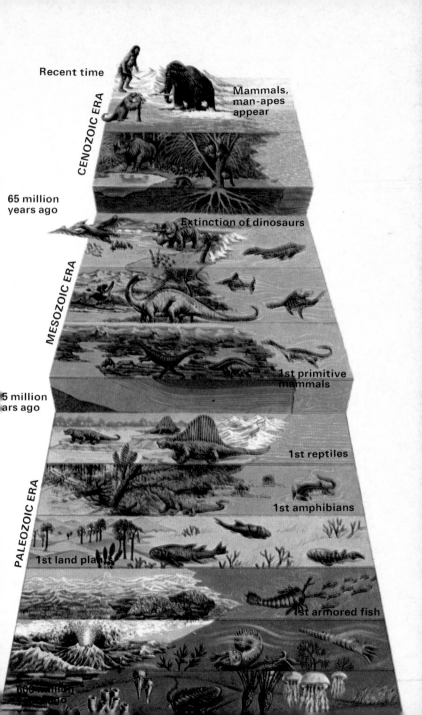

Recent time

Mammals,
man-apes
appear

CENOZOIC ERA

65 million
years ago

Extinction of dinosaurs

MESOZOIC ERA

1st primitive
mammals

5 million
ars ago

1st reptiles

1st amphibians

PALEOZOIC ERA

1st land plants

1st armored fish

600 million
ago

ruled supreme. But when the dinosaurs died out, the little mammals took over and many different kinds developed. Many became extinct during the Ice Ages, when they were killed by a new mammal—man the hunter.

See also DINOSAUR; EVOLUTION; FOSSIL; ICE AGE; MAMMOTH.

PRESIDENT

France, Italy, the United States, and many other countries all have a president. He or she is the head of state, and in the United States, the head of government as well. Other countries have a prime minister as head of government. The president is generally commander-in-chief of the army, navy, and air force.

PRIME MINISTER

A prime minister is a head of government. The prime minister usually leads the political party that has been voted the most seats in parliament. He or she chooses people called ministers to help run the government.

PRINTING

Before the 1400s, the usual way of producing books was to copy them by hand, so they were rare and expensive. About 1450, Johannes Gutenberg made copies of the Bible on a printing press.

Gutenberg's method of printing was to build up his words from separate pieces of *type*, ink the type, then press paper against

▲ **Pages of a book** on a four-color printing press.

it. Printing by inking metal type (called *letterpress*) is still widely used. Many books are now printed by a photographic process (called *lithography*). The words are made up on a piece of film, and flat printing plates are made from the film. The plates are treated so that they pick up the ink only where the words are.

Photogravure, or *gravure,* is the reverse of the letterpress method. Letterpress prints from a raised plate; gravure from a recessed plate. Color printing usually uses three color printing plates as well as black. Most colors can be made by mixing three basic colors.

212

PROTEIN

Proteins are the "building blocks" of life. They are substances in foods that build body tissue and repair cells. They contain carbon, hydrogen, oxygen, and nitrogen. Proteins also provide heat and energy. Most of our proteins come from meat, fish, and cheese. Plants such as peanuts, beans, and peas also contain quantities of protein.

PYGMY

Pygmy people seldom grow much over four feet. One group of Pygmies lives in the Congo basin in Africa. They are nomadic. They build simple shelters to keep out the rain and use poison arrows to kill game.

PYRAMID

The ancient Egyptians buried their pharaohs (kings) in tombs called pyramids. These had four triangular sides meeting in a point at the top. Some are made of more than two million blocks of stone. Thousands of people dragged the huge stones slowly into place. Inside was a tomb where the *mummy* (preserved body) of the pharaoh was laid, surrounded by treasure. The best-known pyramids are a group of three built at Giza about 2680–2565 B.C.

PYTHAGORAS (500s B.C.)

Pythagoras was an ancient Greek astronomer, mathematician, and philosopher. He was one of the first to teach that the earth and the other planets revolved around the sun. Perhaps his best-known contribution to geometry is the Pythagorean Theorem, which states that the square of the hypotenuse of a right triangle (in which one of the angles is 90°) is equal to the squares of the other two sides.

▼ **Thousands** of people slaved to build the pyramids in ancient Egypt.

RABBIT AND HARE

Rabbits are burrowing animals. They live in colonies called warrens. Rabbits breed rapidly. There were none in Australia until the 1850s. Then a few English rabbits were set free. Soon there were rabbits everywhere.

Hares look like rabbits. But they are bigger, with longer ears and legs. Hares are swift runners. Unlike rabbits, they live alone and do not dig burrows. Instead, they live in hollows called *forms*.

▼ **Rabbits** in their burrow.

RACCOON

The raccoon has long gray-brown fur, a short, pointed nose, and a bushy tail tinged with black. Raccoons live in the Americas.

RADAR

Radar stands for *radio direction and ranging*. It is a device that can "see" distant objects by bouncing radio waves off them. The waves travel like echoes back to the radar. They are picked up by the radar antennae, and show up as small dots of light on a screen similar to a television screen. From the position of the dot, the position of the object can be worked out. Ships and planes rely on radar for safety.

RADIO

Radio depends on radio waves. These invisible waves travel as fast as light waves. Radio works because radio waves can carry signals that represent sound.

In a radio broadcasting studio sounds go into a microphone, where they are changed to electrical signals. These signals are combined with a "carrier" wave and transmitted by an aerial.

The aerial of a radio receiver picks up the carrier wave. Circuits in the receiver remove the carrier wave and leave only the electrical signals carrying the sound. These are fed to a loudspeaker, which gives out the same sounds as went into the studio microphone.

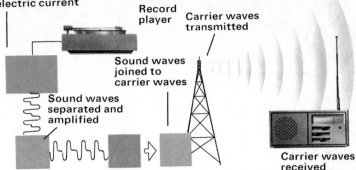

Sound waves turned into electric current

Record player

Carrier waves transmitted

Sound waves joined to carrier waves

Sound waves separated and amplified

Carrier waves received

RADIOACTIVITY

The atoms of most chemical elements do not change. But the atoms of some elements are unstable and emit (give out) atomic particles, or radiation. We call this process radioactivity. Uranium and radium are radioactive elements.

See also ATOM; NUCLEAR ENERGY.

RAILROAD

The first public railroad to use steam locomotives was the Stockton and Darlington line in the north of England. It was opened in 1825. George Stephenson, a self-taught engineer, built the ten-mile track and its first engine, called *Locomotion*. A few years later Stephenson built his most famous locomotive, *The*

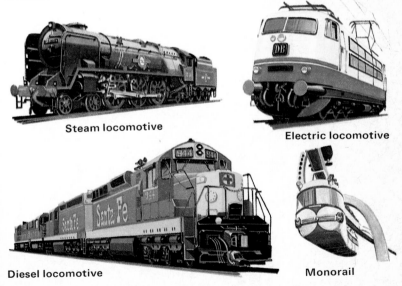

Steam locomotive

Electric locomotive

Diesel locomotive

Monorail

Rocket. It was not long before track was laid so that people and goods could travel right across North America, Europe, and Asia by rail.

Steam locomotives, belching smoke, hauled passenger and freight trains for over a hundred years. But there are few left today. They have been replaced by diesel and electric locomotives, which are cleaner, quieter, and cheaper to run.

Until the beginning of this century the railroads had no rivals. Then the automobile and the airplane were invented. Railroads were used less and less and some lines closed. Now, new trains are in use that travel twice as fast as a car. And hovertrains, which glide on a cushion of air, have been invented.

RAIN
The rain comes from the water in seas, lakes, rivers, and soil. The sun's heat turns some of this water into water vapor which rises in the air. As the rising air cools, some of the water vapor "condenses" or turns back to water droplets, and becomes visible as clouds. As the air rises higher, more and more vapor turns back to water and the clouds grow bigger and darker. Finally, water droplets from the clouds fall to the ground as rain.

See also CLOUD.

RAT AND MOUSE
Rats and mice are rodents. They may eat and spoil our food, and also spread disease. Rats are bigger than mice. There are two main kinds: black and brown.

THE RAIN CYCLE

The water vapor cools and makes clouds.

Clouds release water as rain.

Some rain water flows back into the sea.

The sun heats the water. Water evaporates and rises.

Mice, like rats, breed quickly. The house mouse is a common pest. The wood mouse, the harvest mouse, and the field mouse live in the country.

See also RODENT.

RECORDING
Modern records are discs of plastic that "store" sound in their grooves. Another way of recording sound is on tape. Here, the sound is recorded in the form of a magnetic pattern. Television programs can now be recorded on disc and tape. Movie sound tracks are often recorded as an image on the film.

See also VIDEOTAPE.

RED CROSS
The Red Cross organization helps the victims of wars and disasters. In 1859 the armies of France and Austria fought a terrible battle in Italy. A Swiss traveler, Jean Henri Dunant, saw thousands of wounded soldiers, who had been abandoned. He tried to help them, and wrote a book describing what he had seen. As a result, the Red Cross was formed in Geneva, Switzerland (a country which never takes part in war). Its flag is a red cross on a white background.

REFORMATION
This movement in the 1500s ended the religious unity of western Europe and led to the establishment of the Protestant Churches.

Until 1500 all Christians were Roman Catholics. Martin Luther, a German monk, disagreed with many Church teachings and protested in 1517. Many people agreed with him and a split developed. But not all Protestants believed the same things, and so the movement itself split into the many types of Protestantism today.

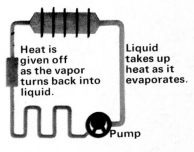

Heat is given off as the vapor turns back into liquid.

Liquid takes up heat as it evaporates.

Pump

▲ **Refrigerators** work on the principle that liquids absorb heat when they vaporize.

REFRIGERATION
Foods last longer when they are kept cool in a refrigerator. Cooling slows down the processes that make food go bad. Freezers, therefore, keep foods fresh even longer.

Refrigerators are worked by electricity or gas. They have a pump that turns a vapor into liquid. The liquid is turned into vapor again inside the freezing compartment. As it does so it takes up heat from the food. In another part of the refrigerator the vapor is changed back into a liquid and recirculated.

RELIGION

A religion is a belief, a way of living, or both. It may mean belief in a god or gods with powers greater than our own, and in another life after this one. It may involve prayer and worship.

All the world's great religions began in Asia. The oldest religion to teach that there is only one god is *Judaism*, the religion of the Jews. Its history is told in the Hebrew Bible, which Christians include in their Bible as the Old Testament.

The followers of *Islam* are called Muslims. Muslims believe in Allah, the one god, and obey the teachings of the Koran, their holy book.

Hinduism is the chief religion of India. Hindus believe people's souls are reborn many times until they are good enough to join Brahma, a supreme power in the Hindu religion.

Buddhism is another important Eastern religion. Its founder, Buddha (the Enlightened One), taught people how to escape from suffering and find peace.

People who follow the teachings of Jesus Christ are *Christians*.

Other important world religions are Confucianism, Taoism, Zoroastrianism, Shintoism, and Sikhism.

See also BIBLE; BUDDHA; CHRISTIANITY; HINDU; ISLAM; JESUS CHRIST; JUDAISM; KORAN; MAGIC; MUHAMMAD.

▲ **Rembrandt** was an old man when he painted this self-portrait around 1660.

REMBRANDT VAN RIJN
(1606–1669)

Rembrandt was a Dutch artist and one of the most famous painters in the world. He was a master of the use of light, color, and mood. His most famous paintings are portraits.

RENAISSANCE

In the 1300s there began a rebirth of learning in Europe. Scholars rediscovered and studied the ancient writings of Greece and Rome. Artists such as Leonardo da Vinci and Michelangelo recaptured the beauty of "classical" Greek architecture and sculpture. Scientists such as Copernicus and Galileo questioned the old ideas about the universe. Explorers brought back new knowledge from their voyages. "Humanist" thinkers taught that people were not just weak creatures ruled by God.

REPRODUCTION

All animals and plants can reproduce. Simple animals and plants can reproduce on their own. They either divide in two (like the ameba) or make special cells that grow into new plants (like the fungi).

More advanced forms of life reproduce sexually by producing special sex cells. When a male cell joins with and fertilizes a female cell, this grows into a new individual. In flowering plants a

REPTILE

Reptiles are cold-blooded animals—their body temperature is the same as the temperature of their surroundings. Because of this, reptiles cannot live in very cold lands. In places where there are cold winters, they hibernate for protection.

Reptiles have tough, scaly skin, and most lay leathery-shelled eggs. Baby reptiles hatch fully developed and most are not cared for by their parents.

▲ **The chameleon** is a reptile. It can change its color to match its background.

male sex cell stored in a pollen grain joins a female sex cell in the carpel. In animals, the male cells are called sperms, and the female cells, eggs.

See also ANIMAL; CELL; FLOWER; GENETICS; HUMAN BODY.

There are four main groups of reptiles: alligators and crocodiles, snakes and lizards, tortoises and turtles, and the very rare tuatara. Most eat insects and small animals, but some eat plants.

See also CROCODILE AND ALLIGATOR; DINOSAUR; LIZARD; SNAKE; TORTOISE AND TURTLE.

RESPIRATION

Respiration is the process in living creatures in which food is converted into energy, using oxygen. Plants and simple animals absorb oxygen directly from the air or water. Higher animals have respiratory organs, such as the gills of a fish and the lungs of human beings. We inhale oxygen into our lungs, where it passes into the bloodstream to be carried to the cells. There *oxidation* takes place, producing energy, carbon dioxide, and water.

REVOLUTION

The word *revolution* means "turn around" or "complete change." If a country has a revolution, its government and laws are overthrown, often by war.

The most famous revolutions in history happened in America, France, and Russia. In 1776 the American colonies broke away from Britain and became an independent republic. The French Revolution of 1789 caused the overthrow of the king and the nobles who ruled France. In 1917 the rule of the Russian czar was ended, and the Soviet Union became the world's first Communist state.

Another kind of revolution is economic. It changes the way people live.

RHINOCEROS

The rhinoceros is the second largest land animal, after the

▲ **Bolshevik revolutionaries** stand their ground in St. Petersburg (now Leningrad) during the Russian Revolution.

elephant. The black rhinoceros and the white rhinoceros live on the African plains. Actually, both are gray. The rhinoceroses of India, Java, and Sumatra live in dense forests. Rhinoceroses eat grass, shoots, and twigs.

RHODE ISLAND

Rhode Island is one of the New England states and the smallest of all the states. It is not an island, though it includes many islands in Narragansett Bay. Once a producer of textiles, Rhode Island today manufactures silverware and jewelry. Offshore is Block Island, a resort island and an important navigation point.

See also page 263.

RICE

Rice is a member of the grass family. Its grains are one of the most important cereals grown. It is a staple food for many people in Asia, though it is grown and eaten in many other parts of the world. Rice is planted in flooded fields called paddies. The young shoots are grown in three to four inches of water. Rice has long, narrow leaves and clusters of flowers that turn into the rice grains.

RIVER

Rivers begin their lives as small streams in hills or mountains. Some begin as trickles of water from melting glaciers. Others bubble up through the ground as springs.

Gravity makes water flow downhill. At first the river rushes along, fed by rain and melting snow. It is narrow but fast-flow-

▲ **Two black rhinos** in Tanzania.

▼ **Rice seedlings** are planted in flooded paddyfields to mature.

221

ing, forming rapids and waterfalls, and carrying along with it stones which help to deepen and widen its course.

When it reaches flatter country, the river flows more slowly. Other streams, called tributaries, may join it. The river valley gradually becomes wider and flatter and it meanders, or loops from side to side. Finally, the river flows into the sea, sometimes through a fan-shaped network of channels known as a delta. The fresh water of many a river meets the salt water of the sea in a river mouth, or estuary.

See also WATER.

ROAD

Roads are made up of layers. Tarmac roads have layers of tar and stones on top of well-pounded soil. Concrete roads are made up of layers of concrete.

John McAdam was a pioneer roadmaker in the 1800s. Italians built the first modern highway in the 1920s. Two thousand years before, their ancestors, the Romans, were building fine roads throughout Europe, North Africa, and the Middle East.

ROBOT

The word *robot* comes from a Czech play about mechanical people. The Czech word *robota* means "work" or "worker." In films and books set in the future, robots often look like metal people and they can walk, talk, and think.

Real robots are very different. They are machines with arms that can move in several directions. Robots are *programmable* machines. This means they can be instructed to carry out different tasks. The instructions, or programs, are stored in the robot's computer brain.

Most robots work in industry and do jobs such as paint spray-

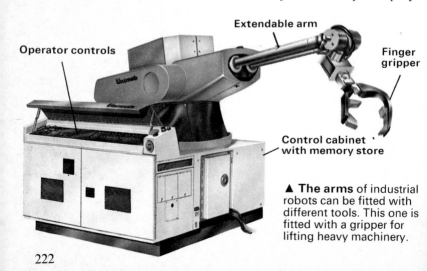

Extendable arm

Operator controls

Finger gripper

Control cabinet with memory store

▲ **The arms** of industrial robots can be fitted with different tools. This one is fitted with a gripper for lifting heavy machinery.

222

ing, welding, and heavy lifting and loading. Some robots work in places that are dangerous for humans, such as nuclear power stations and outer space.

See also COMPUTER.

ROCK

The inside of the earth is a hot, molten mass. But the outer skin, or crust, is made up of solid rock. All rocks belong to three great groups: the *igneous*, the *sedimentary*, and the *metamorphic*. All igneous rocks were once molten (melted) and came from deep in the earth. Sedimentary rocks are formed of layers of materials such as sand and clay which have been cemented together under pressure. Metamorphic rocks are changed from one form to another by heat and pressure.

ROCKET

A rocket is a kind of engine. It works by shooting out a stream of gases backward. As the gases go backward the rocket goes forward. The rocket works like a jet engine. Both burn fuel to make hot gases, which shoot out in a stream. But the rocket carries its own oxygen to burn the fuel. The jet engine gets its oxygen from the air.

See also JET ENGINE.

RODENT

Rodents are mammals that have chisel-like front teeth which are specially adapted for gnawing. There are more than 6,000

▲ **The powerful Saturn rocket** at takeoff.

species of rodent—more than any other kind of mammal. Beavers, squirrels, gophers, hamsters, gerbils, and porcupines are all rodents. They are found everywhere. The smallest rodent is the mouse. The largest is the capybara, which is the shape and size of a pig.

Rodents have many enemies. They are preyed on by hawks, owls, snakes, foxes, and other animals.

See also BEAVER; GUINEA PIG; PORCUPINE; RAT AND MOUSE.

ROME, ANCIENT

According to legend, Rome was founded by twin brothers called Romulus and Remus, who were raised by a she-wolf. At first the Romans were ruled by foreign kings. But in 509 B.C. the people set up a republic in which they elected their own rulers. They fought against their neighbors and built a powerful army. In 217 B.C. the first emperor took power.

Without their army, the Romans would never have conquered and ruled their empire, which eventually stretched from Britain to the Middle East.

The Roman Empire was divided into provinces, ruled by governors. The capital of the Empire was the city of Rome, built on seven hills. To the Romans, Rome was the center of the world. At the height of its power, Rome was a city of great splendor.

In A.D. 295 the Empire was divided into two. One half was ruled from Rome, the other from Byzantium (Constantinople). Rome was no longer strong. Its government was dishonest, and the army could no longer fight off the barbarian raids. Around A.D. 476 the western empire fell, and Rome was destroyed. In the east, the Byzantine Empire lasted until 1453, when Constantinople was captured by the Turks.

See also BYZANTINE EMPIRE; CAESAR; HANNIBAL.

▼ **In Rome,** the wealthy lived in spacious ground-floor apartments in blocks called *insulae.* Above them poor families lived in overcrowded conditions.

RUBBER

Rubber trees grow in tropical countries such as Malaysia and Indonesia. To make rubber, cuts are made in the bark of the tree and a milky sap (latex) oozes out. This is treated with acid to produce crude rubber. Other things are mixed with it, and then it is molded to make soles of shoes, tires, tubes, and many other things. Much of the rubber used now, however, is made by the plastics industry.

RUTHERFORD, Ernest

(1871–1937)

Rutherford was a New Zealand-born British physicist. He was a pioneer of atomic science and his main research was in the field of radioactivity. Rutherford was the first to "split" the atom. He received the Nobel chemistry prize in 1914.

▼ **This Malaysian woman** is tapping latex from a rubber tree.

S

SAINT

A saint is a holy person whom Christians believe came close to being perfect. Some saints, such as St. Francis of Assisi, are remembered for their good lives. Others, such as St. Bernadette of Lourdes, are believed to perform miracles of healing.

To become a saint, a person must be *canonized* with the approval of the Roman Catholic Church. A commission is set up by the Church to examine carefully everything known about the person's life.

SALAMANDER

Like frogs, salamanders are amphibians. They live part of their lives in water and part on land. Most hatch from eggs in water, and the young look like tadpoles. Many adult salamanders, including *newts,* look like lizards, but with moist, slippery skin. The Mexican *axolotl* spends all its life in the water.

SALT

Salts make up a class of chemicals. There are many different salts, but the one we know best is the salt we eat—table salt.

▲ Salt is often produced by flooding land with sea water. As the sun dries the water, the salt is left behind.

It is made up of the two elements sodium and chlorine. Our bodies need salt. There is salt in blood, in sweat, and in tears.

SATELLITE

A satellite is a small body that circles around a larger one. The moon is the earth's satellite. It circles the earth once a month. Most planets have satellites. We often just call them moons.

The earth now has many man-made satellites circling around it. The first artificial satellite, called *Sputnik I,* was launched by the Russians in 1957. To resist the earth's gravity a satellite must travel at over 17,000 miles an hour. Satellites can be very useful. Some help in weather forecasting. Others relay telephone calls and television pictures all over the world.

SAUDI ARABIA

Saudi Arabia is a country that covers most of the Arabian peninsula between the Red Sea and the Persian Gulf. It is mostly hot, dry desert, and is today a rich source of oil. Most Saudis follow the religion of Islam, and they are ruled by a king. The oil boom has brought railroads, highways, and modern schools, hospitals, and homes to the country.

See also page 79.

SCANDINAVIA

This is a region in northern Europe. It includes the countries of Norway, Sweden, Denmark, Iceland, and Finland. History and trade have brought them close together.

The Scandinavian Peninsula is a long strip of land, surrounded by cold seas. There are high mountains, and on the west coast are long, narrow inlets called *fiords.* The northern part of Scandinavia is inside the Arctic

Circle. The people who live there are the Lapps. The forests of Scandinavia produce timber. Farming and fishing are important occupations.

See also VIKING and page 78.

SCIENCE
The word *science* just means knowledge. In science, people try to find out about the world around them by observing things and carrying out experiments. Scientists try to classify new facts and fit them in with what they already know.

Chemistry, physics, and biology are the main branches of science. Chemistry studies the way matter is made up; physics studies the properties of matter and energy; and biology studies living things.

See also CHEMISTRY; ZOOLOGY.

SCOTT, Robert (1868–1912)
Robert Falcon Scott was a British naval commander and explorer. In 1911 he led an expedition to the South Pole, but reached it on January 18, 1912, to find that the Norwegian Roald Amundsen had gotten there first. Scott and the other members of his expedition died on the return journey.

▼ **The Orbiting** Astronomical Observatory (0A0) Satellite gives scientists a clearer view of the stars. Its solar panels change the sun's rays into electricity.

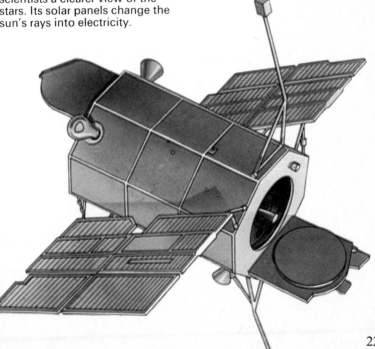

SCOUT

The scout movement for boys was started in 1908 by a British soldier, Robert Baden-Powell. Girl Scouts (called Guides in some countries) began in 1910. Scouts try to help other people and each other. There are more than 17 million scouts in the world.

SCULPTURE

Making models and figures, or statues, is a form of art called sculpture. Sculpture is done in two ways: *carving* and *molding*. In carving, the sculptor cuts into a block of wood or stone with sharp tools. In molding, he or she makes a model in soft clay, then bakes the clay to harden it. From the hard model he makes a mold, and pours into it wet concrete or hot, liquid metal (such as bronze). When this hardens, a "casting" of the model is left.

Today sculptors also use materials such as pieces of glass, metal, and cloth, as well as wood and stone.

SEA HORSE

The sea horse is actually a small sea fish. It gets its name from its horselike head. The sea horse swims in a curious upright position, fanning its dorsal (back) fin. It can cling to seaweed, using its coiled tail.

SEAL AND SEA LION

These mammals spend most of their time in the sea. Their legs

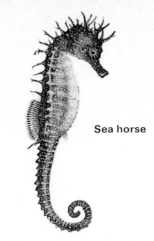

Sea horse

have become flippers, and they are expert swimmers, but they have to come to the surface to breathe. Seals and sea lions catch fish underwater. Seals swim by moving their bodies from side to side. Sea lions use their front flippers like oars.

▼ **A bronze figure** of a cock by the painter and sculptor Pablo Picasso.

228

These animals come ashore to breed. They gather in large colonies on rocky coasts. Seals are slow and clumsy on land. But sea lions can turn their back flippers forward and move quite quickly despite their bulk.

SEASON

The different times of the year are called seasons. They are caused by the way the earth orbits, or travels around, the sun. When the North Pole leans toward the sun, northern lands have their summer and southern lands their winter. At the opposite point of the orbit, when the North Pole leans away from the sun, northern lands have their winter and southern lands their summer. Spring and fall are the points in the orbit when the equator, at the middle of the earth, faces the sun, so northern and southern lands have roughly the same amount of warmth.

SEAWEED

Seaweeds are simple plants of the algae group. They do not have flowers or true roots. Green seaweed grows in shallow water. Brown seaweed grows at greater depth, and red seaweed lives in the deepest water. Seaweeds need sunlight, so none grows deeper than about 250 feet.

Some seaweeds can be eaten. Other kinds are used to make good fertilizers.

SEED

Most plants reproduce themselves by means of seeds. They are formed in the plant's ovary. A seed contains an *embryo*—the plant in its earliest form. Seeds lie dormant or asleep until conditions are right for them to *germinate*. To germinate they need moisture, warmth, air, and darkness. Part of the seed nourishes the young plant while the roots and leaves form.

S

THE SEASONS

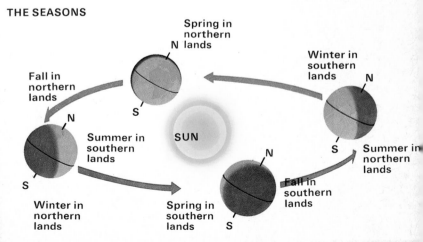

Spring in northern lands

Fall in northern lands

Winter in southern lands

Summer in southern lands

SUN

Summer in northern lands

Winter in northern lands

Spring in southern lands

Fall in southern lands

SEVEN WONDERS OF THE WORLD

1 *The Pyramids of Egypt.* 2 *The Pharos Lighthouse at Alexandria.* 3 *The Colossus of Rhodes.* 4 *The Statue of Zeus at Olympia.* 5 *The Hanging Gardens of Babylon.* 6 *The Temple of Artemis.* 7 *The Mausoleum at Halicarnassus.*

SENSES

Senses tell us what is happening around us and inside us. We have external senses of hearing, taste, touch, sight, and smell. Each sense comes from nerve endings or sense organs that send signals to our brain along the nervous system. For example, nerve endings on our tongue, called taste buds, tell us whether food is salty, sour, sweet, or bitter. Internal senses tell us when we are hungry, tired, or thirsty. And our muscle sense tells us the position of different parts of our body.

SEVEN WONDERS OF THE WORLD

Travelers in ancient times marveled at the Seven Wonders of the World. Of these wonders only the Pyramids can still be seen. The others (illustrated left) have been destroyed.

SHAKESPEARE, William
(1564–1616)

Shakespeare is often called the world's greatest writer. He was born in Stratford on Avon, England. His plays are written in some of the most beautiful poetry in the English language. Some, such as *Richard II* and *Richard III*, are about history. Others, such as *A Midsummer Night's Dream,* are comedies. *Hamlet, Macbeth, Othello,* and *King Lear* are great tragedies. Shakespeare also wrote a series of beautiful short poems, called sonnets.

SHARK

Sharks are the most feared hunters of the sea. Drawn by the smell of blood, they will kill fish, seals, porpoises, and even whales. Some sharks are man-eaters, but most kinds are harmless.

Sharks are strong, fast-swimming fish. Their gaping jaws are full of sharp teeth. Instead of bones, sharks have gristly skeletons.

▼ **Sharks** have skin that is rough, like sandpaper.

SHEEP

Sheep are important farm animals. We make their wool into cloth, eat their meat, and wear their skins. Sheep are easy to keep. They can feed on rough pasture, and their thick coats keep out bad weather. Wild sheep live in the mountains in parts of America, Europe, and Asia.

SHIP

For at least 4,000 years ships have been sailing across seas. They still transport most of the world's cargo between the con-

Kayak

Motor cruiser

Tug

Sailboat

Chinese junk

S

232

tinents, but few carry passengers.

Until about a hundred years ago most ships were propelled by sails. For many years, ships had only one square sail on a single mast. They could only sail well with the wind, and relied on oars to propel them at other times. The Viking longships were an example of this.

By the 1400s ships were being built with several masts, one of which carried a triangular sail. This made sailing easier in all winds. Soon came the three-masted caravels and galleons. Last of the sailing ships were the graceful and speedy clippers, which carried wool or tea from Australia and the Far East.

See also SUBMARINE.

SILICON CHIP

Silicon is the most common element after oxygen in the earth's crust. Silicon chips are tiny pieces of silicon—as small as one square millimeter—made to carry minute electrical circuits which are used in digital watches, electronic calculators and computers, and transistor radios.

See also COMPUTER.

SILK

The beautiful, smooth cloth called silk is made from threads spun by the silkworm. This is actually the caterpillar of a moth. When the caterpillar is fully grown, it wraps itself in a cocoon of fine silk, stuck together with gum. The ancient Chinese were the first to discover how to wash away the gum and unwind the silk onto reels. It was then dyed and woven into cloth.

S

SILVER

Silver is a beautiful, shiny metal which is used to make jewelry and expensive tableware. It can be shaped easily by bending and hammering.

Silver is interesting to the scientist because it conducts (passes on) heat and electricity better than any other substance. It also forms compounds that are sensitive to light. They are used in photography.

SITTING BULL (c.1834–1890)
Sitting Bull was a Sioux chief best known for leading his men in the Battle of the Little Big Horn, the last Indian victory over the whites. He retreated to Canada, but later returned to a reser-

▲ **A silicon chip** mounted in a plastic carrier is shown next to an apple.

vation in South Dakota. He was killed resisting arrest.

See also page 144.

SKELETON
All the bones of your body make up your skeleton. The skeleton supports the soft parts of the body and is an anchor for the muscles. In *vertebrates* (animals with backbones), the skeleton is inside the body. Many *invertebrates* (animals without backbones) have an *exoskeleton*, which is like a hard crust on the outside of the body. Insects and spiders have exoskeletons. There are more than 200 bones in the human skeleton.

SKIING
Skiing has been the main way of getting around on deep snow for thousands of years. Skis from about 3000 B.C. have been found in Sweden. It is only during the last hundred years that skiing has been enjoyed as a sport. Ski racing and ski jumping were developed in Scandinavia about 1860. Downhill and slalom races are also now included in international competitions.

SKIN
Skin is more than just the covering of the body. It helps prevent us from getting too hot or too cold. It helps keep out harmful germs. And it helps the body get rid of waste.

The skin is in two layers. The outer layer is the *epidermis*. It

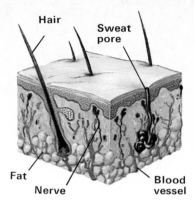

grows all the time. The new cells replace dead skin cells, which are rubbed off.

Underneath the epidermis is a thicker layer called the *dermis*. It contains nerves and blood vessels. Hair grows out of it. The sweat glands are here too.

SKUNK
Skunks live in North America. They are relatives of badgers and weasels, and are animals of the woodlands. They eat insects, birds' eggs, and small mammals. If attacked, the skunk turns its back, raises its bushy tail, and squirts out a foul-smelling spray of liquid from a special gland.

SLAVERY
Slavery means owning people. Slaves were once bought and sold as workers. They were often forced to do hard, cruel work and many died because their owners treated them badly. In ancient Egypt, Greece, and Rome there were a great many slaves.

When Europeans settled in the

New World, they took black people from Africa to work on the plantations. This slave trade was not stopped until the 1800s. All the slaves in the United States were freed in 1865 after the Civil War.

SLEEP AND DREAMS
We spend about a third of our lives asleep. Our minds and bodies do not stop working while we sleep, but they do slow down. Without sleep, we feel tired and cranky, and cannot concentrate.

Part of the brain is active during sleep. Though our eyelids are closed, our eyes move rapidly. When this happens, scientists know we are dreaming.

SLOTH
In the South American forest lives the slow-moving sloth. This strange mammal spends its life hanging upside down in trees. It eats leaves and fruit. The sloth's hooked claws are good for climbing, but useless for walking on the ground. The hair of the sloth hangs downward, so rainwater runs off easily. Sometimes algae grow on the hair, helping to hide the sloth from enemies such as the jaguar.

SLUG AND SNAIL
Slugs and snails are mollusks, but slugs have little or no shell. They both like dark, cool places and die if they get too dry or hot. Slugs and snails are garden pests, eating young and low-lying

▲ **Sloths** sleep most of the day.

plants. Some varieties eat worms and other mullusks.

See also MOLLUSK.

SMELL
Smell, like sight and hearing, is one of the five senses. Mammals, including humans, smell through the nose, which has special cells that pick up scents. These cells send messages to the brain, which interprets the scents. The sense of smell also helps us to taste things. The flavor of food is a mixture of taste and smell.

SNAKE
Snakes are legless reptiles. Unlike lizards, snakes have no eye-

Grass snake swallowing a frog

235

lids. Most snakes lay eggs, but some give birth to live young.

All snakes prey on other animals, such as insects, birds, frogs, and small mammals. Poisonous snakes kill their prey by biting it with their fangs and injecting venom, or poison, into its body. Many snakes have no poison but grab their prey with their sharp teeth. Some large snakes, such as the python, coil their bodies around their prey and crush it until it suffocates.

There are some 2,500 different kinds of snakes, of which only about 150 are dangerous to humans.

See also REPTILE.

Indian cobra

▼ **Children** playing in the snow.

SNOW

Inside a cloud are millions of tiny water droplets. At the top, where the air is coldest, the water freezes to ice. Sometimes the drops of ice melt as they pass into warmer air and they fall as rain. But if the air is cold enough, they fall as snowflakes.

Snowflakes are tiny crystals. Each one has a beautiful pattern and always has six sides. A large snowflake is made of thousands of crystals stuck together.

SOAP

Soap is a substance that helps wash away dirt and grease. The tiny soap particles are able to stick to and surround specks of dirt and float them away in the water. Soap is made by boiling animal or vegetable fat with a chemical called an alkali.

Chemical cleaners called *detergents* are often used today instead of soap.

SOCCER

Soccer is the only kind of football in which handling the ball is not allowed. It is played in many countries of the world and is becoming increasingly popular in the United States. Like football and the British game of rugby, soccer developed from a much rougher ball game played in England as long ago as the Middle Ages.

SOCIALISM

Socialism is a system of economics in which the central government operates state-owned industries and important natural resources. Such industries may include railroads and power, water, and gas companies. Unlike communists, socialists believe in a democratically elected government. Socialist ideals go back to the ancient Greek philosopher Plato; more recent theorists include the British reformer Robert Owen and Karl Marx, though Marx's ideas grew to become more in line with communism. Today socialist ideas are applied in many countries of the world to a lesser or greater degree.

SOCRATES (*c*.469–399 B.C.)

Socrates was an ancient Greek thinker and teacher. He developed the Socratic method, by which he used questions to help his students discover the answers they were seeking. One of his most famous pupils was Plato.

▲ **A dramatic leap** during a final World Cup soccer match between Italy and Germany. Italy won the cup.

SOIL

A handful of garden soil does not look very interesting. But it is alive with millions of tiny plants and animals that help to keep soil fertile.

Soil is made from crumbled rocks. The process of wearing down rocks into small pieces takes millions of years. When plants and animals die, their remains are broken down by bacteria into *humus*. Humus holds moisture in the soil and binds the soil together. Fertile soil holds a lot of water and air.

SOLAR SYSTEM

The solar system is made up of the sun and all the heavenly bodies in orbit around it. The sun's great mass exerts a gravitational pull that keeps the planets, their satellites, comets, and meteoroids moving around it.

The planets closest to the sun—Mercury, Venus, Earth, and Mars—are called the *terrestrial* planets, because they are like Earth. They are all roughly the same size and density. The next four—Jupiter, Saturn, Uranus, and Neptune—are the so-called *giant* planets. They are larger but less dense than the terrestrial planets. Pluto, the ninth planet, is so far away and so small that not much is known about it.

Several planets have satellites—the moon is Earth's only satellite. Jupiter and Saturn have satellites, some as large as the planet Mercury. About 2,000 asteroids have already been recorded, and more are being discovered all the time. The solar system does not, however, end with the planets. It continues as vast, empty space to the limits of the sun's gravitational pull, an area a thousand times as large as the area orbited by the planets.

SOUND

Sound is produced by objects that are vibrating back and forth. If you touch the strings of a violin, you can feel them vibrating. A vibrating string gently nudges the molecules of the air as it goes back and forth. These air molecules nudge other air molecules and a wave spreads from

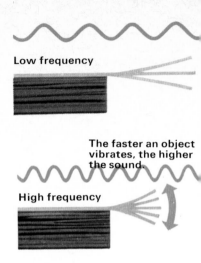

Low frequency

The faster an object vibrates, the higher the sound.

High frequency

the string through the air, just as ripples spread on a pond.

When the sound wave strikes our ears, it causes our eardrums to vibrate and nerves send signals to the brain. This is how we hear. If there were no air, nothing would carry the sound. That is why there is no sound in space.

Sounds are described in various ways. They can be loud or soft, high or low. High sounds, or, rather, high-pitched sounds, are made by things that vibrate rapidly. Low-pitched sounds are made by slow vibrations.

Some things produce ultrasonic sound waves pitched too high for us to hear.

SOUTH AFRICA

The Republic of South Africa lies at the southern end of Africa. It is a warm, sunny land and many wild animals roam in its huge national parks. But there are also

238

large cities, such as Johannesburg, Cape Town, and Durban. South Africa is a rich country. Farming and mining (for gold, diamonds, and uranium) are the chief activities.

Although most South Africans are black, colored (of mixed race), or Asian, the whites control the government. The whites live separately too, part of a policy called *apartheid*, or "separate development."

See also page 78.

SOUTH AMERICA

There are 13 countries in South America. At 6,883,000 square miles, it is the fourth largest continent in the world. It has dense rain forests, barren deserts, wide grasslands, and high mountains.

▲ **Gold is poured into ingots** in South Africa, the world's leader in the production of gold.

▼ **The modern buildings** of Brasilia, Brazil's capital (left) are in sharp contrast to the 17th-century cathedral in Quito, capital of Ecuador.

239

Panama Canal

SOUTH AMERICA

VENEZUELA

Atlantic Ocean

Amazon

PERU

Pacific Ocean

BRAZIL

Gran Chaco

Pampas

ARGENTINA

▲ **Between** the tropical north and cold south, South America has a variety of climates and soils and can produce many kinds of crops. Coffee, cocoa, sugar, and bananas are grown, and fruit, wheat, tobacco, and cotton are also important. The trees of the forest give valuable wood such as mahogany.

Cape Horn

The Andes Mountains, the highest in all South America, stretch for over 4,350 miles down the western side, overlooking the Pacific Ocean. In the center of the continent are vast plains.

They include the forests of the Amazon basin, which cover an area the size of Western Europe, the endless swamps and lakes of the Gran Chaco, and the grassy pampas of Argentina.

South America is rich in minerals, such as copper, tin, iron, bauxite, diamonds, and emeralds. Mining is an important industry everywhere, and there are also large oil fields, particularly off the coast of Venezuela.

Today South America is a rapidly changing continent. Its governments are sometimes democratic, but more often are controlled by military leaders.

See also ARGENTINA; BRAZIL; INCA; and page 79.

▲ The carved heads of Washington, Jefferson, Theodore Roosevelt, and Lincoln at Mt. Rushmore in South Dakota.

niture are also produced. Farms grow tobacco, soybeans, cotton, and peaches.

See also page 263.

SOUTH DAKOTA
South Dakota lies in the center of North America. Its landscape varies from the Black Hills in the southwest to the Badlands, a region of canyons and towering rock formations. Farming and tourism are the state's leading industries. Cattle and corn are raised, as well as wheat. The largest gold-producing mine in the nation is at Lead. Lignite (soft brown coal) is also mined.

See also page 263.

SOUTHEAST ASIA
Southeast Asia is the name given to the group of countries of the Far East south of China. It includes such countries as Vietnam, Laos, Cambodia, Indonesia, and Malaysia. The region has a climate controlled by *mon-*

SOUTH CAROLINA
South Carolina is a southeastern state bordering the Atlantic. The port of Charleston, which once exported rice and indigo, was one of the first American cities to have the cultural refinements of European cities. Textile manufacturing is today the state's leading industry; chemicals, electrical equipment, paper, and fur-

▲ **Rice paddies** in Bali, in Indonesia, typify much of the landscape of Southeast Asia.

soons—winds that bring drenching rain during the summer—and a cool, dry season in winter. Much of the land is covered in jungle and rain forest. Most people are farmers, and many different languages are spoken. Since World War II, Southeast Asia has been torn by conflicts between pro-communist and anti-communist forces.

SPACE FLIGHT
The Soviet Union launched the first spacecraft, *Sputnik I*, in October 1957. The first man went into space in April 1961 when the Russian Yuri Gagarin flew once around the earth. The first woman in space (in 1963) was also a Russian. The United States put the first men on the moon in July 1969.

Today many spacecraft are being sent into space. Some, such as satellites and probes, are unmanned. Satellites carry equipment such as measuring instruments, tape recorders, radios, and cameras. Probes are sent to explore the moon and planets. Probes have already photographed all the planets out to Uranus, and have landed on Venus and Mars.

See also ASTRONAUT; SATELLITE; SPACE SHUTTLE.

SPACE SHUTTLE
The space shuttle is the first reusable spacecraft. Launched into space by a rocket, the winged orbiter goes into its path around the earth. When its mission is complete, the orbiter is slowed until it drops out of orbit. Once back inside Earth's atmosphere, the astronauts maneuver the shuttle like a glider, bringing

▶ **The space shuttle Columbia** is launched by rockets, orbits like a spacecraft, and can land back on earth like an airliner.

242

it to a landing on a runway.

In 1981 the shuttle *Columbia* made its first flight. Many successful flights followed until tragedy struck in January 1986, when the shuttle *Challenger* blew up after launch.

SPAIN

Spain is in southwestern Europe. Much of the center of the country is a high, treeless plateau. Northern Spain is wet and cool, but the south is hot and dry.

Most Spanish people work on farms. Spain is famous for olives, oranges, and onions. Important industries are textiles, steel-making, and engineering. Many tourists visit Spain every year.

In the late 1400s, Spain became rich and strong and built up a huge empire, mainly in South America. Later, however, Spain grew weak and lost its overseas lands.

In 1931 Spain became a republic. From 1936 to 1939 there was a terrible civil war, after which General Franco ruled as a dictator. When he died in 1975 Spain became a kingdom again.

See also page 78.

S

SPANISH–AMERICAN WAR

The Spanish-American War was fought in 1898 between the United States and Spain. It began when the United States went to the aid of Cuba, which was fighting for its independence from Spain. After the U.S. battleship *Maine* was sunk in Havana harbor, war broke out, mainly in Cuba and in the Spanish-governed Philippine Islands in the Pacific. In December a peace treaty was signed. The United States took control of the Philippines, Guam, and Puerto Rico in addition to securing Cuban independence.

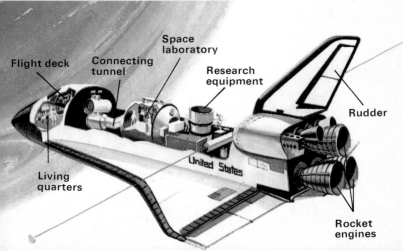

Flight deck

Connecting tunnel

Space laboratory

Research equipment

Rudder

Living quarters

United States

Rocket engines

SPECTRUM

The band of colors that we see in a rainbow, from red to violet, is called the spectrum of colors. White light is not white, but is made up of all the colors of the rainbow, which can be seen when we put a triangle-shaped piece of glass called a *prism* in front of a beam of light.

The spectrum of light in turn is just one section of the electromagnetic spectrum. This includes all forms of radiation, including radio waves, microwaves, infrared rays, light waves, ultraviolet rays, X rays, and gamma rays.

SPIDER

Spiders may look like insects but they are not. Their bodies are made up of two parts (not three) and they have eight legs (not six). They are related to scorpions.

▼ **The trapdoor spider** hides in a hole and waits for its prey to pass. It then leaps out and grabs the creature.

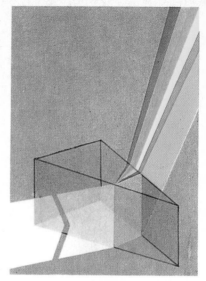

▲ **Passing light** through a prism shows the spectrum of colors.

All spiders make silk inside their bodies. Some spiders use the silk to make webs to trap insects for food. Not all spiders build webs, however. Wolf spiders chase their prey on the ground. Crab spiders lurk inside flowers, and trapdoor spiders lie in wait in holes.

SPINNING AND WEAVING

Spinning is the process of twisting man-made or natural fibers into threads by hand or with machinery.

The most common way of joining the yarns together to make a fabric is called weaving. Weaving is done on a loom. In weaving, one set of yarns (the *weft*) is threaded at right angles under

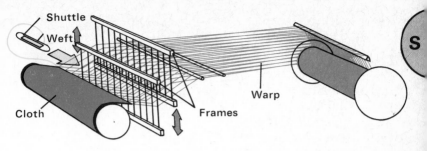

▲ **The shuttle** carries the weft threads back and forth across the warp on a weaving loom.

and over another set (the *warp*). The warp yarns run lengthwise.

STALACTITE AND STALAGMITE

These are two types of mineral deposits found in caves. Stalactites grow down from the roof. Stalagmites grow up from the floor and can be 100 feet high.

Both types are formed by water that seeps into the caves and drips from the limestone ceilings. The water is often saturated with dissolved minerals that are deposited in icicle-like formations. They are sometimes called dripstones.

See also CAVE.

STALIN, Joseph (1879–1953)

Stalin was a revolutionary leader who worked to overthrow the czar of Russia in 1917. As leader of the Soviet Union from 1924 to his death, he helped to turn Russia into an industrialized state. But Stalin was responsible for millions of deaths, and in 1959 he was denounced as a dictator.

STAMP

A stamp can be any sort of official mark, though today we usually think of a stamp as a piece of paper with a special design on one side and glue on the back, for sticking on letters. Each nation has its own postage stamps in varying designs and colors. Many people collect postage stamps—a good specimen of a rare stamp can be worth a great deal of money.

STAR

The stars we see in the night sky are balls of glowing gases. They are so far away that they seem

▲ **The great cluster** in Hercules may contain half a million stars.

245

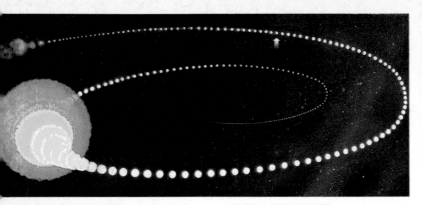

▲ **The life** and death of a star. Stars form from gases. They shine steadily for a long time, then expand into *red giants*. They die away as tiny *white dwarfs*.

very tiny, but if we could get closer, they would look like the sun. The sun is a star, and a very ordinary one. Some stars are much bigger and brighter than the sun; others much smaller and dimmer. Stars shine by nuclear power—heat and light produced when atoms of hydrogen gas fuse, or join together.

See also NUCLEAR ENERGY; SUN; UNIVERSE.

STATUE OF LIBERTY

The Statue of Liberty is one of the United States' best known national monuments. It stands on Liberty Island in New York Harbor. A gift to the United States from the people of France, it was designed by the French sculptor Frédéric-August Bartholdi and dedicated in 1886. It stands as a welcoming symbol to all who enter New York Harbor.

STEAM ENGINE

James Watt built the first really efficient steam engines in the late 1700s and made them suitable for driving industrial machinery of all kinds.

In Watt's type of engine, steam

The Statue of Liberty

pushes a piston back and forth in a cylinder. The piston is connected to whatever is to be driven— for example, the wheels of a locomotive. Steam is produced by burning coal or wood in a furnace beneath a boiler. The hot gases from the furnace pass through tubes in the boiler and heat the water. The steam that is produced drives the pistons.

STONE AGE

This is the name given to the period before people learned to obtain and use metal. Tools and weapons were made from flint and other rocks and wood. The Stone Age probably began about three million years ago.

There are three Stone Age periods: the Old (Paleolithic), Middle (Mesolithic), and New (Neolithic).

At the beginning of the Old Stone Age, hunters made crude stone axes. Thousands of years were to pass before they could chip flint into double-edged blades with which they made more effective implements: knives, scrapers, and weapons.

Middle Stone Age people made more intricate tools and weapons. Many were set in wooden or bone hafts and handles, making them easier to use.

Farming replaced hunting in the New Stone Age. Tools became more refined and more specialized for a particular task.

See also BRONZE AGE; IRON AGE.

▼ **James Watt** built this steam engine in 1788. The steam drove pistons connected to a beam. As the beam rocked, gears turned a drive wheel.

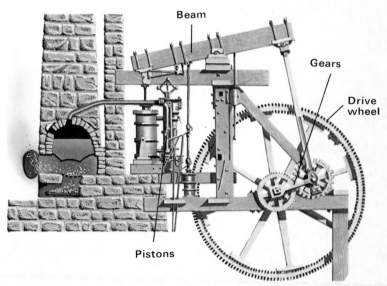

Beam

Gears

Drive wheel

Pistons

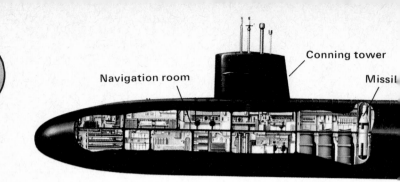

Navigation room

Conning tower

Missil

▲ **This cutaway** drawing of a nuclear submarine shows the navigation room beneath the conning tower, and the nuclear reactor and steam turbine engine in the stern.

SUBMARINE

Ships that can travel underwater are called submarines. A submarine dives by letting water into tanks around the hull (body). This makes it heavier than water. To surface, it blows the water out, making it lighter again. A periscope enables the crew to see above the surface.

Ordinary submarines are propelled under water by a propeller driven by electric batteries. They have to surface when their batteries run down. On the surface they are propelled by diesel engines, which also charge the batteries. Nuclear submarines are powered by a nuclear reactor. They can remain underwater for months at a time.

SUGAR

Plants make sugar for their own food. The sugar that we use to sweeten food, called *sucrose*, comes from sugar beets and sugarcane. Other sugars are *fructose* (from fruits), *glucose* (from fruits, vegetables, and grain), and *lactose* (from milk).

Sugar is a very important food because it supplies energy and heat and helps to form fat.

SUN

The sun is our nearest star. It is a great ball of very hot gases swirling in space. All the time it pours out heat and light as atoms of hydrogen gas join together inside it to form atoms of another gas—helium. Life on earth depends on this heat and light. Without it, the earth would be a dark, cold, dead lump of rock. All living things need warmth, and plants need sunlight to make food.

The sun is very much like many other stars in the sky. It appears bigger and hotter only because it is much nearer than the other stars. But compared with the earth, the sun is very big indeed. You could get more than a million earths inside the sun.

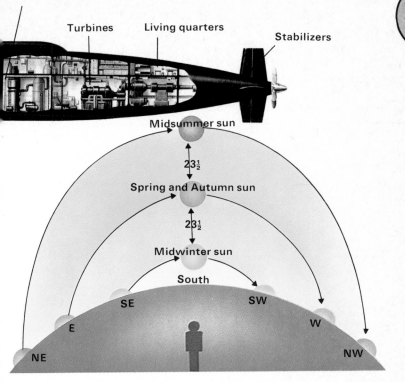

Nuclear reactor

Turbines   Living quarters

Stabilizers

S

Midsummer sun

$23\frac{1}{2}$

Spring and Autumn sun

$23\frac{1}{2}$

Midwinter sun

South

SE   SW

E   W

NE   NW

The earth is part of the sun's family, or solar system. It is one of nine planets circling around the sun.

See also PLANET; STAR.

SWAN

People admire these birds for their grace and beauty. Most kinds are white, but there are black swans in Australia. Swans live on rivers and lakes, and feed on plants and small water animals. They nest by the water. The female swan is called a *pen*; the

▲ **The sun's** daily path across the sky changes at different times of the year. This is because our earth orbits the sun at an angle.

male is a *cob*. Young swans are called cygnets.

SWEDEN

Sweden is one of the Scandinavian countries and the fourth largest European nation. It lies between Norway and the Baltic Sea. It has rich iron mines, and forests that yield timber. Most of Sweden's people live in the south.

▲ **Lake Lucerne,** one of the many large lakes in Switzerland.

Farms near the coast produce milk, meat, grains, and sugar beets.

See also page 78.

SWITZERLAND

This small landlocked country is in central Europe. It borders on Germany, Italy, France, Liechtenstein, and Austria.

Between the spectacular snow-capped Alps in southeastern Switzerland and the Jura Mountains in the northwest is the Swiss Plateau. On this plain are Switzerland's most important towns and large industries. Here, too, most of the country's crops are grown.

Swiss factories produce goods such as machinery, watches, and chemicals. Tourism is also a major industry.

See also page 78.

TALMUD

The *Talmud* is one of the holy books of Judaism. It is a collection of ancient writings that includes many of the laws that govern everyday life for Jewish people and interprets these laws. The *Talmud* and the *Torah*, the other holy book of Judaism, together contain the religious and political laws of Jewish people, wherever they live.

TANK

A tank is a large, armored military vehicle on a continuous "caterpillar" track that allows it to travel over rough ground. It was first used by Britain during World War I. At the top of the tank is a rotating gun turret. The crew is protected inside the body of the tank. Tanks were used during World War II, both by the Germans in their *blitzkriegs* (lightning attacks), and in Allied landing operations in Europe and the Pacific.

See also WAR.

TAX

The government needs money to run the country. It gets this money mainly from the taxes we pay. Taxes pay for the roads, schools, hospitals, and many other services a country needs. Taxes may be levied by federal, state, and city governments.

There are several kinds of taxes. Most people pay tax on their income—the money they earn. Income tax is a *direct tax*. *Indirect* taxes are taxes on goods and services. A sales tax is paid on many goods we buy. Customs duties are paid when goods enter the country. Excise duties are put on goods such as tobacco and alcohol. Property taxes are local taxes paid by homeowners.

TEA
Tea is made by pouring boiling water onto tea leaves. The leaves come from tea bushes, which are grown mainly in India, Sri Lanka, and China. Tea first came to Europe from China in the 1600s. At first it was brewed and stored in barrels, like beer.

TEETH
Teeth cut and chew food into pieces small enough to be swallowed. The kinds of teeth an animal has depends on the kind of food it eats.

Beasts of prey, such as wolves and lions, have long, sharp teeth. They use them to kill their prey and to tear the meat. Rodents, such as squirrels, have gnawing teeth. Grazing animals, such as cattle, have flat grinding teeth.

Human beings have sharp cutting teeth *and* flat grinding teeth.

▲ **Tea pickers** on a plantation in Asia.

This is because we eat both meat and plant food.

TELEPHONE
The first telephone calls could be sent only through wires. Now a telephone call may travel by wire or by radio, sometimes bounced off satellites. When you dial a number, the telephone sends out electrical pulses. They go to an exchange, which automatically connects you to the number you dialed.

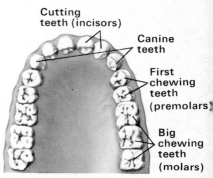

Cutting teeth (incisors)

Canine teeth

First chewing teeth (premolars)

Big chewing teeth (molars)

THE TELEPHONE HANDSET

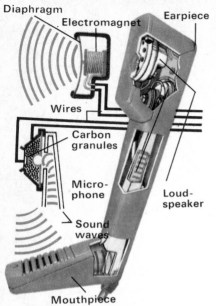

When you talk, a microphone changes your voice into electrical signals. These travel down the wires to the earpiece of the person you are talking to. There they are changed back into the sound of your voice.

TELESCOPE

A telescope is an instrument that makes distant objects appear nearer and larger.

The simplest type, a refracting telescope, consists of a tube containing two lenses which bend the light rays from the distant object and make it appear nearer.

Most astronomers, however, use reflecting telescopes, which have a mirror to collect and bend the light. They are bigger and clearer than refracting telescopes.

As well as light telescopes, astronomers use radio telescopes—large metal dishes that gather radio waves sent out by heavenly bodies.

TELEVISION

Television means "pictures from a distance." Television can show us live pictures of events on the other side of the world.

Two important pieces of television equipment are the *camera* and the *receiver*. The camera records an image of the scene it views on an electrically charged plate. A beam of electrons then sweeps back and forth across this

▼ **A refracting** telescope. The small finder helps to locate objects.

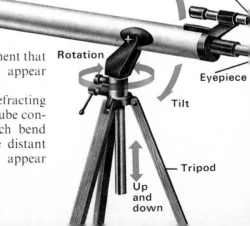

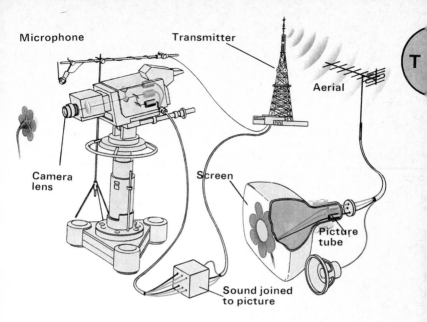

Microphone   Transmitter

Aerial

Camera lens   Screen

Picture tube

Sound joined to picture

plate. The result is electric signals that represent the brightness in different parts of the scene. These signals are combined with a radio wave and sent out into the air by a transmitter to the surrounding area.

The aerial of the television set picks up the wave. Circuits in the set separate the signal from the wave. These signals then go to the picture tube where a "gun" fires a beam of electrons at the screen, causing a spot of light. The television signals alter the strength of the beam and thereby the brightness of the spot. They also make the beam sweep back and forth in a series of lines of spots of varying brightness. The lines are very close together, and our eyes see them as a complete picture.

TENNESSEE

Tennessee is a long, narrow state that reaches from the Appalachian Mountains in the east to the Mississippi River in the west. Once chiefly a farming state, Tennessee is now mainly industrial. Factories produce chemicals, textiles, food, and metal products. Hydroelectric power, mining, tobacco, and cotton are also important. Nashville, the state capital, is also the capital of country and western music.

See also page 263.

TENNIS

When we use the word *tennis* we are usually referring to the game of lawn tennis. This game is played on hard or grass courts. Two people play in a singles match; four people in a doubles match. Tennis today is a form of an old French game.

TEXAS
Texas is a south-central state bordering on Mexico and the Gulf of Mexico. It is the second largest state in the Union. Until 1900, farming and cattle ranching were Texas's main sources of income. But the oil boom that followed helped greatly to develop a manufacturing industry in the state. Today Texas is one of the richest and most heavily populated states in the Union.

See also page 263.

THEATER
The first theaters were in ancient Greece. People sat in the open air on a hillside, while below, actors and dancers performed in a space called the orchestra. Behind the actors was a changing room called the *skene*. This later became a stage, and it gives us our words *scenery* and *scene*.

The modern theater began in Elizabethan England in the 1500s. This had a jutting stage almost surrounded by the audience. Rich people sat under cover. Poor spectators stood in the "pit" and got wet if it rained. But soon all theaters had roofs. Complicated scenery and stage machinery began to be used. And to hide the workings from the audience, a "picture frame" was put around the stage. The audience now sat only in front of it. Some modern theaters have gone back to the old idea.

See also PLAY.

THERMOMETER
A thermometer measures temperature—how hot it is. Most thermometers consist of a thin tube with a bulb of liquid. When liquids are heated, they expand, or grow bigger. So when the liquid in the bulb becomes hot-

▼ **A tropical** thunderstorm near Darwin, Australia.

254

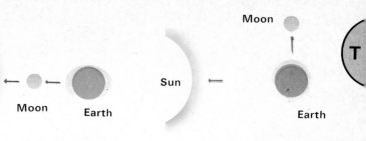

SPRING TIDE   **NEAP TIDE**

▲ **The position** of the sun, moon, and earth at spring and neap tides.

ter, it rises up the tube. The liquid used is generally mercury or colored alcohol.

Every thermometer has a scale marked on it. The most common scale worldwide is the Celsius, or centigrade scale. On this scale, the freezing point of water is 0 degrees, and the boiling point 100 degrees.

THUNDERSTORM

About 44,000 thunderstorms occur each day, mainly in the tropics. Lightning may flash in sheets, in balls, or in forked streaks. The thunder is produced by the sudden expansion of air that has been heated by the lightning flash. Thunder is heard after a flash because light travels faster than sound.

See also LIGHTNING.

TIDE

Tides are caused by the moon and the sun pulling the world's oceans toward them. This is the result of gravity. Because the moon is closer to earth than the sun is, its pull is stronger.

There are roughly two high tides and two low tides every 24 hours. When the moon and sun are on the same side of the earth, their combined pull produces the biggest tides, called *spring tides*. When the moon and sun are pulling at right angles to each other, the smallest tides, called *neap tides*, occur.

TIGER

The tiger is the largest of the big cats. Its home is Asia. Most tigers

▼ **The tiger** is the largest of the big cats.

live in hot forests. But the largest come from cold Siberia.

Tigers hunt alone and at night. They prey on deer, wild cattle, and pigs. Only an old or sick tiger will attack people. The tiger's stripes camouflage it in long grass. Unlike other cats, tigers often bathe to keep cool.

TIME
The day is a natural unit of time. It is the time the earth takes to spin around once in space. Our other main natural unit of time is the year—the $365\frac{1}{4}$ days it takes the earth to travel once around the sun.

The moon circles the earth about every 27 days. This gives us another unit of time—the month. Our calendar has 12 months in each year.

We measure time, or rather the passage of time, with clocks and watches. They help us split each day into 24 hours, each hour into 60 minutes, and each minute into 60 seconds. Day, hour, minute, and second are units of time. We can say what time it is in two ways—by a 12-hour clock or a 24-hour clock.

See also CALENDAR; CLOCK AND WATCH.

TIN
Tin is a common but very important metal. It resists corrosion (being eaten away) by acids and is often used for protective coatings, such as inside cans of food. Its most important use is in alloys such as bronze and brass.

TOBACCO
Tobacco is made from the dried leaves of the tobacco plant. It

▼ **Cigars** must be stored at special temperatures.

originally grew wild in the Americas. In the 1500s the Spaniards brought tobacco to Europe, and today tobacco is grown in Asia, Africa, and Europe as well as the Americas.

Tobacco leaf can be made into pipe, cigar, or cigarette tobacco, or snuff. Smoking is a harmful habit. It is especially bad for the lungs and heart.

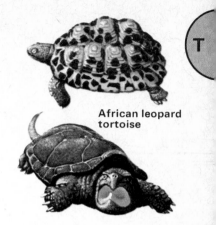

African leopard tortoise

Snapping turtle

TORTOISE AND TURTLE
Unlike other reptiles, tortoises and turtles have hard shells to protect their bodies.

Tortoises are land animals. They live in warm countries and eat plant food. A tortoise cannot run away from an enemy. Instead, it tucks its head and legs into its shell. Some tortoises can live to be much more than a hundred years old—older than any other animal.

Turtles live in water. They have flatter shells than tortoises, and use their legs as paddles for swimming. On land they are very clumsy.

See also REPTILE.

TRADE UNION
Trade unions are organizations or associations of workers. By joining together in a union, workers are better able to negotiate, or bargain, with their employers for higher wages and better working conditions.

Unions began during the Industrial Revolution in the 1700s. Many workers were badly paid, and their work was often unhealthy or dangerous. The unions had a long struggle to improve conditions.

TRANSISTOR
A transistor is a small electronic device used to *amplify* or to strengthen signals in electronic equipment such as radios, computers, and satellites. It is made from crystals of material such as germanium or silicon.

Transistors were invented in 1948. A large number of them can be put in a silicon chip a few millimeters square.

See also SILICON CHIP.

TREE
Trees are the largest of all plants. The world's biggest tree is the California redwood which can reach a height of over 300 feet. Trees grow a little each year. The tips of their branches grow longer, and a ring of tissue in

Beech   Oak   Aspen   Yew

Elm   Bird cherry   Larch   Sweet chestnut

Scotch pine   Wych elm   Alder   Field maple

Black poplar   Sycamore   Ash   Walnut

the main trunk and the older branches produces more cells to make them thicker.

Evergreen trees keep their leaves all year round. Conifers, such as spruce, pine, and fir, are evergreens. They grow in colder climates. Their leaves are thin and hard and look like needles. Conifers do not have flowers; instead, they have winged seeds hidden inside cones.

Many tropical trees are also evergreen. But they have broad

leaves and flowers. Broad-leaved trees grow in cool countries too. Those that shed their leaves in autumn are called *deciduous*. Other broad-leaved trees, such as hollies and live oaks, are evergreen.

TSUNAMI

When an earthquake occurs on the ocean floor it produces great waves called tsunamis. They travel long distances at speeds of up to 500 miles per hour. In the open ocean they may be only a few feet high, but when they run into shallow water and slow down they rise rapidly to heights of 30 to 100 feet.

▼ **Women harvest grain** by hand in Turkey. Cotton and tobacco are also important crops. Along the Aegean coast farmers grow figs and other fruit.

TURKEY

Turkey is a country that straddles both Europe and Asia. The largest city, Istanbul (once called Constantinople), is in the European part. Much of Turkey is mountainous, but the coastal plains are fertile and farming is the main industry. Once part of the vast Byzantine Empire, Turkey became a Muslim country under the Ottoman emperors.

See also page 79.

TWAIN, Mark (1835–1910)

The great American novelist and travel writer was born Samuel Langhorne Clemens. He grew up on the Mississippi River and later wrote about life on the Mississippi. His best known works include *The Adventures of Tom Sawyer* and *The Adventures of Huckleberry Finn*.

ULTRAVIOLET RAY

Light from the sun can be split by a prism into a *spectrum* of color. Red is at one end of the spectrum, violet at the other. Ultraviolet rays are found beyond the violet end of the spectrum.

These rays are very useful and important, although we cannot see them. They produce vitamin D in our bodies, necessary for growing bones. Ultraviolet rays can be used to kill bacteria.

UNITED KINGDOM

England, Scotland, Wales, and Northern Ireland together make up the United Kingdom of Great Britain and Northern Ireland. The head of state is the queen, but parliament makes the laws. The government is led by the prime minister.

The climate is mild, with plenty of rainfall. In this rather crowded country, most people live in towns. Farming is important, but the farmers cannot produce enough, so food has to be imported.

There is coal underground, and natural gas and oil offshore beneath the sea. Together these fuels help to provide power for the nation's many industries. Heavy industries are mainly in northern England, South Wales, and Scotland. Many people live in and around London, the capital and business center.

England was conquered by the Romans and later by the Normans. In the 1200s the English conquered Wales. From 1603 England and Scotland had the same king; and from 1707 they shared a single parliament. Ireland joined the union in 1801, but southern Ireland broke away in 1921 and later became a republic.

See also page 78.

UNITED NATIONS

In the present century there have been two terrible world wars. The United Nations was set up in

◄ **The Queen** opens Parliament in London.

1945 to try and prevent wars.

The U.N. tries to settle quarrels between countries peacefully. It helps refugees and children, and sends experts to fight hunger, disease, and ignorance in poor countries. The headquarters of the U.N. are in New York City. Here the General Assembly and the Security Council meet to discuss world problems.

UNITED STATES OF AMERICA

Fifty states make up the United States of America. This huge

▲ **Fall in Vermont** is a patchwork of color

▼ **A New Orleans steamboat** on the Mississippi River.

country consists of the middle part of North America, Alaska in the far north, and Hawaii in the Pacific Ocean.

The climate varies from region to region. Some areas are hot in summer and cold in winter, but the south and west coasts have mild winters. Most regions get good rainfall.

The United States has very great natural resources. Its farmland is fertile. Huge crops of wheat are grown on the prairies, and corn, tobacco, cotton, fruit, and vegetables are also grown. From the forests comes timber, and underground are valuable

	STATE	CAPITAL	POPULATION	STATE BIRD	STATE FLOWER
1.	Alabama	Montgomery	3,943,000	Yellowhammer	Camellia
2.	Alaska	Juneau	438,000	Willow ptarmigan	Forget-me-not
3.	Arizona	Phoenix	2,860,000	Cactus wren	Saguaro (Giant cactus)
4.	Arkansas	Little Rock	2,291,000	Mockingbird	Apple blossom
5.	California	Sacramento	24,724,000	California valley quail	Golden poppy
6.	Colorado	Denver	3,045,000	Lark bunting	Rocky Mountain columbine
7.	Connecticut	Hartford	3,153,000	Robin	Mountain laurel
8.	Delaware	Dover	602,000	Blue hen chicken	Peach blossom
9.	Florida	Tallahassee	10,416,000	Mockingbird	Orange blossom
10.	Georgia	Atlanta	5,639,000	Brown thrasher	Cherokee rose
11.	Hawaii	Honolulu	994,000	Néné (Hawaiian goose)	Hibiscus
12.	Idaho	Boise	935,000	Mountain bluebird	Syringa (Mock orange)
13.	Illinois	Springfield	11,448,000	Cardinal	Native violet
14.	Indiana	Indianapolis	5,471,000	Cardinal	Peony
15.	Iowa	Des Moines	2,905,000	Eastern goldfinch	Wild rose
16.	Kansas	Topeka	2,408,000	Western meadowlark	Sunflower
17.	Kentucky	Frankfort	3,667,000	Kentucky cardinal	Goldenrod
18.	Louisiana	Baton Rouge	4,362,000	Brown pelican	Magnolia
19.	Maine	Augusta	1,133,000	Chickadee	White pine cone and tassel
20.	Maryland	Annapolis	4,265,000	Baltimore oriole	Black-eyed Susan
21.	Massachusetts	Boston	5,781,000	Chickadee	Arbutus (Mayflower)
22.	Michigan	Lansing	9,109,000	Robin	Apple blossom
23.	Minnesota	St. Paul	4,133,000	Common loon	Pink and white lady's slipper
24.	Mississippi	Jackson	2,551,000	Mockingbird	Magnolia
25.	Missouri	Jefferson City	4,951,000	Bluebird	Hawthorn
26.	Montana	Helena	801,000	Western meadowlark	Bitterroot
27.	Nebraska	Lincoln	1,586,000	Western meadowlark	Goldenrod
28.	Nevada	Carson City	881,000	Mountain bluebird	Sagebrush
29.	New Hampshire	Concord	951,000	Purple finch	Purple lilac
30.	New Jersey	Trenton	7,438,000	Eastern goldfinch	Purple violet
31.	New Mexico	Santa Fe	1,302,981	Roadrunner	Yucca
32.	New York	Albany	17,659,000	Bluebird	Rose
33.	North Carolina	Raleigh	6,019,000	Cardinal	Flowering dogwood
34.	North Dakota	Bismarck	670,000	Western meadowlark	Wild prairie rose
35.	Ohio	Columbus	10,791,000	Cardinal	Scarlet carnation
36.	Oklahoma	Oklahoma City	3,177,000	Scissor-tailed flycatcher	Mistletoe
37.	Oregon	Salem	2,649,000	Western meadowlark	Oregon grape
38.	Pennsylvania	Harrisburg	11,865,000	Ruffed grouse	Mountain laurel
39.	Rhode Island	Providence	958,000	Rhode Island Red	Violet
40.	South Carolina	Columbia	3,203,000	Carolina wren	Carolina jessamine
41.	South Dakota	Pierre	691,000	Ring-necked pheasant	American pasqueflower
42.	Tennessee	Nashville	4,651,000	Mockingbird	Iris
43.	Texas	Austin	15,280,000	Mockingbird	Bluebonnet
44.	Utah	Salt Lake City	1,554,000	Sea gull	Sego lily
45.	Vermont	Montpelier	516,000	Hermit thrush	Red clover
46.	Virginia	Richmond	5,491,000	Cardinal	Flowering dogwood
47.	Washington	Olympia	4,245,000	Willow goldfinch	Coast rhododendron
48.	West Virginia	Charlestown		Cardinal	Rhododendron
49.	Wisconsin	Madison	4,765,000	Robin	Wood violet
50.	Wyoming	Cheyenne	469,557	Meadowlark	Indian paintbrush

Name	Location	Area in acres
Acadia	Maine	38,632
Arches	Utah	73,379
Badlands	South Dakota	243,302
Big Bend	Texas	708,118
Biscayne	Florida	173,274
Bryce Canyon	Utah	38,835
Canyonlands	Utah	337,570
Capital Reef	Utah	241,904
Carlsbad Caverns	New Mexico	46,753
Channel Islands	California	124,740
Crater Lake	Oregon	160,290
Denali	Alaska	4,700,000
Everglades	Florida	1,398,000
Gates of the Arctic	Alaska	7,500,000
Glacier	Montana	1,013,595
Glacier Bay	Alaska	3,225,198
Grand Canyon	Arizona	1,218,375
Grand Teton	Wyoming	310,516
Great Smoky Mountains	North Carolina and Tennessee	517,369
Guadalupe Mountains	Texas	76,293
Haleakala	Hawaii	28,655
Hawaii Volcanoes	Hawaii	229,177
Hot Springs	Arkansas	5,826
Isle Royale	Michigan	571,796
Katmai	Alaska	3,716,000
Kenai Fjords	Alaska	670,000
Kings Canyon	California	460,136
Kobuk Valley	Alaska	1,750,000
Lake Clark	Alaska	2,874,000
Lassen Volcanic	California	106,372
Mammoth Cave	Kentucky	52,452
Mesa Verde	Colorado	52,085
Mount Rainier	Washington	235,404
North Cascades	Washington	504,781
Olympic	Washington	908,781
Petrified Forest	Arizona	93,493
Redwood	California	109,027
Rocky Mountain	Colorado	263,809
Sequoia	California	402,023
Shenandoah	Virginia	194,826
Theodore Roosevelt	North Dakota	70,416
Virgin Islands	Virgin Islands	14,695
Voyageurs	Minnesota	219,128
Wind Cave	South Dakota	28,292
Wrangell-St. Elias	Alaska	8,945,000
Yellowstone	Wyoming, Mon-tana, Idaho	2,219,823
Yosemite	California	760,917

Each state's capital city is indicated by a black dot on the map below.

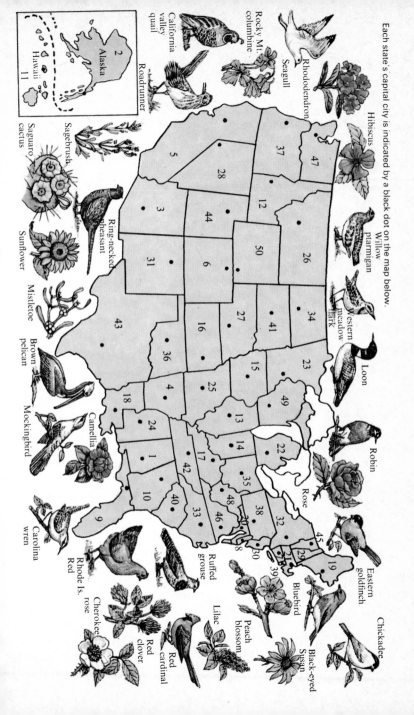

U

▲ **An assembly line** at the Ford Motor Company. Automobile manufacturing is an important industry in Detroit, Michigan.

minerals, including coal, oil, natural gas, iron, gold, copper, and uranium. Many rivers and lakes have been dammed to produce electricity.

More than half the people live in towns and cities, for the United States is the greatest industrial country in the world. Its factories make aircraft, cars, computers, machines, and many other kinds of goods.

The first Americans were the Indians, who lived by farming and hunting. But after Columbus's discovery of the New World, Europeans began to settle in America. Beginning in the 1600s, the British set up thirteen colonies on the east coast. But the colonists wanted to govern themselves, and in 1776 they broke away from Britain and became an independent republic, the United States of America, with George Washington as the first President.

The republic grew into a union of fifty states. Many poor people from European countries came to the United States. Industry developed so quickly that Americans soon enjoyed a higher standard of living than any other people in the world.

See also page 79.

UNIVERSE

When we talk of the universe, we mean everything that exists. This includes the air, the sea, the earth, the other planets, the moon, the stars, and space.

Years ago people thought that the earth was the center of the universe. Now we know that the earth is only a tiny speck in the universe. It belongs to the sun's family of stars called the galaxy. The galaxy belongs to a family of galaxies. And there are millions of such families in the universe. But most of the universe is just empty space.

URANIUM

This element is a rare whitish metal. It is radioactive; that is, it gives off rays that cannot be seen but which will darken film.

Although it was discovered in 1789, uranium had very few uses until 1940. Then a method of obtaining energy from it was discovered. When uranium is bombarded with neutrons its atoms become unstable. They split and give off energy. This splitting process is called fission. Uranium is used for nuclear power and in atomic bombs.

See also NUCLEAR ENERGY.

U.S.S.R.

U.S.S.R. stands for the Union of Soviet Socialist Republics, the official name of the Soviet Union. Many people still call this vast country Russia, though Russia is only one of the 15 republics that make up the U.S.S.R. Soviet culture is a rich one, and Russians are fond of sports, art, and dance. People everywhere enjoy the works of famous Russian writers such as Tolstoy, Dostoevsky, and Solzhenitsyn. Russia was a monarchy ruled by *czars* (emperors) until 1917, when a communist revolution established a communist government led by Vladimir Lenin.

The Soviet Union has a varied landscape and climate, from the frozen wastes of Siberia to the warm resorts on the Black Sea. It is rich in natural resources such as coal, oil and natural gas, iron, chromium, lead, and manganese. Soviet farmers grow wheat, rye, barley, vegetables, fruit, tea, and cotton. Most farms are owned and run by the government. At the beginning of the century Russia was a nation of farmers. Today the Soviet Union is a major industrial power, and head of the Eastern bloc of communist nations. Disagreements between the Eastern bloc and the nations of the West after World War II led to the Cold War, a state of mutual mistrust that has existed for more than 30 years.

See also page 78.

UTAH

Utah is a mineral-rich western state divided down the center by the Rocky Mountains. To the west is the Great Salt Lake, one of the largest lakes in the United States. Lying at the foot of the mountains is Salt Lake City, the capital, founded by the Mormons, the first permanent settlers in Utah.

See also page 263.

▲ **St. Basil's Cathedral** is in Moscow, capital of the U.S.S.R.

U

265

now gaining popularity. Some of these are pre-recorded tapes of movies or video games that can be played on a videocassette recorder (VCR) attached to an ordinary TV set. Others are blank tapes that can be used to record TV programs.

VEGETABLE
Many of the plants we eat are called vegetables. Vegetables are good food, supplying energy or body-building substances.

Various parts of vegetables are eaten. Potatoes are root vegetables, spinach is a leaf, Brussels sprouts are leaf buds, and broccoli is a flower. Some fruits, such as tomatoes, are eaten as vegetables.

VERMONT
Vermont is a New England state that lies between New Hampshire and New York. The state is divided down the center by the Green Mountains and is known for its beautiful rolling country and lovely old villages. Camping, hiking, and skiing attract many tourists. The state produces maple syrup, apples, dairy products, asbestos, and marble.

See also page 263.

VIDEOTAPE
Videotape is a means of recording sound and pictures on tape. Many television programs are recorded on videotape to be sent across a network or for relaying at a later time. Home videos are

VIETNAM WAR
The Vietnam War was fought in the 1960s and early 1970s when the United States intervened to back South Vietnam in its struggle against communist North Vietnam. It was fought mainly as a guerrilla war, and American involvement in the conflict caused much controversy in the United States. In 1973, when President Nixon called for the withdrawal of American troops, the war's dead included more than 57,000 Americans, about 200,000 South Vietnamese, and over 2,000,000 people in all.

VIKING
In the 700s fierce Vikings from Scandinavia began raiding the coasts of Europe.

In their longships (wooden boats with oars and square sails) they crossed the Atlantic Ocean to settle in Iceland and Greenland. They probably reached America around A.D. 1000. The Vikings also settled in Ireland, France, Russia, and England.

VIRGINIA
Virginia is a historic southern state named after Queen Eliza-

beth I of England, the Virgin Queen. The first English settlers in North America arrived in Virginia in 1607, establishing Jamestown. Today Virginia is a manufacturing state, though it is also an important tobacco producer. Many eminent Virginians, including Patrick Henry, Thomas Jefferson, and George Washington, played an important part in the years before and during the Revolutionary War.

See also page 263.

VITAMIN

Vitamins are chemicals our bodies need for healthy growth. We get vitamins from food. From lettuce, carrots, butter, and eggs comes *vitamin A*. It helps us grow. There are several kinds of *vitamin B*. We eat them in cereals, milk, meat, vegetables, and fruit. *Vitamin C* is found in fruit. *Vitamin D* prevents a bone disease called rickets. Egg yolks and liver are rich in vitamin D.

VOLCANO

Volcanoes occur where the earth's crust is being squeezed or stretched as new mountains are formed. The enormous pressures melt the solid rock to liquid magma. When the pressures become too great, gases and hot liquid rock, called *lava,* may burst through the center of a volcano and out of a pit or crater at the top.

Volcanoes are usually cone-shaped with a crater at the top. Active volcanoes erupt for short periods and then remain dormant for long periods. If the lava remains bubbling in a lava lake, eruptions are just overflows. If, however, the lava solidifies, the next eruptions will explode.

▼ **Inside a volcano.**
Hot lava and melted rock spout up from the central vent. The mountain is made from layers of cold ash and lava.

WAR

People have always found it difficult to live together in peace. From prehistoric times envy and greed have made one tribe attack another, in order to steal its land or animals. Later great empires were founded by conquest.

In ancient Greece and Rome foot soldiers, or infantry, made up the largest part of an army. The Roman armies were so well trained that for hundreds of years they were unbeatable.

Horsemen, or cavalry, played an important part in wars throughout the Middle Ages. Knights in armor, helpless on foot, battered their way through enemy ranks on horseback.

Gunpowder came into use in the 1300s. From then on wars were fought increasingly with guns. But it took many years before soldiers had guns light enough to carry easily.

By 1914 guns were so powerful that soldiers had to dig trenches for protection. During World War I whole armies were bogged down in trenches. The tank, first used in 1916, was a powerful new weapon. Even more deadly was the airplane. For the first time civilians were attacked in their homes by bombs dropped from planes in the air.

World War II was a war of rapid movement. Submarines sank many ships with their torpedoes. The war against Japan ended with the dropping of the

▼ **Civilians** are often the victims in today's wars, fought with efficient tanks and missiles.

first atomic bombs on the cities of Hiroshima and Nagasaki. These nuclear weapons are the most terrible ever known in warfare.

See also CIVIL WAR; REVOLUTION; VIETNAM WAR.

WASHINGTON

The state of Washington lies in the Pacific Northwest, on the border of Canada. The Cascade Range of mountains runs down the center of the state. Between the mountains and the Pacific, it is green and rainy. To the east, the country is mainly dry. The state's chief industries produce

▲ **The White House,** a Washington landmark.

aircraft, minerals, food, and lumber. Seattle, Spokane, and Tacoma are the largest cities.

See also page 263.

WASHINGTON, D.C.

Washington, D.C. (District of Columbia), is the capital of the United States and the center of government. It is named after George Washington, who chose the site of the new city in 1791, and was laid out by the French engineer Pierre L'Enfant. Much of it was burned by the British during the War of 1812 but was rebuilt by 1819. Places to visit include the Capitol, the White House, the Supreme Court Building, the Lincoln Memorial, the Library of Congress, and the Smithsonian Institution.

See also DISTRICT OF COLUMBIA.

WASHINGTON, George
(1732–1799)

George Washington, the first U.S. president, was a farmer

W

269

from Virginia. Having fought bravely in the French and Indian War (1756–1763), Washington became a national hero as leader of the American forces during the Revolutionary War (1775–1783). In 1789 he became president, although he did not consider himself fit for such an important task.

WASP
Wasps are related to ants and bees. They are hunting insects, and many wasps will sting if annoyed.

Social wasps live in colonies. Inside the nest, the queen lays eggs, and workers care for the eggs and larvae. Adult wasps eat nectar. But the larvae are fed insects and caterpillars. In the autumn all the wasps die, except for the young queens. They hibernate, and start new nests in the spring. Solitary wasps live alone and build small nests.

WATER
Water is the most precious liquid on earth, for without it, nothing can live.

▼ **A potter wasp** molds mud into a pot-shaped nest.

Water is the only mineral that is liquid. It is made up of the chemical elements hydrogen and oxygen. Its molecules contain two atoms of hydrogen (H) to one atom of oxygen (O). We write this as the chemical formula H_2O.

Water plays an important part in our weather. The sun warms the earth's water, changing some of it into vapor. The vapor rises and as it does so, condenses and falls back to the ground as rain or snow. This continuous process of evaporation and condensation is called the water cycle.

Water also shapes the earth. Rain, ocean waves, and rivers weather and erode the land. Glaciers gouge paths through rocks and soil.

Water power helps people. Great dams can harness the power of water to make electricity. We call this form of power hydroelectricity.

See also ENERGY; GLACIER; ICE AGE; LAKE; OCEAN; RAIN; RIVER.

WATERFALL
A waterfall is caused by water wearing away rock at different speeds. If a river flows over hard rock and onto soft rock, it wears away the soft rock more quickly and makes a deep "step." Some waterfalls are quite small, but in some places wide rivers fall over huge cliffs. The most famous waterfalls are Niagara, between Canada and the United States, and the Victoria Falls in Africa.

▲ **At 3,212 feet,** Angel Falls in Venezuela is the highest in the world.

The highest is Angel Falls in Venezuela.

WATT, James (1736–1819)
Watt was a Scottish engineer who invented a more efficient steam engine than any before. He devised a condenser and several methods of changing the motion of a piston into the rotating motion of a wheel.

WAVE
If you drop a stone into a pond, it pushes the water out of the way in a wave. The energy in this wave moves along to make another wave, and in this way moves across the water. Sound is also carried by waves. Light waves, X rays, radio waves, and other forms of radiation are all types of electromagnetic waves.

WEATHER
The earth's atmosphere moves constantly, driven by the sun's heat. Huge masses of warm and cold air flow between the tropics and the polar regions. As these air masses meet, rise and fall, and heat and cool, they cause weather. When cold and warm air masses meet, a giant spiral of air called a depression results. A depression brings clouds, rain, or storms. The meeting line between two air masses is called a *front*. Fronts usually bring changes in the weather.

▼ **Wind blows** as air moves between areas of high and low pressure.

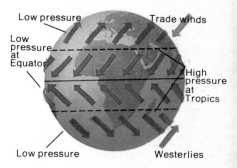

Low pressure

Trade winds

Low pressure at Equator

High pressure at Tropics

Low pressure

Westerlies

WEST INDIES
The islands known as the West Indies lie between the Caribbean Sea and the Atlantic Ocean. The many islands are divided into more than 20 countries. The largest are Cuba, Jamaica, Haiti, and the Dominican Republic.

Most of the islands have a tropical climate and people grow

▲ **Blue whales** have baleen instead of teeth. The rows of bony plates filter water and trap lots of tiny shrimplike animals.

sugar, tobacco, cocoa, coffee, coconuts, bananas, and other fruits. There is not much industry but iron ore, bauxite, and asphalt are mined. Many islands have a busy tourist industry.

The West Indies were discovered in 1492 by Christopher Columbus. Spain conquered the islands in the 1500s and later the British, French, and Dutch set up colonies there. African slaves were brought to work on plantations. Today most islands run their own affairs.

See also page 79.

WEST VIRGINIA

West Virginia is a mountainous mining state in the eastern United States. Only Kentucky produces more coal each year. Once part of Virginia, West Virginia became a separate state in 1863. Today coal mining is second only to manufacturing as the state's chief industry. Most West Virginians live in the river valleys, where land is fertile and transportation is good.

See also page 263.

WHALE

Although whales spend all their lives in the sea, they are mammals, not fish. Whales are warm-blooded. They have skin, not scales. The females give birth to live young and feed them on milk. Although a whale can dive to great depths, loading its blood with enough oxygen to last for up to 45 minutes, it must surface to breathe. Whales swim by beating their tails up and down.

There are two families of whales: toothed whales, and whalebone or baleen whales.

WHEEL

The wheel is one of the most important inventions. A great deal of human and animal energy is saved through using it.

No one knows when the wheel was invented. Its first use was probably as a potter's wheel in Mesopotamia about 5,000 years ago. Wheels were next used on carts. These wheels were solid, made by cutting slices off large tree trunks.

Without wheels, advanced transportation systems would not be possible. They are essential to the operation of most machines and engines.

WILLIAM THE CONQUEROR (*c*.1027–1087)

In 1066 William, Duke of Normandy, landed with his army in England and defeated and killed the English King Harold. He was crowned William I, the first Norman king of England.

William was an efficient administrator. He caused a great survey of the land to be made. It is known as the Domesday Book. William's descendants ruled England for many years after his death.

WIND

Wind is the movement of air over the earth's surface. The chief cause of wind is the unequal heating of the earth's surface. At the equator, which gets the most heat from the sun, air becomes warm and rises. At the poles, which are the coldest places, cold air sinks. As the warm air rises, cool air moves in to take its place. This causes the trade winds that blow over tropical oceans. Changing temperatures over the sea and land also affect the pattern of the winds.

Winds are named after the direction from which they come; so a north wind blows from the north, and so on.

WINDMILL

Windmills are used to grind corn, pump water, and generate electricity. Their source of power is the wind. Sails or blades are fixed to a shaft. The shaft is connected to the machinery to be driven. As other forms of energy become expensive, windmills may again become popular. A light steel type has been devised for use on farms.

WISCONSIN

Wisconsin is a midwestern state bordering Lake Michigan and Lake Superior. It is known as America's Dairyland and is famous for its cheeses. Other industries include manufacturing, transportation, and communications. Wisconsin's Great Lakes ports are among the busiest inland ports in the world. Campers and hikers enjoy the lakes, streams, and forests.

See also page 263.

▼ **An egg-beater** windmill in Albuquerque, New Mexico.

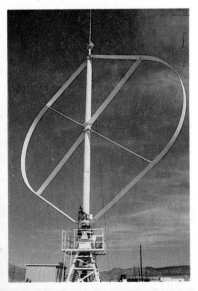

273

WOLF

Wolves belong to the dog family. They are strong, intelligent animals and often hunt together in packs. They will chase a deer for many hours until the prey is exhausted. Wolves also eat smaller animals, and will attack cattle and sheep. The gray timber wolf of North America, Europe, and Asia is the largest wolf. All kinds are now quite rare.

Timber wolf

WOOD

Wood is used in building and in making furniture, and is burned as fuel. Cut wood is called timber. The timber we get from coniferous trees, such as pine, is called softwood. The timber we get from deciduous trees, such as oak, is called hardwood. Softwoods are used mainly in building construction, hardwoods for furniture.

Wood is also made into paper, textile fibers, plastics, explosives, and several other chemicals. The main chemical substance in wood is cellulose.

WORLD WAR I

World War I (1914–18) involved Europe, America, and much of the Middle East, and so became known as a "world war." France, Britain (and her empire),

▼ **A recruiting poster** from World War I.

▼ **British soldiers** in the trenches during World War I.

I WANT YOU
FOR U.S. ARMY
NEAREST RECRUITING STATION

the United States, and Russia were on one side. On the other were Austria-Hungary, Germany, and Turkey.

The war reached a stalemate in northern France, where the front lines of both sides hardly moved for several years. In the east, the Germans fared better. Because of this and its own internal problems, Russia was forced to withdraw from the struggle in 1917.

The United States was at first reluctant to be drawn into the conflict, but after repeated German attacks on U.S. shipping, the United States declared war on Germany. The Allied armies slowly pushed the Germans back, until in November 1918 peace was declared.

WORLD WAR II

In September 1939, Adolf Hitler's German armies invaded Poland, an early step in his planned conquest of Europe. Within weeks, Germany, Italy, and then Japan had entered into a war with most of the major nations of the world. Before the war was over, battles had been fought from the North Atlantic and Europe to the tropical jungles of the Pacific islands in the Far East.

At first the Germans were successful in their sweep across Europe, and into North Africa and Russia. In December 1941, however, the United States entered the war after the Japanese

▲ **Churchill, Roosevelt,** and Stalin at the Yalta Conference in 1945, just before the end of World War II.

bombed the Pacific Fleet at Pearl Harbor in Hawaii, and the tide began to turn. By June 1944, Allied forces had landed in France. Germany surrendered the following spring.

In the Pacific, Japan had invaded China, Malaya, and Indonesia and had captured many Pacific islands. Victories by the U.S. Navy and finally the dropping of atomic bombs on the Japanese cities of Hiroshima and Nagasaki forced Japan to accept Allied surrender terms.

WORM

Worms are animals with soft bodies. Some live underground or in water, others as parasites inside plants or other animals.

There are about 20,000 dif-

275

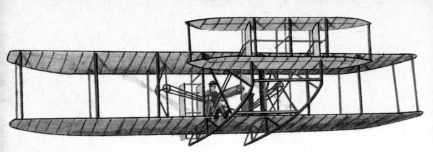

ferent kinds of worms. One group includes *flatworms* which have flat, ribbon, or leaf-shaped bodies. The harmful parasites, the tapeworm and the liver fluke, are flatworms. Threadworms, roundworms, and hookworms are found in another group. Many of these are also parasites. *Segmented worms* are not harmful. Their bodies are made up of segments or rings. They include ragworms, lugworms, and the earthworm.

WRIGHT, Orville (1871–1948) and Wilbur (1867–1912)

These two brothers made the first motor-powered, heavier-than-air flight in 1903.

They taught themselves about flight by making and flying kites and gliders. By 1903 they were ready to attach a four-cylinder, 13-horsepower engine to a biplane glider. On December 17, Orville took off, reached a speed of 30 mph, and flew 120 feet. The flight took 59 seconds.

WYOMING

Wyoming is a Rocky Mountain state in which the average height of the land above sea level is more than 6,500 feet. Yellow-

▲ **The Wright brothers** were the first to build and successfully fly an airplane.

stone National Park, with its hot springs and geysers, is in the northwestern corner of Wyoming. The mining of oil, natural gas, iron ore, and uranium is Wyoming's most important business; cattle, sheep, and horse ranching comes next.

See also page 263.

X RAY

Like light waves, X rays are invisible waves of energy. They can pass through and into most materials. They pass through flesh, for example. In hospitals doctors take X-ray photographs to look inside the body. A patient stands in front of a photographic film and X rays are passed through him. When the film is developed, the patient's bones show up. This is because the bones block some of the rays and cast a shadow on the film. The doctors can see if any of the bones are broken. Some new X-ray machines can photograph body organs as well.

X rays were discovered by the German scientist Wilhelm Röntgen in 1895.

YAK

Yaks live in the cold, high mountains of central Asia. Yaks are among the largest wild cattle, yet they climb as nimbly as goats. The yak can live on poor pasture and is very useful to the people of the Himalayas. It gives milk, butter, and meat, its skin is made into leather, and its long hair is woven into cloth.

YUGOSLAVIA

The great river Danube flows through the north of this mountainous country in southeastern Europe. Farmers here grow wheat, barley, olives, and grapes. Different groups live in the country, such as the Slavs and Croats, and each group has its own language. Belgrade is the capital.

See also page 78.

ZAIRE

This hot, rainy country is in central Africa. The Zaire River, once called the Congo, runs right through the rain forest. Cobalt, copper, and diamonds are mined in Zaire but most of the people work on farms.

See also page 78.

ZAMBIA

Zambia is a landlocked country in southern Africa. Copper mining is very important—nearly a quarter of all the copper in the world comes from Zambia.

The Zambezi River, which Zambia shares with Zimbabwe, has been dammed to form Lake Kariba.

See also page 78.

ZEBRA

The zebra is a relation of the horse. Its distinct black stripes help to camouflage it in the shadowy high grass of the African plains on which it lives. Zebras roam in herds, and gallop off at great speed if attacked by lions, their main enemy.

◄ **The yak's** shaggy coat keeps it warm in its mountain home.

ZIMBABWE

Most people in this country are farmers. They grow food crops and crops such as sugarcane, tobacco, and fruit to sell to other countries.

For a long time Zimbabwe was a British colony called Rhodesia. It became the republic of Zimbabwe in 1980.

See also page 78.

ZOO

A zoo is a place where wild animals are kept in captivity. People enjoy going to zoos to see animals from other countries. But more important, zoos help to save rare animals from becoming extinct. Zoos around the world exchange animals for breeding.

In the past, kings collected wild animals in zoos. The first public zoos began in the 1800s. Often the cages were too small for the animals and the bars made it hard to see them.

Today zoos have enclosures in which the animals feel more at home. Ditches, moats, and glass keep the animals and visitors apart. Birds fly around inside large aviaries. In special darkened buildings, people can see animals that are normally active only at night.

ZOOLOGY

This is the science that deals with the study of animals. Zoologists find out about animals' bodies, growth patterns, and habits. About a million different species, or kinds, of animals have been described by zoologists and sorted into groups.

The study of zoology helps us to understand animals, to control animal pests and diseases, and to improve the quality of farm animals.

▼ **Children** feed elephants at a zoo.

Index

Page numbers in **bold** type denote main entries; page numbers in *italic* type refer to illustrations and charts.

A

Aardvark, **5**, *5*
Abacus, 49, *146*
Aborigine, **5**
Abstract art, 23
Abyss, 194, *194*
Acetic acid, 5
Acid, **5**
Aeneid, 207
Africa, **5–7**, *5, 6*
AIDS, **7**
Air, **7**
Air-cushion vehicle, **7–8**, *7*
Aircraft, **8–9**, *8, 9, 41*
Airfoil, 9
Alabama, **10**
Alaska, **10**
Aldrin, Edwin, *27*
Alexander the Great, **10**, 20
Alexandria, 10
Algae, **10**, *10, 162, 205,* 229
Alligator, **82**
Alloy, **10–11**, 76
Alphabet, **11**, *11,* 71
Aluminum, **11**, 22, *172*
Alzheimer's disease, **11**
Amazon River, 45, *240,* 241
American history, **11–13**
Ameba, 58
Amphibian, **13**, *13,* 14, 115–16, 210, *211*
Amundsen, Roald, *104,* 105, 227
Andes Mountains, 60, 165, 210, 240
Aneroid barometer, 33
Anesthetic, 172
Anglo-Saxon, **13**
Animal, **14**, *14, 15*
Ant, **14–16**, *16*
Antarctica, **16**, *16*
Antelope, **16**
Antibiotic, 92, 172
Antony, Mark, 66
Ape, **16–17**, *17*
Apollo spaceflight, 54
Aqualung, 91
Archaeology, **17–18**, *18*
Arch bridge, *46*
Archery, **18**, *19*
Archimedes, **18**, *146*

Architecture, **18–20**, *21,* 62
Arctic, **20**
Argentina, **20**
Aristotle, **20**
Arizona, **20–2**, *20*
Arkansas, **22**
Armadillo, **22**
Armor, **22**
Armstrong, Neil, 26
Art, **22–24**, *22, 23*
Artery, *41*
Artificial intelligence, 24
Asia, **24–6**, *24, 25*
Astronaut, **26–7**, *26–7*
Astronomy, **27**, *27*
Atahualpa, 143
Athens, 127, *127*
Athletics, **28**
Atlantic Ocean, **28**, 128, *129*
Atmosphere, 7, 95
Atom, **28**, *28,* 99, 100, 148, 192–3, 215
Australia, 5, **29–30**, *29*
Austria, **30**
Automobile, **30–1**, *30*
Axolotl, 225
Aztec, 31, *31*

B

Bach, J.S., **31**
Bacteria, **31**, *31,* 90
Bactrian camel, 51
Baden-Powell, Robert, 228
Badger, **32**, *32*
Ballad, 207
Ballet, **32**
Balloon and airship, **32–3**, *32*
Barley, 59, *59*
Barometer, **33**
Baroque style, 19
Barter, 178
Bartholdi, Frédéric-August, 246
Baseball, **33**
Basketball, **33**
Bat, **33–4**, *33,* 96
Battery, 99
Bauxite, *11,* 22, *172*
Bear, **34**, *34*
Beaver, **34**, *35*
Becquerel, Henri, 84
Bee, **35**, *35*
Beethoven, L. van, **36**
Beetle, **36**, *36*
Belgium, **36**
Bell, A.G., **36**, *37*
Bible, **36**, 62, 152
Bicycle, **37**, *37*

Bill of Rights, **37**, 75
Biology, **38**, *38*
Bird, 14, *15,* **38–40**, *39,* 210
Bison, **40**, *40*
Black hole, **40**
Black Sea, *24*
Blériot, Louis, **40–1**, *41*
Blitzkrieg, 250
Blood, **41–2**, *41,* 140, *140*
Bone, **42**, *42*
Book, **42–3**
Booth, John Wilkes, 163
Boron, *28*
Boston, *169*
Boston Tea Party, **43**, *43*
Botany Bay, 29, 75
Bow, 18, *19,* **43**
Boxing, **43**, *43*
Brachiosaurus, 89
Brahms, Johannes, **44**
Braille, **44**, *44*
Braille, Louis, 44
Brain, **44**, *44*
Brasilia, *239*
Brazil, **45**
Breathing, **45**, *45,* 220
Bridge, **45–6**, *45, 46*
British Isles, *102*
Bronze, 10, 46
Bronze Age, **46**
Buddha, **46–7**, *46*
Buddhism, 26, 218
Buffalo, **47**
Buffalo (bison), *see* Bison
Bulb, **47**, *47*
Bulgaria, **47**
Butler, Edward, 182
Butterfly, **47–9**, *48,* 146, *175*
Byzantine Empire, **49**, *49,* 224

C

Caesar, Julius, **49**, 66
Calculator, **49**
Calendar, 27, **49–50**
California, **50**, *50*
Camel, **50–1**, *50*
Camera, **51**, *51, 203*
Camouflage, **51–2**, *52–53*
Canada, **52–3**, *53,* 190–1, *191*
Canadian Shield, 190, *191*
Canal, **53**
Cancer, **53–4**
Canterbury Tales, The, 59
Cape Canaveral, **54**
Carbohydrate, 112
Carbon, **54**, 87
Carbon dioxide, 119, 131,

160, 203
Caribou, 86, 175
Cartoon, **54**, *54–5*
Cartridge, **54–5**
Caspian Sea, *24*
Cassette, **54–5**
Castle, **55**, *54–5*
Castro, Fidel, 83
Cat, **56**, *56, 57*
Caterpillar, 47, 49
Cathedral, **57**, *57*
Cattle, 40, *40*, **57**
Cave, **58**, *58*
Cell, **58**, 91
Cenozoic era, *211*
Census, 209
Centipede, **58**, *58*
Cereal, **59**, *59*, 125
Cerebellum, *44*
Cerebral cortex, 44, *44*
Cézanne, Paul, 23
Challenger, 243
Chaplin, Charlie, *181*
Charcoal, 54
Charlemagne, **59**
Chaucer, Geoffrey, **59**
Cheese, **60**
Cheetah, **161–2**, *161*
Chemistry, **60**
Chess, **60**, *60*
Chile, **60**, *60*
Chimpanzee, *17*
China, *25*, 26, 53, **61**, *61*
Chivalry, 156
Chlorophyll, **62**, 160, 203, 205
Christianity, 36, **62**, *62*, 152–3, 218
Christmas, 62
Chromosome, 119, 172
Chrysalis, 49
Church, **62**
Churchill, Winston, **62–3**, *275*
Circus, **63**, *63*
Citric acid, 5
City, **63–4**, *63*
Civilization, **66**
Civil rights movement, **64**, *64*
Civil War, American, 13, **64–5**, *65*, 163, *269*
Clemens, Samuel L., 259
Cleopatra, **66**
Climate, **66–7**
Clock, **67**
Clothing, **67**
Cloud, **67–8**, *67, 68*, 216, *216*
Coal, **68**, *68*, 116

Cockerell, Christopher, 8
Coffee, **69**
Coin, **69**, 178, *178*
Coke, 54, 68
Cold War, **69**, 265
Collarbone, *42*
Colombia, **69**
Color, **69–70**, *69, 70, 162*, 163, 244
Colorado, **70**, *70*
Colorado beetle, 36, *36*
Columbia, 243, *243*
Columbus, Christopher, **71**, 77, 90, 105, 272
Combustion, 116
Comet, **71**, *71*
Commonwealth, **71**
Communications, **71**
Communism, **72**, 160, 169
Composers, *184*
Compounds, **100**
Computer, 24, 72, **72–3**, *72*
Concrete, **73**
Confederate States of America, 64
Confucius, 61
Congress, U.S., **73**, *73*, 125
Conifer, **74**, *74*, 258
Connecticut, **74**
Conservation, **74**
Constantine, Emperor, 49, *49*
Constellation, **74–5**, *74–5*
Constitution, U.S., 37, **75**
Continental shelf, 194, *194*
Cook, James, 29, **75**
Copernicus, Nicolaus, **75–6**
Copper, 10, **76**
Coral, **76**, *76*
Corn, 59, *59*, 77
Cortés, Hernando, 31, **77**, *77*
Costa Rica, **77**
Cotton, **77**, *77*
Countries of the world: chart, **78–9**; map **80–1**
Crab, *38*, **82**, *82*
Crocodile, **82**, *83*
Cromwell, Oliver, **82**
Crusades, **82–3**, *82*
Crustacean, 82
Crystal, **83**, 236
Cuba, **83**
Cubism, 23, 203
Curie, Marie and Pierre, **84**, *84*
Custer, George, **84**
Cybernetics, 24
Cyclone, **84**
Czechoslovakia, **84**

D
Daguerre, Louis, 202
Daimler, Gottlieb, 30, *30*, 182
Dam, **85**
Darwin, Charles, **85**
Da Vinci, Leonardo, *see* Leonardo da Vinci
Declaration of Independence, **85–6**, *85*, 115
Deer, **86**, *86*
Delaware, **86**
Delta, 222
Democracy, **86**, 125, 127
Dendrochronology, 18
Denmark, **87**
Depression, Great, *see* Great Depression
Dermis, 234
Desert, **87**, *87*
Dialect, 158
Diamond, 54, **87–8**, 119
Dickens, Charles, **88**
Dicotyledon, 205, *205*
Diesel engine, **88**, 101
Digestion, **88**
Dike, 187
Dinosaur, **89–90**, *89*, 210, *211*
Diplodocus, 89
Disease, 31, **90**
Disneyland, *50*
Disney, Walt, **90**
District of Columbia, **90**
Diving, **90–1**, *90*
DNA, **91**, 119
Dog, **91–2**, *91*
Dolphin, **92**, *92*
Dragon, **92**
Drake, Francis, 101
Dream, **235**
Drugs, **92**
Duck, **93**, *93*
Dunant, Jean Henri, 217
Dye, **93**, *93*
Dynamite, **93**

E
Eagle, **94**, *94*
Ear, **94**, *94*, 238
Earth, **95**, *95*, 204, *204*, 238
Earthquake, **96**
Earthworm, **96**
Easter, 62
Echo, **96**
Eclipse, **96**, *96*
Ecology, 38, **97**
Ecuador, **97**

280

Edison, Thomas A., **97**, *97*, *147*, 148
Egg, **97**
Egypt, **97–8**
Egypt, ancient, 42, 56, 64, 66, *66*, **98**, *98–9*, 133
Einstein, Albert, **98**
El Salvador, **98**
Electricity, **98–9**
Electron, 28, *28*, 99
Electronics, **99**
Element, **100**, *121*
Elephant, **100**, *100*
Elizabeth I, **100–1**, *155*
Empire State Building, *21*
Energy, **101**
Engels, Friedrich, 72
Engine, 88, **101**, *101*
ENIAC, 73
Epic, 207
Epidermis, 234
Eskimo, 20, **101**
Estuary, 222
EURISKO, 24
Europe, **102**, *102–3*
European Economic Community, 36, **102–3**
Evolution, 85, **103–4**
Exoskeleton, 234
Explorer, **104–5**, *104*
Eye, *104*, **105**

F
Falkland Islands, 20
Farming, **105**
Fat, *112–13*
Feminism, **105–6**, *106*
Femur, *42*
Fern, **106**, *106*, *205*
Fertilizer, **106**
Feudal system, 174
Fiber optics, **107**, *107*
Fibula, *42*
Film, 51, *51*, 54
Fingerprint, **107**, *107*
Finland, **107**
Fish, 14, *15*, 45, **107–8**, *108*, 210, *211*
Fishing, **109**, *109*
Fission, 193, 265
Flag, **109–10**, *110*
Flea, **110**
Florence, *21*
Florida, **111**, *111*
Flower, **111–12**, *112*
Fly, **112**, *112*
Fog, **112**
Food, **112–13**
Food web, 97
Football, **113**

Ford, Henry, 30, **113**
Forest, **113**
Fossil, 113–14, *113*
Fox, **114**, *114*
France, *102–3*, **114–15**, *114*
Franklin, Benjamin, **115**, *115*
French and Indian War, 12, 269
Freud, Sigmund, **115**
Frog, 13, *13*, **115–16**, *115*, *116*
Fruit, **116**
Fuel, 101, **116**
Fuji, Mount, *152*
Fungus, 162, 183, *183*, 205, *205*

G
Gagarin, Yuri, 26, **117**
Galaxy, **117**, *117*
Galileo, 67, **117–18**, *118*, *146*, 218
Gama, Vasco da, **118**
Gandhi, M.K., *102–3*, *118*
Garibaldi, Giuseppe, **118**
Gas, **118–19**
Gasoline, **119**
Gem, **119**, *119*
Gene, 120
Generator, 99, *99*
Genetics, **119–20**, *120*
Genghis Khan, 120
Geology, **120–1**, *121*
Geometry, 170, 213
Georgia, **121**
Germany, *103*, **121–2**, *121*
Germany, East, **96**, 121–2
Germany, West, 121–2
Geyser, **122**, *122*
Gibbon, *17*
Gill, 45
Giraffe, **122–3**, *122*
Girder bridge, *45*
Glacier, *16*, **123**, *123*, 142
Glass, **123**
Goat, **123**, *123*
Gold, **124**, *124*, *239*
Golden Gate Bridge, 46, *46*
Gold Rush, **124**
Golf, **124–5**, *124*
Goose, **93**, *93*
Gorbachev, Mikhail, 69
Gorilla, *17*
Gothic style, 19, *21*, *57*, 62
Government, **125**
Grand Canyon, 22
Grand Coulee Dam, 85
Grant, Ulysses S., 65
Grass, **125**, *125*

Grasshopper, **125–6**, *126*
Gravity, **126**
Great Barrier Reef, 29, *29*
Great Depression, **126**, *126*
Great Wall of China, 61, *61*
Greece, *103*
Greece, ancient, 10, 19, *21*, 28, 64, *66*, 125, **126–8**, *127*, 185, 254
Gregorian calendar, 50
Guatemala, **128**
Guinea pig, **128**
Gulf Stream, 28, **128**, *129*
Gun, **128–9**
Gutenberg, Johannes, 43, 71, **129**, *146*, 212
Gymnastics, **129**, *129*

H
Halley's Comet, 71, **130**, *130*
Handel, George Frideric, **130**
Hannibal, **130**
Hare, **214**
Hargreaves, James, 147
Harvey, William, **130**
Hawaii, **130**
Hearing, 94
Heart, 41, **130–1**, *131*
Helicopter, **131**, *131*
Helium, 32
Henry VIII, 100–1
Heraldry, **131–2**
Hercules, **132**
Heredity, 119–20, 172
Hesiod, 185
Hibernation, **132**, *132*
Hieroglyphic, **133**
Himalaya Mountains, *25*, 143, 182
Hindu, 26, **133**, 143, 218
Hippopotamus, **133**, *133*
History, **133**, *134–7*
Hitler, Adolf, **138**
Hockey, **138**
Holocaust, **138**
Holy Roman Empire, 59
Homer, **138**, 185
Homo sapiens, 139
Hoover Dam, 20
Horse, **138–9**, *138–9*
House of Representatives, 73
Hovercraft, *7*, 8
Hovertrain, 216
Human being, **139–40**, *139*
Human body, **140**, *140*
Hummingbird, *39*, **140**, **141**
Hydrochloric acid, 5
Hydrofoil, **141**, *141*

281

Hydrogen, 28, 32, 119, **141**
Hyena, **141**
Hypothalmus, 44, *44*

I

Ice Age, **142**, 212
Iceberg, **142**
Idaho, **142**
Ides of March, 49
Igneous rock, 95, 223
Iliad, 138, 207
Illinois, **143**
Inca, **143**
India, *25*, 26, 118, **143**, *143*
Indiana, **144**
Indian, American, **144–5**, *144–5*, 192
Indonesia, *25*
Industrial Revolution, 64, 67, **145**, *145*, 257
Insect, 14, *14*, 45, **146–7**, *146*
Instinct, 14
Instrument, musical, *see* Musical instrument
International Date Line, **147**
Intestine, 88
Invention, **147–8**, *146–7*
Inventors, *146–7*
Invertebrate, 14, 210, 234
Ion, **148**
Iowa, **148**
Iran, **148**, *148*
Iraq, **148–9**
Ireland, **149**
Iron, 28, **149–50**, 172
Iron Age, **149**
Irrigation, **150**, *150*
Islam, 26, **150**, 156, 180, *180*, 183, 218
Israel, **150**, *151*, 175
Istanbul, *21*
Italy, 118, **151**, *151*

J

Japan, *25*, 26, **152**, *152*
Jefferson, Thomas, 86
Jenner, Edward, **152**
Jerusalem, *151*
Jesus Christ, 37, 62, **152**
Jet engine, 9, **153**, *153*
Joan of Arc, **153**
Judaism, 36, **153**, **218**, 250
Jupiter, 204, *204*, 238

K

Kabuki, *207*
Kalahari Desert, *6*, 7
Kangaroo, 30, **154**, *154*
Kansas, **154**

Kennedy, John F., **154**
Kennedy Manned Space Flight Center, 54
Kentucky, **154**, *155*
Kenya, Mount, 5
Kilimanjaro, Mount, 5
Kiln, 210
Kinetic art, 24
King, **155–6**, *155*
King, Dr. M.L., Jr., 64, *64*, **154–5**
Kiwi, **156**, *156*
Knight, **156**, 174
Knot, **156**, *157*
Koala, 30, **156**, *157*
Kohoutek, Comet, *71*
Koran, **156**
Korea, *25*, 26
Korean War, **157**
Kremlin, **157**
Kublai Khan, 168
Ku Klux Klan, **157**

L

Lactic acid, 5
Lake, **158**
Language, **158**
Lao Tse, 61
Laser, 107, **158**, *158*
Latitude, 66, **159**, *159*
Latter Day Saints, **159**
Law, **159**
Lead, **159–60**
Leaf, **160**, *160*
League of Nations, **160**
Lee, Robert E., 65
Lenin, Vladimir, **160**
Lens, 51, *51*, **160–1**, 163
Leonardo da Vinci, *22*, 23, **161**, 218
Leopard, 52, **161–2**, *161*
Letterpress, 212
Libya, **162**
Lichen, **162**
Light, 160–1, **162–3**, *162*, *163*, 174, 244
Lightning, **163**
Lincoln, Abraham, 64, *65*, **163**
Lindbergh, Charles, **163**, *163*
Lion, 56, **164**, *164*
Lister, Joseph, **164**
Lithography, 212
Liver, 88
Lizard, **164–5**, *165*
Llama, **165**
Locomotion, 215
Locomotive, 215–16, *215*
Longitude, **159**, *159*

Lorenzo the Magnificent, 171
Louisiana, **165**
Louisiana Purchase, 12, 13, 22
Lumière brothers, 180
Lungs, 41, 45, *45*
Luther, Martin, **165**, 217

M

Machine, **166**, *166*
Magellan, Ferdinand, 105, **166**
Magic, **166**
Magnet, 99, **167**
Maine, **167**
Maine, U.S.S., 243
Malaria, 180
Malaysia, *25*
Mammal, 14, *15*, **167**, 210, *211*
Mammoth, **167**, *167*
Maori, 189
Mao Zedong, 61, **168**
Map, **168**, *168*
Marconi, Guglielmo, **168–9**
Marco Polo, 104, **168**
Mars, 204, *204*, 238
Marsupial, 30, **169**, *169*
Marx, Karl, 72, **169**, 237
Maryland, **169**
Massachusetts, **169**, *169*
Mathematics, **170**
Maya, **170**
Mayflower, **170**, *170*
McAdam, John, 222
Measurement, **170–1**
Medicine, **171–2**, *171*
Medicis, **171**
Mediterranean Sea, *102–3*
Medulla, 44, *44*
Mendel, Gregor, **172**
Mercury, 204, *204*, 238
Mercury barometer, 33
Mesa Verde, *70*
Mesozoic era, *211*
Metal, **172–3**, *172*
Metamorphic rock, 223
Metamorphosis, 147
Meteor, **173**
Metric system, **173**
Mexican War, 22, *269*
Mexico, 31, 77, **173**, *191*
Michelangelo, 23, **173–4**, *173*, 218
Michigan, **174**
Microscope, **174**, *174*
Mid-Atlantic Ridge, 28
Middle Ages, **174–5**
Middle East, 24, *24*, **175**

Migration, **175**–**6**, *175*
Millipede, **58**, *58*
Mimicry, 52
Mineral, **176**
Mining, 68, *68*, **176**
Minnesota, **176**, *176*
Missile, **176**–**7**, *177*
Mississippi, **177**
Mississippi river, 22, *177*, 191, *261*
Missouri, **177**
Model T Ford, 30, *30*
Molecule, 100
Mollusk, **177**
Monastery, **177**–**8**
Money, 69, **178**, *178*
Mongols, 120
Monkey, **178**–**9**, *179*
Monocotyledon, 205, *205*
Monsoon, 241–2
Montana, **179**
Montgolfier brothers, 32, 33
Moon, 26, 27, 96, **179**–**80**, *179*
Moose, 86
Moraine, 123
Mormon, *see* Latter Day Saints
Moscow, 157
Mosque, **180**, *180*
Mosquito, **180**
Moss, **180**, *205*
Moth, **47**–**49**, *48*
Motion picture, **180**–**1**, *181*
Motorcycle, **181**–**2**, *181*
Mountain, **182**, *182*
Mouse, **216**–**7**
Mozart, W.A., **183**
Muhammad, 150, 156, **183**
Mushroom, **183**, *183*
Music, **183**–**4**, *184*, 196
Musical instrument, **184**–**5**, *185*, 196
Muslim, 82–3, 150, 156
Mythology, 132, **185**

N

Napoleon Bonaparte, **186**
Nasser, Gamal A., **186**
Nazis, 138
Nebraska, **186**
Nelson, Horatio, 186
Neptune, 204, *204*, 238
Nest, *186*, **187**
Netherlands, *186*–**7**, **187**
Neutron, 28, *28*
Neutron star, 40
Nevada, **187**
New Cornelia Tailings Dam, 85

New Hampshire, **187**
New Jersey, **188**
New Mexico, **188**, *188*
Newt, 13, *13*, 225
Newton Isaac, 70–71, **189**
New York, **188**, *189*
New Zealand, **189**
Niagara Falls, **189**
Nigeria, **189**–**90**, *190*
Niger River, 6, *6*
Nile River, 5, 6, *6*, 97, 98
Nirvana, 47
Nitroglycerin, 93
Nobel, Alfred, 93
Nobel Prize, 93, **190**
Nomad, **190**
Norse myth, 185
North America, **190**–**2**, *191*
North Carolina, **192**, *192*
North Dakota, **192**
North Pole, 20, 229
Norway, **192**, *193*
Nuclear energy, **192**–**3**
Nuclear reactor, 193
Nuclear weapon, 69, 193
Nucleus, 28, *28*
Nut, **193**, *193*
Nymph, 146

O

Oasis, **194**, *194*
Ocean, 28, 95, **194**–**5**, *194*
Octopus, **195**
Odyssey, 138, 207
Ohio, **195**
Oil, **195**, *195*
Oklahoma, **196**
Olympic Games, 28, 128, **196**
Opal, 119, *119*
Opera, **196**
Orangutan, *17*
Orchestra, **196**–**7**, *196*
Oregon, **197**
Ovum, 97
Owl, **197**, *197*
Oxygen, 28, 41, 45, 119, 131, **197**

P

Pacific Ocean, **198**
Painters, *198*
Painting, 22, 23, *22*, *23*, **198**–**200**, *199*
Paleozoic era, *211*
Pampas, 20
Panama, **200**
Panama Canal, 53, *91*, 200
Pancreas, 88
Panda, **200**, *200*

Paper, **200**, *201*
Papyrus, 200
Parachute, **200**–**1**
Paris, *114*, 115
Parliament, 125
Pasteur, Louis, **201**
Pearl, 119
Pearl Harbor, **201**, 275
Peary, Robert, 105
Pelvis, *42*
Penguin, 16, **201**–**2**, *202*
Penicillin, 92, **202**
Pennsylvania, **202**
Perfume, **202**
Periscope, **202**
Petroleum, 116, 195
Pharaoh, 98
Philippines, **202**
Photography, 51, 72, **202**–**3**, *203*
Photogravure, 212
Photosynthesis, 62, 160, **203**, 205
Picasso, Pablo, 23, *198*, **203**, *228*
Pig, **203**
Pilgrims, 170
Pirate, **203**
Planet, **204**, *204*
Plankton, **204**
Plant, 45, 47, 58, 62, **205**, *205*
Plasma, 41
Plastic, **206**
Plato, 20, 237
Platypus, 30, **206**, *206*
Play, **206**–**7**, *207*
Playwrights, *206*
Pluto, 204, *204*, 238
Poe, Edgar Allan, **207**
Poetry, **207**–**8**
Poison, **208**
Poland, **208**
Polar bear, 34, *34*
Pollen, 112, 219
Pollution, **208**, *208*
Polyp, 76
Pope, **208**–**9**
Population, **209**
Porcupine, *208*, **209**
Portugal, *102*, **209**
Post office, **209**
Pottery, **210**, *210*
Prehistoric animal, 89–90, **210**–**12**, *211*
President, 125, **212**
Prime minister, **212**
Printing, 43, 71–72, **212**, *212*
Prism, 69, *162*, 163, 244,

283

244
Program, computer, 72–73
Protein, 113, **213**
Protestant, 217
Proton, 28, *28*
Protoplasm, 58
Pygmy, **213**
Pyramid, *31*, 98, **213**, *213*
Pythagoras, **213**

Q
Queen, **155–6**, *155*
Quito, *239*

R
Rabbit, **214**, *214*
Raccoon, **214**
Radar, 96, **214**
Radiation, 215
Radio, **214**, *215*
Radioactivity, 84, **215**
Radiosondes, 33
Radio wave, 214, *215*, 244
Radium, 84, 215
Railroad, **215–16**, 215
Rain, 67–68, **216**, *216*
Raphael, *198*, *199*
Rat, **216–7**
Recording, 54, 55, **217**
Red Cross, **217**
Red Sea, *24*
Reformation, 165, **217**
Refraction, 163
Refrigeration, **217**, *217*
Reindeer, 86
Religion, **218**
Rembrandt, 23, **218**, *218*
Renaissance, **218**
Renoir, Pierre Auguste, 23
Reproduction, **219**
Reptile, 14, *15*, 210, *211*,
  219, *219*, 235–6
Respiration, **220**
Revolution, **220**, *220*
Revolutionary War, 12, *12*,
  43
Rhinoceros, **220**, *221*
Rhode Island, **220**
Rib, *42*
Rice, 59, *59*, **221**, *221*, *242*
River, **221–2**
RNA, **91**
Road, **222**
Robot, **222–3**, *222*
Rock, **223**
Rocket, **223**, *223*
Rocket, The, 216
Rocky Mountains, 190
Rodent, **223**
Roman Catholic Church,

151, 165, 208–9, 217,
  225
Romanesque style, 19, 62
Rome, ancient, 19, *21*, 49,
  50, 63, 64, *66*, *150*, 185,
  224, *224*
Romulus and Remus, 224
Rosetta Stone, 133
Rubber, **225**, *225*
Rutherford, Ernest, **225**
Rye, 59, *59*

S
Sahara Desert, *6*, 7, 87
Saint, **225**
Saladin, 83
Salamander, 13, *13*, **225**
Salt, **225–6**, *226*
Satellite, **226**, *227*
Saturn, 204, *204*, 238
Saudi Arabia, **226**
Scandinavia, *103*, **226–7**
Schumann, Robert, 44
Science, **227**
Scott, Robert, **227**
Scout, **228**
Sculpture, 23, *23*, 24, 228,
  228
Sea horse, **228**, 228
Seal, **228**
Sea lion, **228**
Season, **229**
Seaweed, 10, *10*, 205, **229**
Sedimentary rock, 95, 223
Seed, **229**
Seismometer, 96
Senate, 73
Senses, **231**
Seven Wonders of the
  World, *230*, **231**
Shakespeare, William, 101,
  206, 207, **231**
Shark, **231**, *231*
Sheep, **231**
Ship, **231–3**, *232*
Silicon chip, 73, 99, **233**,
  233, 257
Silk, **233**
Silkworm, 47, 233
Silver, **233**
Sitting Bull, *144*, **233–4**
Skeleton, 42, *42*, **234**
Skiing, **234**
Skin, **234**, *234*
Skull, *42*
Skunk, **234**
Slavery, **234–5**
Sleep, **235**
Sloth, **235**, *235*
Slug, **235**

Smallpox, 152
Smell, **235**
Smith, Joseph, 159
Snail, **235**
Snake, **235–6**, *235*, *236*
Snow, 68, **236**, *236*
Soap, **236**
Soccer, **237**, *237*
Socialism, **237**
Socrates, **237**
Soil, **237**
Solar system, 76, 204, *204*,
  237–8
Sonar, 96
Sound, **238**, *238*
South Africa, **238–9**, *239*
South America, **239–41**,
  239, *240*
South Carolina, **241**
South Dakota, **241**, *241*
Southeast Asia, *25*, **241–2**,
  242
South Pole, 16, 227
Space biology, 38
Space flight, **242**
Space shuttle, **242–3**, *243*
Spain, *102*, **243**
Spanish-American War, **243**
Sparta, 127–8
Spectrum, 70, **244**, *244*
Sperm, 97, 219
Spider, **244**, *244*
Spine, *42*
Spinning, **244–5**
Spore, 106, 180
Sputnik I, 226, 242
Squid, **195**
Stalactite, *58*, **245**
Stalagmite, *58*, **245**
Stalin, Joseph, **245**, *275*
Stamp, 209, **245**
Star, 40, 74–5, *74–5*, **245–
  6**, *245*, *246*
Statue of Liberty, **246**, *246*
Steam engine, 101, **246–7**,
  247
Steel, 10, 11, **149–50**, *149*
Stephenson, George, 215
Steppe, 24
Stomata, 160
Stone Age, **247**
Submarine, **248**, *248–9*
Suez Canal, 53, 186
Sugar, 83, 160, **248**
Sulfuric acid, 5
Sumter, Fort, 64
Sun, 96, **248–9**, *249*
Suspension bridge, *46*
Swan, **249**
Sweden, **249–50**

Switzerland, **250**, *250*
Sydney, Australia, *21*

T

Talmud, **250**
Tank, **250**
Tasman, Abel, 189
Tasmania, *29*
Tax, **250–1**
Tea, **251**, *251*
Teeth, **251**, *251*
Telephone, 36, *37*, 158, **251–2**, *252*
Telescope, 27, **252**, *252*
Television, **252–3**, *253*
Tennessee, **253**
Tennis, **253–4**
Tenochtitlán, 31
Texas, **254**
Theater, **254**
Thermometer, **254–5**
Thorax, 146
Thunderstorm, **254**, **255**
Tibia, *42*
Tide, **255**, *255*
Tiger, 56, *57*, **255–6**, *255*
Time, **256**
Tin, 10, **256**
Toad, 13, **115–6**
Toadstool, **183**, *183*
Tobacco, **256–7**, *256*
Torah, 250
Tortoise, **257**, *257*
Trade union, **257**
Transistor, 99, **257**
Tree, **257–9**, *258*
Troposphere, 95
Tsunami, **259**
Turkey, **259**, *259*
Turtle, **257**, *257*
Twain, Mark, **259**
Tyrannosaurus, 89

U

Ultraviolet ray, 244, **260**
United Kingdom, **260**, *260*
United Nations, 157, **260–1**
United States of America, 190–1, *191*, **261–4**, *261*, *262–3*, *264*
Universe, **264**
Uranium, 215, **264–5**
Uranus, 204, *204*, 238
U.S.S.R., *24*, *25*, *103*, 157, **265**, *265*
Utah, **265**

V

Vaccination, 152, 172
Vatican, 151, 209
Vegetable, **266**

Venice, 53
Venus, 204, *204*, 238
Vermont, *261*, **266**
Verrazano-Narrows Bridge, 46
Vertebrate, 14, 42, 167, 210, 234
Videotape, **266**
Vietnam War, **266**, *269*
Viking, 104, **266**
Virgil, 207
Virginia, **266–7**
Virus, 90
Vitamin, **267**
Volcano, *152*, **267**, *267*

W

Wallaby, *169*
War, **268–9**, *268*, *269*
War of 1812, 13, 269
Washington, **269**
Washington, D.C., 90, **269**, *269*
Washington, George, 12, *12*, **269–70**
Wasp, **270**, *270*
Watch, **67**
Water, 28, 67–68, **270**
Waterfall, **270–1**, *271*
Waterloo, Battle of, 186
Watt, James, 145, 246, **271**
Wave, **271**
Weather, **271**, *271*
Weaving, **244–5**, *245*
West Indies, **271–2**
West Virginia, **272**
Whale, 92, **272**, *272*
Wheat, 59, *59*
Wheel, **272**
White dwarf, 40
White House, *269*
Whittle, Frank, 153
William the Conqueror, **273**
Wind, *271*, **273**
Windmill, **273**
Wisconsin, **273**
Wolf, **274**, *274*
Wood, **274**
World Series, 33
World War I, 13, 268, *269*, **274–5**, *274*
World War II, 13, 62–63, 138, 152, 201, 268–9, *269*, **275**, *275*
Worm, **275–6**
Wright brothers, 8, 9, 148, **276**, *276*
Wyoming, **276**

X

X ray, 172, 244, **276**
Xylem, 160

Y

Yak, **277**, *277*
Yellowstone National Park, 276
Yugoslavia, **277**

Z

Zaire, **277**
Zaire River, 6, *6*
Zambia, **277**
Zebra, *4*, 52, **277**
Zimbabwe, **278**
Zinc, 10
Zoo, **278**, *278*
Zoology, **278**

ACKNOWLEDGMENTS

Photographs: Nature Photographers 4; Connecticut Historical Society (top), Robert Hunt Library 12; ZEFA 16; Service de Documentation, Paris 22; Jeu de Paume, Paris (top), Tate Gallery 23; ZEFA 31; Mansell Collection 37; Heather Angel 38; Nature Photographers 40; RNIB 44; Dave Collins 46; Sonia Halliday 49; Dave Collins (top), Geoscience Features 50; ZEFA 53; Sonia Halliday 57; ZEFA 60; ZEFA 61; Sonia Halliday 62; Japanese Tourist (top), ZEFA 63; Photosource 64; Peter Newark (top), BBC Hulton Picture Library 65; ZEFA 70; N.H.P.A. 76; Mansell Collection 84; U.S. Capitol Historical Society 85; ZEFA 92; ZEFA 93; Mary Evans Picture Library 106; Metropolitan Police 107; Barbara Taylor 111; Pat Morris 113; J. Allan Cash 114; Mansell Collection 115; N.H.P.A. 116; NASA 117; Associated Press 118; Geological Museum 119; J. Clapham 121; New Zealand House 122; D & J. Wright 123; SATOUR (top), Allsport 124; Michael Chinery (top), Bettman Archive 126; ZEFA 129; Westland Helicopters 131; ZEFA 140; Michael Holford 142; ZEFA 143; J. Allan Cash 145; Geosceince Features 148; Alabama Bureau of Publicity (bottom) 151; ZEFA (top), National Portrait Gallery 155; Mansell Collection 163; Novosti 167; Australian News & Information Bureau (top), ZEFA 169; Siemens Ltd.; Ames Europe Ltd. 172; Italian Institute 173; Memphis Chamber of Commerce (bottom right) 177; Irak Tourist 180; National Film Board (top left), B.F.I. 181; ZEFA 188; B. J. Cruickshank 189; Camera & Pen 190; ZEFA 192; ZEFA 193; Adrian Sington (left) 194; Shell U.K. Ltd. 195; Pitti Gallery, Florence (top left); Tate Gallery (top right), Kunsthistoriches Museum, Austria 199; Science Museum 203; Japanese Information Service 207; U.S. Environmental Protection Agency 208; Mauritshuis, The Hague 218; ZEFA 219; Novosti 220; Nature Photographers (top) 221; ZEFA 226; Tate Gallery 228; SATOUR (top), ZEFA (both) 239; ZEFA 241; J. Allan Cash 242; U.S. Naval Observatory 245; Ceylon Tea Centre 250; Met Office 254; Tampa Chamber of Commerce 256; Sonia Halliday 259; Press Association 260; ZEFA (both) 261; ZEFA 264; ZEFA 265; Frank Spooner Pictures 268; Geoscience Features 269; Sandia Laboratories 273; Imperial War Museum (left) 274; Press Association 275; ZEFA 277; ZEFA 278.